*The Art of Ancient Mexico*

Paul Westheim was born in 1886 in Germany where he studied art history under Heinrich Woelfflin. He edited a series of books on art, *Orbis Pictus*, and founded and edited the expressionist art magazine, *Das Kunstblatt;* he also edited a graphics art magazine, *Die Schaffenden*. He is the author of numerous books about art, published in Germany. Among these: *Die Welt als Vorstellung* (*The World as Representation*), *Das Holzschnittbuch* (*The Book of Wood Etching*), *Für und Wider* (*Pro and Contra*), *Künstlerbekenntnisse* (*Artist's Confessions*), *Helden und Abenteurer* (*Heroes and Adventurers*), and, together with Carl Einstein, he edited the *Europa-Almanach,* in collaboration with such artists as Gide, Léger, and Le Corbusier. From 1933 to 1939 he lived in Paris, and from 1941 to November 1963, in Mexico where he devoted himself to studies on the esthetics of ancient Mexican art. He was invited by the Ford Foundation to study modern art for a year in Berlin but his studies were cut short by his death in December of 1963. Paul Westheim's books, published in Mexico, include *Ideas fundamentales del arte prehispánico en México* (*Fundamental Ideas of the Art of Prehispanic Mexico*), *La Calavera* (*The Skull*), *Tamayo, El grabado en madera* (*Wood Etching*), *La cerámica del México antiguo* (*Ceramic Art of Ancient Mexico*), and *La escultura del México antiguo* (*The Sculpture of Ancient Mexico*), which Doubleday published in the Anchor Edition (A335), in Spanish with English translation. *The Art of Ancient Mexico* was published in Mexico as *Arte antiguo de México*.

# The ART of ANCIENT MEXICO

## PAUL WESTHEIM

*Translated from Spanish into English*
by URSULA BERNARD

Anchor Books
Doubleday & Company, Inc.
Garden City, New York

*The Art of Ancient Mexico* was first published in Spanish, translated from the original German by Mariana Frenk, as *Arte Antiguo de México* by the Fondo de Cultura Económica in Mexico in 1950.

The Anchor Books edition is published by arrangement with the author.

Library of Congress Catalog Card Number 64–19224

To
Wilhelm Worringer
Esteemed Teacher and Friend

Until we thoroughly understand the inevitability and the orderliness of its expression, every work of art is to us a closed book.

Worringer, *Form in Gothic*

## Preface to the Second Edition

Octavio Paz has graciously permitted me to quote the following lines from a letter of his: "For me, your books on Mexican art have been a font in the true sense of the word: they have slaked my thirst, they have awakened and enriched my spirit, and they have enchanted me. Thank you for your books." This was the purpose that guided me in writing my books about ancient Mexico: to help the reader see the artistic beauty of pre-Cortesian works, to enable him to convert an historic past into an encounter with the eternal present of the art.

There has appeared meanwhile, also from the Fondo de Cultura Económica, my book, *Ideas fundamentales del arte prehispánico en México*, which complements *The Art of Ancient Mexico*. The two make up a unity. I think I can say without boasting that these works constitute a base for an insight into the aesthetic phenomena of a unique and great artistic world.

For this second edition, the text has been carefully revised. Some chapters were rewritten. There are additional illustrations and some of the earlier ones have been replaced by new photographs in which the artistic structure stands out with greater clarity.

I am grateful to the Instituto Nacional de Antropología e Historia, to the Museo Nacional de Antropología, to the Völkerkundemuseum of Berlin, as well as to several friends—all of whom gave me photographs.

On the publication of this new edition, I feel it incumbent on me to express my gratitude to the Fondo de Cultura Económica and especially to its director, Dr. Arnaldo Orfila Reynal, whose interest in my work and encouraging understanding have been a valuable stimulus.

*Mexico, January 1963*                              *Paul Westheim*

## Preface to the First Edition

In 1921 I published in Berlin, in the series *Orbis Pictus* which I edited, a work entitled *The History of Ancient Mexican Art*. The author was Walter Lehmann, a disciple of Seler who had taken part in the explorations of Teotihuacán. At the same time, the publishing firm of Crès in Paris brought out the French edition.

When, twenty years later, I had the good fortune to come to this country to see personally the masterworks of ancient Mexico, I sought a book that would introduce me to this art from its spiritual and creative bases. There are many well-illustrated publications with descriptions of the different works; there are very important studies by archeologists, especially Mexican archeologists, which in the last fifty years have established the foundations for an understanding of the pre-Columbian cultures. But I did not find what I was looking for, an esthetics of pre-Columbian art. I found in the discontinued magazine *Universidad de México* a fundamental essay by Eulalia Guzmán, "Caracteres esenciales del arte antiguo mexicano." Meanwhile, there was published Salvador Toscano's excellent work, *Arte precolombino de México y de la América Central,* which proposes another important task: to present a clear and methodical survey of the evolutionary course of pre-Cortesian art. Since the book I was seeking did not exist, I decided to write it, for myself and for all those who are interested in grasping artistic phenomena from their spiritual and psychic bases. I understood from the first that to do this I would have to start from the myth, the religion, the conception of nature, and the social structure of the pre-Columbian peoples. The result, after some seven years of intense work, is the present book.

Possibly the reader will say that it is a book of many quotations. In the literature on ancient and even modern Mexico, many authors give free rein to their fantasy. Therefore I believed it necessary to base my thesis, wherever possible, on sources that are considered to be trustworthy. Quotations and illustrations are my witnesses.

I wish to state my appreciation to the Museo Nacional de Antropología and particularly to its director, Dr. Daniel Rubín de la Borbolla, for the very kind assistance he gave me. I would also like to express my gratitude to my friend, Dr. Ernest Rathenau, who was kind enough to let me use his handsome, unpublished photographs, the fruits of a trip to Mexico for photographic studies. No less warmly do I thank my friends Albrecht Viktor Blum, Enrique A. Cervantes, Arnold Deutsch, J. Rodolfo Lozada, Dr. Kurt Stavenhagen, and Lic. Salvador Toscano (who, tragically, died a few months ago) for the photographic material, equally interesting and unpublished, that they placed at my disposal; and to Don Jorge Enciso for the kind execution of some drawings taken from his work, *Design Motifs of Ancient Mexico*. And finally, I thank Señora Mariana Frenk for the comprehensive translation and the valuable assistance she gave me in checking the work.

It gives me deep satisfaction and great honor that Dr. Wilhelm Worringer, my esteemed teacher, has accepted the dedication of this book. His fundamental work, *Form in Gothic*, has been my model, criterion, and stimulus.

*October 1950*                                        *P. W.*

# Contents

# List of Plates

*Plates 89–122*
*Follow page 220*

*List of Figures*

*Figure*

# PART ONE

# The Conception of the World

FIG. 1. The Sun, the planet Venus, the Moon, the Earth. *Borgia Codex,* 71

In this drawing Xólotl offers a quail to the sun god, who sucks up the river of blood pouring from the bird. Sahagún writes: "Every day of their lives they offered blood and incense to the sun; then when he appeared in the morning they offered him blood from their ears and blood from quails, which, when their heads had been torn off and they were dripping blood, they raised to the sun as if offering that blood to him, and doing this, they said: now the sun has come out . . . ; we do not know how he will complete his path this day, nor do we know if some misfortune will happen to the people. And then they addressed their words to the sun himself, saying: Our Lord, perform your duty successfully!"

## The Theogonic System

Almost all religious systems must face the contradiction that the world, created, arranged, and ruled by God, is not perfect, but is oppressed with misery and misfortune. How is this possible? God is the All-Powerful; everything happens according to His Will and against His Will "not a bird falls from the sky." And yet. . . .

Judaism places this conflict in the human soul and conscience. The world is full of violence because men are headstrong, because they are dominated by the *Jezer horah* or evil instinct, because they sin and deny God. "For the imagination of man's heart is evil from his youth" (Genesis 8:21). God is all powerful, but man is weak, much too weak, and because of his weakness (sin), there is evil in the world.

Christianity creates the concept of original sin. In Paradise, before the Fall, man was the image of God until original sin inflicted a curse upon all humanity and changed the world into a vale of tears. It is the mission of man to expiate this primordial guilt. Jesus Christ, the Redeemer, carried the cross, the guilt of man, but man has not been saved from falling into sin again. He has to struggle against his sinful nature, to which he is continually succumbing. Why is salvation given to him only as a promise? Christianity invents the Devil, the "Enemy," who with cunning and perfidy sows the seeds of unhappiness, and man falls into his trap. St. Augustine tries to elude this contradiction by excluding the criterion of reason, for reason was also corrupted by original sin and is not a trustworthy guide. The goal of all human efforts, wherein also lies the solution of all these contradictions, is communion with God.

The people of ancient Mexico found a solution of inspired simplicity. Since they could neither deny nor suppress the contradiction, they incorporated it into their religious system. The gods, creators and masters of the world, are of course gifted with superhuman forces; but one god confronts another, quarrels with another, the constructive god against the destructive, in an eternal, continual, never-ending struggle, forming and transforming the world, dominating nature, and determining the existence of man. In the Tro-Cortesianus Codex is a scene in which Chac, the rain god, is nurturing a young tree. Behind him, Ah Puch, the death god, breaks the tree in two (Fig. 2).

FIG. 2. The rain god nurturing a tree, the god of death breaking it in two. *Tro-Cortesianus Codex.*

Dualism is the essential principle of the pre-Cortesian world, governing its conception of the gods, of nature, and of art. The solution to the cosmic enigma lies in a clash of opposing forces. As represented on the "Stone of the Sun," or "Aztec Calendar," the epochs of the world are an unending succession of destructions. Four suns, i.e., four worlds, were destroyed. According to myth, our present world will be annihilated by earthquakes.

The Biblical Deluge is a punishment for man's impiety.

Only Noah and his family escape destruction. The motivation for this catastrophe is ethico-religious: evil and perversity must be destroyed. In the Mexican myth, the destruction of the four worlds is the result of a struggle for power between the two great godly adversaries—Quetzalcóatl and the black Tezcatlipoca. The latter created the first world and made himself the sun. When Quetzalcóatl attacked him with a club, he fell into the water, transformed himself into a tiger, and devoured the giants then populating the earth. Quetzalcóatl created a new world, which was struck down by the claws of the tiger, Tezcatlipoca. The creating gods then chose Tláloc, the rain god, to be the sun, but this third world was destroyed by a rain of fire. Next Quetzalcóatl selected as the sun Chalchiuhtlicue, goddess of water and sister of Tláloc, and Tezcatlipoca demolished this fourth world with torrents of water. "The struggle of these two gods is the history of the universe; their alternating victories so many other creations" (Alfonso Caso).

FIG. 3. The jaguar devouring the Sun. Petroglyph in the area of Tenango. Drawing according to Del Moral.

Properly speaking, being does not actually exist. Only birth and death exist. Being is a transitory state between birth and death, and life is no more than this. The dead "awakened from a dream in which they had been living." According to Sahagún (*Historia general de las cosas de Nueva España*), this was the interpretation of life. There is neither duration nor security in this life. Tezcatlipoca—

also called "he who does as he wishes"—was feared because "he was constantly seeking opportunities to take
away what he had given" (Sahagún, *op. cit.*). He represented the law of nature, the impossibility of knowing
the future. His symbol was the jaguar, "he who destroys."

Sowing and harvest, day and night, birth and death.
Eternal birth, eternal death. Childbirth is considered a
combat in the womb of the woman giving birth (Eduard
Seler: *Gesammelte Abhandlungen*). A part of her being
dies there so that the new life can begin, just as a grain
of maize dies in the earth so that a new plant can spring
up. This polarity is the primitive root, the primordial
meaning, of all being and happening. Attraction and re-
pulsion keep everything in a state of equilibrium, subject
to magic conjuration. Celestial bodies—the sun, the moon,
the morning star—whose movements are thought to affect
all human events, are the cosmic confirmation of this be-

FIG. 4. The Sun in the womb of the Earth. *Borbonicus Codex,* 16

lief. It is necessary to recognize the existence of this cosmic order wherein any irregularity is interpreted as misfortune, but the most important fact to be learned from this observation of the heavens is that the celestial bodies are subject to the same law of birth and death. The sun sets, "is devoured by the jaguar" (Fig. 3), "buried in the womb of the earth," the lower world. The moon (see Chapter 4, "The Conception of Nature" Fig. 3) is crushed and killed by the sun in order to reappear as a full moon. Each region of the realm of the dead is governed by one of the "destructive animals." The bat reigns in the East. The Vaticanus B Codex represents it with a human head in each claw: in the Borgia Codex it is seen pulling the heart from a skeleton. The North belongs to the jaguar: in the codices we see it destroying a man. In the West, an alligator tears off one of Tezcatlipoca's feet. The eagle reigns in the South. The codices show it clutching a rabbit that appears between the jaws of a serpent.

What we are concerned with here are monumental struggles and cosmic dramas, in which the actors are the gods.[1] These are the reflections of a dynamic concept of

[1] The fact that the ball game symbolizes a combat of the antagonistic cosmic forces explains the great importance attributed to it by all cultures. The priests celebrated it as a ceremonial ritual. It is pictured in all the codices and, with the exception of Teotihuacán, ball courts have been found in every great ceremonial center: Monte Albán, Xochicalco, Tula, Chichén Itzá, Copán, etc. Seler affirmed that this game had a mythological significance: it represents the disappearance and the resurgence of the moon, "the moon alternately succumbs, i.e., disappears as a new moon, and triumphs, i.e., becomes a full moon." It is the struggle between light and darkness. Seler explains that the movement of the ball is the path traversed by the sun from the clear half (of the sky) toward the dark half (of earth), and vice versa. The ring through which the player must throw the ball symbolizes the earth's opening into which the sun disappears when it sets. "The presence of the Xiuhcóatl, the serpent-guide of the sun in its course, in the rings of the ball game at Chichén Itzá, seems to be a reference to this belief" (Salvador Toscano, *Arte precolombino de México y de la América Central*). Xólotl is expressly designated as the god of the ball game, and the game itself should be interpreted as a combat between Xólotl, god of twilight and of the setting sun,

the world, based not on an ethical ideal, but on the recognition of elemental forces of nature that obey no law other than that of their own inherent energy.

This dualism is manifested in concrete, expressive form in the very name of Ometecuhtli, father of the creator gods. Ometecuhtli means "Two Lord." The first interpreter of the Telleriano-Remensis Codex identifies him with Tonatecuhtli, "God, lord, creator, ruler of all, Tloque Nahuaque . . . the one who is god, of whom it was said that he had created the world, and thus was he depicted, with the crown of a king as master of all." Sahagún writes: "They said that upon that great Lord depended the existence of all things and that he authorized the divine grace and warmth by which children were begotten in the wombs of their mothers." In the scene that represents Tlazoltéotl as a woman giving birth, we see footprints over the head of this earth goddess, the footprints of the child descending from the thirteenth heaven in order to enter into his mother's womb (Fig. 5). Ometecuhtli ("Two Lord") must be considered the origin and primordial source of all individual being. His wife is Omecíhuatl ("Two Lady"). Fundamentally, these two deities are one, embracing the opposing principles of the masculine and the feminine and, in general, incarnating the governing dualism of the whole ancient Mexican universe. Ometecuhtli lives in Omeyocan, "the two place." "It is seen that the word contains a mystical and transcendental significance" (Walter Lehmann).

According to ancient Mexico's representation of the world, only one thing is eternal: the revolution of the heavenly bodies in their orbits, silent, and distant from all human events and desires. Or, expressed more concretely, the cyclical recurrence of phenomena, the unchanging rhythm of natural events: day and night, sunrise and sunset, the dry season and the rainy season.

---

and Quetzalcóatl, god of the morning star and of the rising sun. Preuss sees in it an *Analogiezauber* (magic practice based on analogies).

FIG. 5. Tlazoltéotl giving birth to the maize god. *Borbonicus Codex*, 13

"Therefore, to discover what those rhythms were and follow their complicated but regular beat would, in Aztec philosophy, ensure the safe survival of the community. . . . Thus rhythm and form become an essential part of worship and found their outlet in ritual and religion, art, philosophy, and science" (George C. Vaillant, *The Aztecs of Mexico*).

The cycle of the seasons, i.e., the constant renewal of the procreative force of the earth, its ability to nourish men and through men the gods, is determined by the stars, as is likewise determined the life of each individual. Man does not shape his own life; it is formed by those sacred forces. The day of birth is a decisive factor in the infant's destiny. There are lucky and unlucky men; the former "were born under a good star." Those born on the day of the "serpent's head" are destined to be fine workers, good farmers, strong warriors, fortunate merchants, etc. Those born on a "serpent" day will be poor, homeless beggars who will live as naked as the serpent. Sahagún tells us that those born under the sign of the fire god, thought to be especially propitious, were considered

FIG. 6. Quetzalcóatl and the worm. Representation of Heaven
and Earth. *Tonalámatl of the Aubin Collection,* 13

foresighted and cautious; they accumulated fortunes for
their descendants; they were countrymen, hard-working
tillers of the soil, who knew how to turn everything to
advantage.

For people of Western civilization, who think scientifically, or, let us say, who believe in scientific thought, the
miraculous is the unexpected, the unforeseen, and the
unforeseeable. To be able to establish the regularity of a
natural phenomenon and to calculate it in advance is
scientific knowledge. Anything that our science is unable

to solve is disturbing and mysterious. But for the pre-scientific man (interpreting the word "scientific" in the sense that we use it today) these things have an opposite meaning. Defenseless, he confronts a nature that, with its passion for destruction, its unforeseeability and its lack of order, he must find chaotic. In its workings, on which depend his well-being and oftentimes his life, he sees neither meaning nor law, but chance and capriciousness. And then above this chaos he discovers the world of heavenly bodies where chance does not rule, but, mysteriously and inconceivably, an eternal order established since time immemorial in such form that it is possible to foresee and foretell its phenomena even far into the future. For those men who live in the midst of happenstance, that which is not hazard—the order, the rhythm, the cyclic-periodic recurrence of the same phenomenon—is the "miracle," exciting and exalting his imagination. It is a revelation of the divine, in which is manifested the true, supreme meaning of every cosmic happening. The calendar established by "the ancients" is the interpretation of that order, that rhythm. "Mathematics is religion," said Novalis. The observation of the stars, their appearance and disappearance, regularity and aberrations—this is the basis of all knowledge of life, of all thought, particularly all religious thought. Nothing else is important.

The Mexican pantheon is peopled by innumerable deities. According to López de Gómara (*Historia general de las Indias,* 1552), it was said that they "reached two thousand in number." At first glance this appears to be an impenetrable virgin forest through which one will never find his way, but in reality it is not only a very clear and logical system but, as we shall see, one of strict geometric structure.

We must distinguish between the so-called creator gods who made and maintain the universe and the countless gods who personify the forces of nature and to whom the people turned for help with the difficulties of daily life and for special purposes: for planting and harvesting, when rain was needed, and when it rained to excess. The pantheon created by their fantasy was peopled by very different spirits, who nevertheless were blended and mixed, were superposed and compenetrated, and who formed, on the basis of relations and affinities, certain distinct groups of divinities. They venerated the divinities of the earth and of death, the gods of rain, vegetation, fertility, the goddess of water and of salt, the four hundred gods of pulque—one for each type of drunkenness—and many, many more. One particular deity for every physical and metaphysical phenomenon, for all the events of life, for all human activities.

It is not possible to compare those Mexican gods, for example, with the agrarian divinities of the Romans, each of whom presided over a definite phase of agriculture. Ernst Cassirer (*An Essay on Man*) says of these latter: "They are not a product of religious imagination or inspiration; they are conceived as the rulers of particular activities. They are, so to speak, administrative gods who have shared among themselves the different provinces of human life. They have no definite personality; but they are clearly distinguished by their office, and upon this office their religious dignity depends." Cassirer believes that the typical aspects of the Roman spirit can be seen in this system, the robust, energetic mentality of a people skilled in the organization and co-ordination of all their forces. The gods of Mexico, on the other hand, are the creations of magic thinking that attributes everything that takes place to the work of spirits, divine beings on whose help or opposition all depends fatally.

The primordial god, Ometéotl, Ometecuhtli, Tloque Nahuaque, is the supreme principle who begot all: the world, the gods, and men. (One of his aspects is the fire god,[2] "he for whom all live," the ancient spirit, who ex-

[2] Xiuhtecuhtli, the fire god, "the old lord," is represented as ancient in all Mesoamerican cultures. According to Plancarte (*Prehistoria de México*), the Otomís and the Chichimecs, the two tribes whose existence in the Valley of Mexico can be proved from the earliest ages, had only this one god, "the father," as they called him. Sahagún says that fire and heaven were the father, and the earth, which is fertilized by the sun's rays or "arrows," the mother. Tezcatlipoca, Quetzalcóatl, Xipe Tótec, and Huitzilopochtli ruled over the four cardinal points;

FIG. 7. The five regions of the Universe. *Fejérváry-Mayer Codex*, 1

isted in the dawn even before the birth of the sun.) Tloque Nahuaque Ometecuhtli lives in the highest of the thirteen heavens and also in the center of the three worlds: heaven, earth, and the lower world. He represents the vital principle, corresponding more or less to the "divine breath" of religions with which we are familiar. He remains in the background during the different stages of creation. It is stated in *Historia de los mexicanos por sus*

---

the fifth region of the world (the center, up and down) belonged to the fire god, the "god of things close by," who lived in the navel of the earth just as the hearth is found in the center of the home.

*pinturas* that the creation is the work of Quetzalcóatl and Tezcatlipoca.

Ometecuhtli and his wife Omecíhuatl—philosophico-theological concepts—are the sustainers of the universe. Just as they did not intervene in the creation, neither do they intervene directly in human happenings as do, in contrast, the other spirits, like the gods of the sun, wind, and rain. Pedro de Ríos, interpreter of the Vaticanus A Codex, observes in his notes that not one temple was erected in honor of Ometecuhtli, nor were sacrifices offered to him, because of the belief that the god did not want them.

In Mictlan, the lower world, live the gods of death, similarly grouped around four principal deities.

Ometecuhtli and Omecíhuatl had four sons, the creator gods: the powerful black Tezcatlipoca; Quetzalcóatl, the priest god and wind god; Xipe Tótec, also called the Red Tezcatlipoca, god of sowing, to whom men owe sustenance; and Huitzilopochtli, god of the sun and of war. In the beginning it was they who determined human events. Sacrifices had to be offered to them, for on them depended the well-being of the community.

The creator gods not only characterize the four points of the compass, but they symbolize colors as well: Tezcatlipoca, "the most evil," lives in the North and his color is black; Huitzilopochtli, whose color is blue, is the god of the South; Xipe Tótec, the red god, represents the East; and Quetzalcóatl, white, dwells in the West. The colors of the serpents on the four sides of the Tenayuca Pyramid corresponded to those of the points of the compass. "One of the fundamental concepts of the Aztec religion was the grouping of all beings according to the four cardinal points of the compass and the central direction, or up and down. . . . Not only were colors and gods grouped in this manner. Also animals, trees, days, and man, according to the day on which they were born, belonged to one of the four regions of the world" (Caso).

As a result of these conceptions, the universe is constructed geographically according to the four points of the compass, and geometrically in the horizontal and vertical sense. In the center is the earth, believed to be a flat surface; beneath it, the lower world; and above it, the heavens, or, thirteen heavens, stepped like the bodies of the pyramids—the "thirteen mantles of clouds," in Maya phraseology. A system that might be graphically described as three circles, one above the other. Each of the four cardinal points is the dwelling place of a deity and the center or axis of the three circles, so to speak, is the abode of Tloque Nahuaque, making thirteen gods in all, five of whom belong to the earth circle.

The number "four" is the magic, sacred, fundamental, and cosmic number. "To the Mexican, the number 'four' was the number in which things were fulfilled completely and in many ways" (Seler). There are four destructions of the world, four regions of the sky, of the earth, and of the lower world. Four corners of heaven and of earth, four roads toward the center of the earth, each a different color (*Libro de los Libros de Chilam Balam*). Four sections of the court for the ball game, four gods who raise the sky when it has fallen to earth, and four gods who hold up the heavens. Quetzalcóatl remains four days in the lower world. At the end of four years the souls of dead warriors are transformed into hummingbirds; the trip of the dead to Mictlan lasts four years. There are four kinds of maize: black, yellow, red, and white. There are four kinds of water that the Tlaloques, the helpers of the rain god, send down to earth: the first is good for sowing and for grain, the second withers the plants, the third freezes them, and the fourth dries them (*Historia de los mexicanos por sus pinturas*). According to the *Libro de Chilam Balam de Chumayel*, the Maya had thirteen gods of the "katunes" (the katún was one of their periods of time: 20 × 360 days = 7200 days, or approximately twenty years). The supreme god was Itzamná. The four Paualtin held up the earth, like atlantes, and the four Bacab, the sky. In the four corners of the sky lived the Chac, gods of wind and rain. The axis of the world formed the trunk of a gigantic tree, Yaxché, whose branches extended in the four directions and whose top formed the canopy of heaven. In another

Maya version, the sky assumed the shape of a turtle's shell.

In order to understand this cosmogonic system with its very well-planned theological structure, it is of some help to consider the large number of saints of the Catholic Church to whom the believer turns in special situations, while the concept of God is limited exclusively to the Trinity. (Without a doubt, that multiplicity of saints helped convert the natives to Catholicism and induced them to embrace it with fervent devotion.)

Alfonso Caso says that "there was among the uneducated classes a tendency to exaggerate polytheism." It appears, on the other hand, that the thinkers and the people of increased spirituality gradually drew away from this polytheism that gave the masses an opportunity to demonstrate their religiosity in feasts, sacrificial ceremonies, dances, in the mortifications to which they submitted, etc. The most impressive and at the same time best-known example of this new form of religion is Netzahualcóyotl, "the hungry coyote" (1431–72), the Chichimec prince of Texcoco and a man of refined culture.

Netzahualcóyotl was certainly an exceptional figure, a sort of Mexican Solomon, a poet who wrote hymns, a wise formulator and interpreter of the law, whose counsel in difficult questions was sought by other sovereigns, including the powerful king of the Aztecs (Alfonso Toro, *Historia de la Suprema Corte de la Nación*), a scholar with a great knowledge of astronomy, and the founder of an academy of music that was actually an academy of arts and sciences. The great public buildings that he built in Texcoco and Texcotzingo were destroyed in 1539 by order of Zumárraga, the first archbishop of Mexico. A religious philosopher, preoccupied with changing the existing theological speculation, he was so advanced in his philosophical concepts that he erected a temple to the "invisible god." It was a ten-zone pyramid with a black roof decorated on the exterior with stars and incrusted with stones inside. No images were allowed there, nor any bloody sacrifices, the only offerings permitted being the perfume of flowers and the fragrant smoke of copal. On the other hand, Netzahualcóyotl did not prevent the people from practicing human sacrifice according to the traditional rites. There is no doubt that this sovereign and the "select minority" who were close to him had arrived at monotheism. No less interesting is that he was not attacked by being branded a heretic and a seducer of the public, as was the Egyptian king, Amenhotep.

In his description of the presents sent by Montezuma to Cortes, Sahagún mentions the "suit that was worthy of him," although actually this consisted of the garments of four different gods. Seler (*Das Tonalamatl der Aubin'-schen Sammlung*) infers from this that at least in the cultured and governing circles the multiple gods of the Mesoamericans were particular manifestations or different aspects of only one god. Pedro de Ríos, attempting to explain why no sacrifices were offered to Ometecuhtli, arrives at a similar conclusion. Ometecuhtli was the only *god*, while all the others were no more than men or demons.

Ernst Cassirer (*An Essay on Man*) states that in the evolution of human culture it is impossible to establish the point where magic ends and religion begins. Religion is imbued in each of its phases with mythical ideas, and myth, even in its most primitive form, anticipates religious ideals. Cassirer rejects the fairly arbitrary supposition of Sir James George Frazer (*The Golden Bough*) that the failure and overthrow of magic smoothed the road toward religion. If further refutation of Frazer's hypothesis were needed, the religion of ancient Mexico would provide it. Without any doubt, those people succeeded in creating a true religious system and in raising it to a high level of perfection. But this system rested on magic conceptions, which formed its pith and essence, magic based not on the personal magic force of the individual, but an impersonal magic converted into religious ritual. That religion impregnated with magic touched every phase of material and spiritual life in a unity so closely knit, an order so systematic and built with such perfection, that there was room for little deviation. It was the work of priests, of philosophico-religious thinkers who with admirable strictness dominated and knew how to regulate the religious thinking of the community.

The religion of the ancient Mexicans is distinguished from monotheistic religions not only by its polytheism, but also by its faith in the forces of magic and the belief that it is possible to influence those forces by means of magic conjuration. From this arises a markedly different relationship with God, with the universe, and with nature, as well as a very different attitude of man in the presence of the suprasensible and the suprareal.

In monotheistic religions, God is the incarnation of an ethical ideal. God is just. The concepts of good and evil come into play, for not only are good actions decisive, being commanded by God and pleasing to Him, but perhaps even more important is the intention that motivates them. Sin is an infraction of divine mandates, and the worst and most reprobate sin is to deny God. Apostasy does not exist in the magic religion of ancient Mexico. It is inconceivable, since the deity will act whether or not the individual believes in him. It is a natural force that is operating, which can be conjured, turned aside, or propitiated by magic. The working of the divinity does not have an ethical character, nor do ethical concepts determine it, just as magic conjuration is not based on ethical conduct but is the exercise of a certain ritual to which is attributed the power of influencing, in the desired manner, the acts of the deity. If the virtue of a religious man rests in his conformance to the Will of God (and, further, in confidence in divine justice), the man of magic convictions does not lack this conformity— everything that happens is destiny, unavoidable fatality, which he accepts with resignation—but at the same time there exists in him a desire to confront this destiny and to resist misfortune with the weapon that he believes he possesses: magic conjuration. This is his defense, and it is even more—it is action, an offensive against the hidden forces that pursue or that might pursue him. Man dares to fight the deity and its malevolence, i.e., its will. From the point of view of monotheistic religions, this is not only superstition but presumption, impiety, rebellion against God. Since according to magic thinking the acting of the deity is determined not by ethical norms but mechanically, as the effect of an inherent demoniacal force subject to no law but that of its own nature, neutralization of this demoniacal force through the opposing force that is conjuration cannot be considered sin. In the religious conception of the people of ancient Mexico is perceived a widespread interpenetration of these two tendencies: conformity to the will of the gods, subjection to their supernatural powers, and at the same time the belief that by means of magic one should and could channel this power in terms of human necessities and desires. "In the first place, therefore, ritual acts are applications of magic, efficient in themselves and intended on one hand to intensify man's own force of magic in the performance of ceremonies (fasts, chastity, consumption of certain foods having magic power); and on the other hand to influence the cosmic forces and the incarnations of these forces: the demons and gods whose power is maintained and strengthened by means of the sacrifices. In the second place, the ritual acts are considered as a means of devotion to the gods, who are thereby disposed to help man. But even in this second case, the help is independent of divine will because the gods themselves are only forces of nature . . . and are limited in their actions. Only the creator gods and a few tribal deities rise above this limitation" (K. Th. Preuss: *Mexikanische Religion*).

In monotheistic religions God is a promise, a goal, a finality; it is man's duty to try to approach Him. Man, subject to error, by his very nature a sinner, is constantly in search of God. St. Thomas and St. Teresa are two examples of the restlessness of the soul that desires to attain God. But compliance with the Will of God bestows on the soul an inner security and a hopeful deliverance of itself to its Creator. Daniel walked unharmed from the lions' den, therefore, because nothing could happen to him. Without God's willing it, not a hair can fall from the head. The man of magic thinking lacks this inner security. Placed in a hostile world against which he must protect himself with insufficient forces, he sees himself everywhere surrounded by dangers: the serpent that treacherously attacks him, the boulder that crushes him, the lightning that strikes him, the drought that destroys his crop and, in consequence, the hunger and the danger of dying from starvation. It is of vital importance to him to know the hidden forces inherent in things. Their exterior appearance is of no importance to him. He is not concerned with this, just as a geologist in search of oil or magnesium deposits is not concerned with the appearance, beauty, and charm of a landscape. To defend himself against the supernatural powers he has only one defense, the spiritual weapon of magic. He cannot place confidence in the gods, but he gains confidence in himself through the possibility of magic conjuration, the undertaking that pits his own forces against those of the spirits, of the divine beings. "Here he no longer feels himself at the mercy of natural or supernatural forces. He begins to play his own part, he becomes an actor in the spectacle of nature. Every magical practice is based upon the conviction that natural effects to a large degree depend on human deeds" (Cassirer, *op. cit.*). Without this intervention, without the magic influence that emanates from himself, he cannot believe that a grain of maize could germinate, grow, and bear fruit. Technical methods to increase crops through systematic husbandry are almost undeveloped, for it is not sufficient to plant the seed—it must also be fertilized. This is the meaning and the purpose of the feast of Ochpanitzli, "Sweeping of the Road," celebrated in the eleventh month of the year: to assure, by means of the symbolic fertilization of the maize seed, that the new crop will be a good one. It is then a feast consecrated to the harvest. The patron of this feast is therefore Tlazoltéotl, goddess of the earth and also of sexual love. At midnight the virgin chosen to be sacrificed in the goddess' honor is carried to the temple on the shoulders of a priest, "as the bride is brought to the house of the bridegroom." As shown on Plate 30 of the Borbonicus Codex and on Plate 33 of the Aubin Collection, the goddess, accompanied by her Huastecs (the Huastecs were

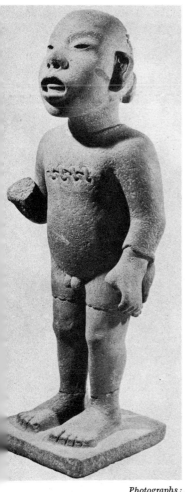

Photographs: Irmgard Groth-Kimball, Mexico City.

PLATE 1. Xipe Tótec, dressed in the skin of a sacrificial victim. Stone. Aztec. Private collection.

PLATE 2. Xipe Tótec, same as Plate 1, seen from the back.

PLATE 3. Xipe Tótec. Ceramic (detail). Teotihuacán. Teotihuacán Museum.

PLATE 4. Dancers. Stone relief. Monte Albán.

PLATE 5. Dancers. Stone relief. Monte Albán.

*Photograph: Walter Steinkopf, Berlin.*

PLATE 6. Tláloc. Stone. Aztec. Völkerkundemuseum, Berlin.

PLATE 7. Pyramid Quetzalcóatl. Teotihuacán.

PLATE 8. Pyramid Quetzalcóatl. Tula. Toltec.

PLATE 9. Jaguar and eagle. Pyramid Quetzalcóatl. Tula.

PLATE 10. Tajín, Vera Cruz.

*Photograph: Ruth Deutsch de Lechuga, Mexico City.*

*Photograph: Irmgard Groth-Kimball, Mexico City.*

PLATE 11. Parrot's head. Stone. Marker for the ball game from Xochicalco. National Museum of Anthropology, Mexico City.

PLATE 12. Head of an eagle warrior. Stone. Aztec. National Museum of Anthropology, Mexico City.

PLATE 13. Bottom, interior of a vessel for hearts with the sign Ollin. Stone. Aztec. Naturhistorischen Museum, Vienna.

Photograph: *National Institute of Anthropology and History, Mexico City.*
PLATE 14. Cuicuilco. Pyramid. Preclassic.

Photograph: Compañía Mexicana Aerofoto, S.A. Mexico City.

PLATE 15. Pyramid of the Sun. Teotihuacán.

*Photograph: Ernest Rathenau, New York City.*

PLATE 16. Frieze of the plumed serpent. Xochicalco.

*Photograph: Ernest Rathenau, New York City.*

PLATE 17. Frieze of the plumed serpent (detail). Xochicalco.

Photograph: *Ernest Rathenau, New York City.*

PLATE 18. Frieze of the plumed serpent (detail). Xochicalco.

*Photograph: National Institute of Anthropology and History, Mexico City.*

PLATE 19. Pyramid of Quetzalcóatl. Calixtlahuaca.

PLATE 20. Structure of the Pyramid of Quetzalcóatl. Teotihuacán.

Photograph: Albrecht Victor Blum.

PLATE 21. Pyramid. Aztec. Tepezteco.

Photograph: Ernest Rathenau, New York City.

PLATE 22. Pyramid. Aztec. Teopanzalco.

PLATE 23. Pyramid with belt of serpents. Tenayuca.     *Photograph: Ernest Rathenau, New York City.*

*Photograph: Ernest Rathenau, New York City.*

PLATE 24. Serpent's head. Tenayuca.

PLATE 25. Mask. Stone. Teotihuacán. Diego Rivera Collection, Mexico City.

*Photograph: from the museum.*
PLATE 26. Dog with mask. Ceramic. Colima. National Museum of Anthropology, Mexico City.

*Photograph: Ferdinand Anton, Munich.*
PLATE 27. Mask. Stone. Mezcala. Kurt Stavenhagen Collection, Mexico City.

PLATE 28. Mask of Xiuhtecuhtli. Mosaic. Aztec. Ethnographic Museum, Rome.

*Photograph: National Museum of Anthropology, Mexico City.*
PLATE 29. Mask. Mosaic. Aztec. British Museum, London.

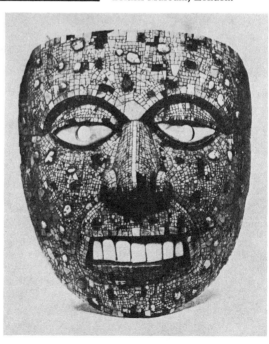

considered highly immoral and of great sexual potency),
runs to the temple of Huitzilopochtli pursued by the warriors who challenge her to combat. In the temple she lies
on her back at the feet of the god, and turning to face him,
opens her arms and legs (Sahagún). The child who is
born is the young god of maize. The finale of the feast
takes place when a captive, tied to a board with his arms
and legs extended, is shot to death with arrows. This
ceremony has the same symbolic significance: copulation,
fecundation. All fires are extinguished at the end of the
fifty-two-year cycle and at midnight, in a ceremony of
great solemnity celebrated in the temple, the priests kindle
the new fire with twigs, on the chest of a prisoner. This
is not only a matter of lighting the new fire, the life-giving
element of the community; no less transcendental is the
fact that it is man who succeeds in lighting the fire, that
it is man's magic force that ensures his existence for another such period. In this sense and only in this sense
magic is also science. The goal of natural sciences too is
to place the forces of nature at the service of human
necessity. Only the method is different: science makes
use of rational investigation, magic of mythico-poetic conceptions.

The man of magic thinking lives in the universe as in
a closed entity. Every object, man, animal, plant, stone,
and star is possessed by and ruled by hidden forces, by
spirits, demons, and gods. What characterizes phenomena
and gives them their existence is not matter, but the spirits
inherent in matter. These spirits are in no way a property
of matter as, for instance, the radioactivity of certain substances is a property of those substances. They cannot be
perceived by the senses for they are as minute as an atom.
They can abandon any object they have chosen to inhabit
and transport themselves to another. Also, they can be
carried off or exorcised. They are representations. But
since the man of magic thinking considered these representations as more real than anything perceived by his
senses, these hidden forces were reality to him.

Therefore, there is no division into a sensible and a
suprasensible world, into organic and inorganic nature.

The occult powers are not only incorporeal, but also above the limitations of time and space. Past, present, and future are fused into one unity. The theological distinction between beings with a soul and beings without a soul is not conceivable, since the spirits live in and act through everything that exists. Nor does man occupy a privileged place in this cosmic communion. He is one part of nature, worth neither more nor less than any other creature. He is not considered the peak of creation, he does not believe that he is destined to figure in the foreground and dominate all other beings. The Bible says: "Be fruitful, and multiply, and replenish the earth and subdue it: and have dominion over the fish of the sea, and over the fowl of the air, and over every living thing that moveth upon the earth" (Genesis 1:28). The man of magic thinking knows that he and everything else is dominated by the spirits, which cannot be classified as superior or inferior spirits according to the places where they are found. In the *Popol Vuh,* the book of Quiché-Maya legends, in whose text, edited after the Conquest, are gathered—in all probability unconsciously—various strange ideas as much Christian as Toltec, the fact that animals do not speak in the language of man is explained as follows: "It was said [by the gods] to the deer, the birds, jaguars, and serpents: *Speak, then, our names, praise us, your mother, your father. . . . Speak, invoke us, adore us,* they were told. But they could not make them speak like men; they only hissed and screamed and cackled. . . . For this reason they were sacrificed, and the animals which were on earth were condemned to be killed and eaten." This could be a theological justification of the fact that animals serve as food for man. Myth does not recognize such condemnation of animals. The gods transform themselves into animals and appear in animal guise: Tezcatlipoca as a jaguar, Huitzilopochtli as a hummingbird, Xólotl, "who guides the dead to hell," the "animal of lightning," as a dog, the gods of pulque as rabbits. There are animals such as the serpent who are adored as gods, although naturally a distinction is made between the animal itself and the spirit living in it.

Likewise, with the exception of Tloque Nahuaque or Ometecuhtli, enthroned far from the world in the thirteenth heaven, the gods are similar to man in that they too need food and are exposed to the dangers of age and debilitation. They must fight, they are defeated, annihilated, die, and are resurrected.

Another characteristic of this religious system, compared with monotheistic religions, is the idea of death and the beyond, based on that conception of the universe.

Biblical Judaism does not embody the idea of life after death. Man continues to live in his male progeny, which explains the direst of all divine threats: "I will extinguish thy name," and, "For I the Lord thy God am a jealous God, visiting the iniquity of the fathers upon the children unto the third and fourth generation of them that hate me" (Exodus 20:5): a threat that annihilates not only the sinner but also his descendants after him. This explains the command that if a man die without sons, his brother marries the widow so that the *Schem*, the name of the deceased, will not be extinguished. Living after death through one's descendants is the idea of Judaism. "The dead praise not the Lord, neither any that go down into silence" (Psalm 115:17).

Paradise and hell are the concepts through which Christianity won souls. This conception of a paradisiacal beyond, in which the pious and the just will enjoy a second existence of inconceivable joy, was a promise of captivating seduction. Future life was promised as a compensation —we are almost tempted to say, as a social compensation —especially to those who were excluded from earthly pleasures and riches, to the disinherited masses, the proletariat, the slaves, the poor, the weak, and the sick; while the impious and the powerful, those favored here on earth who "enjoyed life" without thinking about salvation, were condemned to the eternal pains of hell. "For it is easier for a camel to go through a needle's eye, than for a rich man to enter into the kingdom of God" (Luke 18:25). Seen in the perspective of those times, this is the revolutionary element inherent in Christianity. The social order of this world cannot be changed, but this world counts for nothing. In the minds of the rich and the powerful, this was an attempt against the existing order within which they occupied so privileged a position. The comfortable ruling class suddenly had an attack of conscience. If what this new sect claimed were true, was not all that they possessed and enjoyed worthless? Were they not paying too highly for earthly possessions and power if because of them they lost the blessings of the future? This explains the bitter and bloody persecutions of the first era of Christianity. The privileged classes did not wish to be disturbed or hindered in the enjoyment of their privileges by a faith that condemned them to the torments of purgatory and hell.

A lofty ethical ideal governs these conceptions: to win afterlife through one's descendants or resurrection in a paradise after death in exchange for a just, devout, and holy life.

To the people of ancient Mexico, death is only another state of being, only a transformation, a continuation of existence under different conditions and with different hypotheses, a "duplicate of life," as Swedenborg called the future life. Just as birth is important for the course that life will take, so also "where a man's soul went after death was not determined by his conduct in this life . . . but rather by the manner of his death and his occupation in life" (Caso). There existed, so to speak, a "death according to one's class."

The superior and privileged class of souls consists of the warriors who died in combat or on the sacrificial stone. They joined Huitzilopochtli's following, for they had fought for him in life and continue fighting for him after death, except that the battle takes place in another sphere, the "Eastern Paradise" situated in the North.

To this category of privileged dead belong also the women who die in childbirth, who go to the "Western Paradise" and participate as midwives in the birth of the sun each morning. This homage to woman is a manifestation of the highest respect for motherhood.

Those who died a natural death have to travel to Mictlan, the realm of the god of death. Mictlan is not an inferno or a place of punishment, but neither is it a place of joy. The journey, which lasts four years and during which one must undergo "a series of magical trials" (Caso), is most fatiguing. The dead person, guided by a yellowish dog, must cross nine great rivers and nine deserts. He must traverse a place where a wind blows "that cuts as though it bore blades of obsidian" and he has to endure still other tribulations.

The third place is Tlalocan, the "Earthly Paradise" of Tláloc. There the dead find themselves in a state of happiness, as depicted in the fresco discovered at Teotihuacán. They amuse themselves by playing ball, they hunt butterflies, enjoy the abundant fruit, swim and bathe in the river. Below and to the right, a man is weeping copiously. Caso explains that this is a new arrival and that he is still crying over the misery and pain he suffered on earth and from which he has but lately escaped. The "Earthly Paradise" was reserved solely for those under the protection of Tláloc: those who died of an incurable disease, such as leprosy, who in this world had to suffer more than others and whose lives had been nothing but affliction, grief, and torment. Also admitted here were those killed by lightning. Tláloc took pity on these beings mistreated by life and spared them the journey to Mictlan, and—once again I am tempted to speak of a social compensation—he gathered them into his paradise. Therefore, it is not a reward for virtue, devotion, and a life pleasing to God as in the Christian paradise, but a compensation for excessive suffering.

The Borgia Codex, describing the five regions of the world, shows, after the destructive forces, the creative forces symbolized by the pair of gods, shown in the act of copulation, who dominate each region. In the South, the place of death, the god and goddess of death are seen thus (Plate 52 of the Borgia Codex). Death in the act of giving life! A vision inconceivable to our minds and alien also to the romantic conception that the baroque age formulated of death and that it expressed in its art and literature, but perfectly natural for a world that sees death as only another form of life.

This cosmic unity also determines the artistic conception. The purpose of pre-Cortesian art is not and cannot be the representation and embodiment of the optic phenomenon. In that artistic world, the authentic and genuine reality that must be represented is what acts as the vital element within things, the hidden mythico-magic forces. To give them plastic expression and to convert into Form the spirits that animate things, the essence and meaning of things, to shape the significance rather than the visual aspect—this is the aim of that artistic creating and this is where all esthetic appreciation must start. It is thought expressed in symbolic images, in contrast to realistic-objective thought (Westheim, *Ideas fundamentales del arte prehispánico en México*, Chapter "Realismo Mítico").

If the art is a reflection and condensation of the magico-mythical representations, then sacrifice, and particularly human sacrifice (like the ritual dance), is a translation of these representations into action, a collective mobilization of magic conscience and magic energy for the purpose of influencing the gods. Sacrifice was not originally an ethico-religious duty but only became so in the course of evolution. In offering to the gods the heart and blood of man, magic substances par excellence, the decisive motive was the preservation of their strength and power. Certainly there also existed the intention of propitiating them—because the religious idea was sufficiently developed for that —although not as yet in the general form of divine benevolence, but first and foremost to obtain from them certain benefits of vital importance: timely and abundant rain, germination of seeds, good harvests, protection from dangers, triumph in war. "Thus the Mexican sacrifices to the sun were magical rather than religious, being designed, not so much to please and propitiate him as physically to renew his energies of heat, light, and motion" (Frazer, *The Golden Bough*). Toward the end of the Aztec Empire, when it became more and more difficult to dominate the subjugated tribes, the fear that the tribal deity might lose his powers acquired the proportions of a psychosis. Multitudes of human beings were sacrificed to the gods on every imaginable occasion. The temples of Huitzilopochtli became slaughterhouses. The goal was sought by dint of quantity.

From the legends concerning the introduction of sacrifice, we infer that the only way to induce the gods to carry out certain actions indispensable for the collective good was to offer sacrifices to them. We are almost tempted to use the expression *"quid pro quo."*

The Teotihuacán legend describing the birth of the fifth (or current) sun and of the moon through the self-sacrifice of Nanahuatzin, the syphilitic god (another instance of one who suffered in this world), and of Tecciztécatl, the rich god, who became the moon god, relates that these recently created stars refused to perform their functions. Neither the sun nor the moon shone in the firmament. They demanded food. In other words, the gods went on strike, which lasted for four days until the other gods, assembled at Teotihuacán, decided to sacrifice themselves to the sun and the moon. And then the latter began to fill their cosmic roles. In order for the sun to shine, give heat, and fertilize the earth, it must be nourished with the blood and hearts of men.

In the *Popol Vuh, Las antiguas historias del Quiché,* human sacrifice is the *"quid pro quo"* for the gift of fire. The Quichés obtained the first fire from Tohil, their tribal deity, the thunder god, who was able to produce fire from his sandals. The other tribes lacked this element. When they begged for fire, Tohil declared: "Would they then agree to be united [to me]? Do they want me to embrace their hearts . . . ?" And when they brought a few men as tribute, the Quichés sacrificed them to their gods.

This might explain why no sacrifices were offered to Ometecuhtli, that most important god. As he in no way intervened in earthly affairs, it was not necessary to use magic conjuration with him. Nor were sacrifices offered to Mictlantecuhtli, the lord of the lower world, as it was obviously believed that he only received the dead, while the decision over life and death rested with Coatlicue, the feared earth goddess.

War, too, which plays such a predominant role in the imagination and the life of the peoples of ancient Mexico,

is of magic origin. The brave warrior's heart and blood
were the preferred food of the gods and possessed the
greatest magic efficacy. Sacrifice of a prisoner of war was
not punishment, defamation, or penalty as a "war crimi-
nal," but a distinction and a high honor, because by being
sacrificed he too was accepted into Huitzilopochtli's following and became a star, a god. (In this respect it seems
that there was not any nationalism that reserved such an
honor to members of their own people, as in the case of
the German warrior who is welcomed to Valhalla, quite
astounding in a world in which the concept of the tribal
deity was transcendental.) Tlalhuicate, a Tlaxcaltecan
warrior of very noble lineage, had the misfortune to fall
into the hands of the Aztecs during battle. Montezuma
wished to grant him his life and freedom, but, believing
this to be a dishonor, he begged to be sacrificed. This
was his right, his glory. In the codices, the victim is always
identified with the *chalchíhuitl* glyph, "precious stone,"
the most precious of all.

The fact that the captive was considered the most desired spoil, reserved for the gods, probably has its origin
in certain beliefs related to a primitive agrarian cult from
remotest times that fertilizing the fields with human blood
favors the development of the grain. Seler (*Das Tonalamatl
der Aubin'schen Sammlung*) thinks that "probably the
belief that fields should be fertilized with human blood
constituted here as elsewhere the principal motive for human sacrifice." Xipe Tótec, god of the planting of maize,
is one of the gods of war; he is frequently represented in
the codices with the emblems of the warrior. Speaking of
the earth goddess, Sahagún says that the gods decided
that from her (the earth) should come forth food. "That
at times she shouted at night, demanding human hearts,
and then would not be pacified until they were given to
her, and would not be fruitful until she was drowned with
human blood."

What is related in the *Anales de Cuauhtitlán* about the
introduction of the sacrifice by shooting a war captive with
arrows (a rite already mentioned in the description of the
feast of Ochpaniztli) gives clear evidence of this fact. "In

this year [Eight Rabbit] arrived the demons, the Ixcuiname, the devil women. . . . And in the place called Cuextécatl ichocayan [where the Huastec cries], there they gathered the prisoners they had captured in the Huasteca and informed them of their death, saying to them: 'We wish to go to Tollan, with you we will celebrate the feast. Because never until now have men [prisoners] been killed by arrows, we will be the first to do so, and we will kill you with arrows.'" On the other hand, in order to form a man, the gods resorted to maize, a product of the soil, "the substance which should enter into the flesh of man . . . this was his blood" (Popol Vuh).

War, therefore, is the origin of everything, wherein is expressed once again the basic principle of that order of the world: battle, destruction of all that exists, so that the new might come forth. "Before creating the sun, the gods introduced war. For this reason they created the stars and the moon, the men of the sky, who warred against each other" (Preuss). How otherwise would the sun have been able to shine? And Preuss adds: "In this way the sun had for food the hearts of those killed in war." The Teotihuacán legend states that it was necessary to create war so that the sun could continue on its way. This is why, among the Aztecs, Huitzilopochtli, the sun god, is also the war god, and Tezcatlipoca, god of the setting sun, is the warrior who brings the victims whose blood fertilizes the earth (Historia de los mexicanos por sus pinturas). This same work relates that when the four hundred cloud serpents had risen, the sun god gave them arrows (the arms of war) and commanded: "Bring food and drink to me with these." But they shot for pleasure, and when they had killed a jaguar they slept with their wives and drank too much pulque. Then the sun god sent for five other cloud serpents. A combat ensued, and for the first time the sun could eat (hearts) and drink (blood).

But the gods not only have to be fed—the sun, in order to rise; the earth goddess, to retain her fertility; the Tlaloques, not to parch the lands; and the maize god, so that there is no lack of food. Man also fears that the gods might grow old, might be overcome by the weakness of age and

lose the ability to perform their functions. . . . They must
be rejuvenated again and again. This is a terrible fear
crushing the heart, which might be termed an obsession
with youth or a complex against old age.

Eternal youth was attributed only to Tezcatlipoca, who
is pictured as an adolescent. He is "the eternally young
god, whose youth is renewed annually by kindling a fire
with twigs." But even he preserves his youth only because
each year in May when the sun passes through its zenith
an adolescent is sacrificed to him, the new Tezcatlipoca
who comes to substitute for the old, so that the god is born
again. Sahagún gives a detailed account of this ceremony.
The priests chose the most handsome of the youths, whom
everyone worshiped for a whole year as if he were Tezcatlipoca himself. He received special teaching. He had to
learn to walk with dignity, to greet people, to carry flowers
and incense burners gracefully, and to play the flute. An
entourage of eight youths accompanied him everywhere
and never left him. He also wore the dress of the god, the
headdress of white turkey feathers, little bells of gold on
his sandals, and his left leg was painted black to the thigh
(like that of Tezcatlipoca, who had only one foot). When
he appeared in public, the people prostrated themselves
before him and kissed the ground. Even the king paid
him divine honors, sending him precious garments and the
emblems of Tezcatlipoca. In the final month he was mar-
ried to four young girls who were given the names of the
fertility goddesses: the goddess of flowers, the goddess
of tender corn, "our lady above the waters," and the goddess of salt. When the year ended, he crossed the lake in
a royal canoe, carrying his flutes in his hands and accompanied by his wives. He landed near Ixtapalapa, where
the women left him. He climbed the steps of the small
pyramid, on each step breaking one of his flutes, the marks
of his greatness. At the summit, the priests seized him and
sacrificed him.

Xipe Tótec, the maize god, also had to be rejuvenated
in the spring before planting time. The victim was flayed
and during twenty days, i.e., one month, the priest wore
the victim's skin over his shoulders, and we see Xipe Tótec

represented in this way, covered with the skin (Plates 1 and 2). During the sacrificial ceremony women danced with their hair hanging loose, so that the maize would grow as high as their hair was long.

The skin of the victim draped over the shoulders symbolizes the new garment, the new verdure of the earth, the new sprouting of the maize in the spring. Frazer (*The Scapegoat*) believes that the skin signifies that the dead god immediately comes back to life. "If that was so," he writes, "we may infer with some degree of probability that the practice of killing a human representative of a deity has commonly, perhaps always, been considered merely as a means of perpetuating the divine energies in the fullness of youthful vigor, untainted by the weakness and frailty of age, from which they must have suffered if the deity had been allowed to die a natural death."

Rejuvenation of the gods. . . . The concept of the eternal disappears completely before that of the dynamics of birth and death, the creative power that determines and explains every cosmic occurrence. The gods are also subject to this development. Cosmic creation is not something that happened only once: it has to happen constantly, over and over again. Every day is a day of creation. The activity of the gods must not cease, nor must that of man. The blood myth is likewise rooted in this conception: there must be sacrifice of what is most precious—life—to ensure the continuation of the community and of the Universe.

## Collective Art

In the *Popol Vuh*, the book of the sacred traditions of the Quiché Maya Indians, we read:

"In heaven all was invisible and immobile. There existed nothing that was built. . . . Then came the word. . . . Then the Dominators, the Powers of Heaven, conferred about life and light, what they would do so that there would be light and dawn, who it would be who would provide food and sustenance. . . . *Thus let it be done! Let the emptiness be filled! Let the water recede and make a void, let the earth appear and become solid.* Thus they spoke."

Thus they created earth, mountains, plains, trees, deer, birds, reptiles. "Say our names aloud, praise us," they demanded. "But the creatures could not speak like men. . . . When the Constructors, the Builders, heard their impotent words, they said to each other: *"They could not say our names, the names of their Creators, their Shapers. It is not well. . . ."*

*"What shall we do to be invoked, in order to be remembered on earth?"* they asked themselves. And they decided to create man, so that he would adore them, call upon them, feed them.

First they created a man of mud, but it could not move its head, its sight was blurred, and its speech senseless. Therefore they destroyed their creation.

Then they made figures of wood. These multiplied, but ". . . they did not have souls nor minds, they did not remember their Creator, their Maker; they walked on all fours, aimlessly. . . . *Why do you not give us our nourishment? Why do you not use your reason? Why do you not think about your own existence?"* the Founders reproached them. "And their death was this: they were drowned. . . . Their descendants are the monkeys which now live in the forests."

Then they created a generation of giants who in turn had to be destroyed because they were too proud in the presence of their Creators.

Finally, out of maize and blood, they made men of flesh and bone. "They immediately saw all that was in the world . . . and then gave thanks to the Creator and the Founder. *We see the large and the small in the sky and on earth. We give you thanks for having created us, oh, Creator and Maker!"*

The thunder god, who gave fire to the Quichés, orders them: "First of all give thanks; do what is necessary to bleed your ears, prick your elbows, and make your sacrifices."

This is what might be termed the "social contract" of pre-Cortesian humanity. The gods create man so that he might adore, maintain, and nourish them, so that they might retain their power. Their *quid pro quo* is to exercise their functions, which is indispensable to the preservation of the world. "Creation was not a gracious gift to man from the gods, but in the nature of a contract carrying an obligation for man to worship the gods continually" (Alfonso Caso: *The Aztecs, People of the Sun*). The world and humanity can exist only if the gods are maintained, and that maintenance is the duty of man. It is his eternal obligation, the one task he must fulfill in the world, the end and meaning of his existence.

This is a collective task, beyond the forces of any one person, and only the community, in which are joined the forces of all individuals, is able to fulfill it. The well-being of the individual is not at stake, nor, as in Christianity, individual salvation. It is uniquely and exclusively a matter of the well-being of the community, without which the individual does not and cannot exist. The individual climbs to the sacrificial stone and offers his life, heart, and blood to the gods, not in order to participate in grace, but to ensure the continuity of the community and to forestall the dangers that threaten it: drought, poor harvests, and the disappearance of the sun. Individual life, happiness or unhappiness, are of no importance. What is necessary is that the community survive, and through the strength of the community, the Universe.

The sacrifice is a collective one. "Is it possible that we could cause our creator, our maker, to be hungry?" asks the *Historia tolteca chichimeca*. If human slaughter is offered to the sun god, the sacrifice is made for the good of all humanity.

The faith is a collective faith and a collective obligation. He who might wish to avoid this obligation—something unthought of—would not only be an impious, accursed sinner condemned to the pains of hell, but a noxious, asocial element placing the existence of the community in jeopardy.

Religion is not a metaphysical superstructure built on a profane civil life, because a private life not at the service of the gods does not exist, or at least does not count for anything. The Bible says that after original sin, God cursed the earth so that it would produce thorns and thistles and so that man would earn his bread by the sweat of his brow. Pre-Hispanic man did not consider labor, the cultivation of the soil, a punishment from God, but a religious duty and ritual act. Planting is a ritual act prepared for by specific ceremonies, sacrifices, burning of copal, fasts, sexual abstinence. One sheet of the Fejérváry-Mayer Codex devotes no less than four drawings to the agricultural ritual. Idols of the gods of maize, earth, rain, and so forth, were placed in the ground so that they would help the germination of the seed and the maturing of the fruit. The merchant went to the temple to consult the priest, who in turn consulted the calendar, before concluding an important piece of business or undertaking a journey. Often he had to postpone the business or the journey for a long time, until a day of good omen. War was waged so that food for the gods would not be lacking from the sacrificial stones. Joyce believes that the fall of the Aztec Empire can be attributed to this complete subjection of life to religious conceptions and especially to the legend of Quetzalcóatl, in which the god promised to return in a year *Ce Ácatl* (One Reed). Because the arrival of the Spaniards coincided with such a year, the Aztecs identified this with the return of Quetzalcóatl in accordance with his divine promise. "Indeed," Joyce says, "but for this legend it is more than doubtful whether the almost incredible exploit of Cortes would have been successful."

All science was a search for the divine, serving the community spiritually and opening to it extremely vast horizons. As an astonishing, unique phenomenon, J. E. Teeple ("Maya Astronomy," *Contributions to American Archaeology*, Vol. I, No. 2) notes that a civilization developed in America that did not have the lathe or other technical inventions, but in which mathematics had advanced to a degree not achieved by the primitive races of the rest of the world. On the other hand, he adds, the ancient cultures of the Old World did invent the lathe, but their progress in mathematical sciences was most tenuous. The knowledge possessed by the peoples of ancient Mexico in the field of medical science even today astounds many experts on the subject whose free judgment has not been curtailed by orthodox medicine, and even they have to apologize when they make use of certain facets of this knowledge. However, cures were not attributed to medical procedures but to magic, psychic powers. We can apply here what Lévy-Bruhl says about the medicine of primitive people: if the magician effects a cure, it is the spirit of the remedy that works on the spirit of the illness. Recovery is attained not through a physical process but a mystical one. The infirmity is interpreted psychically, as an abandonment of the body by the soul. In the pre-Columbian world, the natural sciences, technique, and technical progress were all unworthy of being studied for themselves. Its science was a science of the spirit, the spiritual was a knowledge of the divine, as it is in the imposing logical structure that St. Thomas formulated on the base of Christian doctrine. And religion constituted at the same time the basis of their social and political order. Since the early centuries of the Christian Era, almost everyone has lived under a theocratic regime. A passage of the Matritense Codex of the Real Academia de la Historia (Sahagún) in Madrid, which extols the "wise man," says of him: "His is the red and black paint, the codices are his work." Thus the "wise man" is, in the mentality of ancient Mexico, the priest. The codex is his book; by means of his interpretation of the Tonalámatl, he becomes a "guide," even in the sphere of human affairs.

Aztec agriculture was a collective agriculture. It can almost be called an agrarian communism. The towns were divided into "neighborhoods." In Tenochtitlan there were twenty of these neighborhoods, called *calpulli* ("large house"). The land was the property of the *calpulli* (except for some lands that were the property of the sovereign). A "council of elders" was charged with dividing the lands among families. César Garizurieta ("Aspecto histórico y económico del ejido," in the *Revista Jurídica*, 1939) calls the council "a kind of agrarian comity, which administered the *calpulli*. . . ." Each year this council of elders redivided the soil, in all probability taking into account the changes that had occurred in family circumstances. Distribution of the parcels of land was by lot, and in general, families continued as the proprietors of their own lands, passing them from father to son. Fields that remained uncultivated for two years were given to another family. Sale of land was prohibited. In résumé, Garizurieta says it was a matter of "an usufruct, with the obligation of planting and cultivating [the land]. It was one community, constituting a corporation with a certain moral personality for the defense of common interests." In the Aztec Empire, therefore, no one could die of starvation. Everyone was assured of a "bare subsistence level," of whatever was indispensable to sustain life, provided only that he tilled his parcel of land. If in the wake of poor crops or natural phenomena victuals were scarce, the hunger that followed was, in a manner of speaking, collective hunger.

This system remained in force among the Aztecs until conquests enriched the Empire with the land of subjugated tribes. Itzcóatl, the fourth Aztec king, of whom it is said in the Ramírez Codex that "he did only what

Tlacaélel [the great military chief] advised," decreed that these lands be conferred as rewards upon certain fortunate generals. The first to receive them was Tlacaélel, victor in the war with Azcapotzalco (1439) that marked the rise of the Aztec Empire. "They gave to him," writes Durán (*Historia de las Indias de Nueva España*), "all of these lands, and he was chosen over the others because the entire victory was attributed to him and to his ability." Previously, after the overthrow of Coyoacán and Xochimilco, Tlacaélel had received a considerable part of the spoils, while the other chiefs had to be satisfied with only a small portion of the conquered land (called *pilalli*). And since such eminent generals did not work their own lands, nor were they able to cultivate such immense areas, but required help, i.e., slaves, this was the birth of feudalism. Paul Kirchhoff ("Land Tenure in Ancient Mexico," *Revista Mexicana de Estudios Antropológicos,* Vol. 14, 1954) expresses it as follows: "With the formation of this new nobility, the place of the *calpullis* in the total socio-economic structure changed completely. . . . With this subordination of the representatives of the old order, based on kinship, to those representing the new one, based on property, society ceased to be tribal and had begun to take on a class character."

Not only was ownership of the land collective, but cultivation of the soil was, too. Joyce says that the Maya used a system of "co-operative labor in the preparation of the fields, for weeding and for sowing. . . ." "They followed the custom of forming groups of sixteen to twenty people to clear and plow each member's parcel of land in succession. The head of each family selected a part of the forest to cultivate, usually choosing a new location each year. . . ." (Thomas W. F. Gann and J. Eric S. Thompson: *The History of the Maya, from the Earliest Time to the Present Day.*) After clearing one section of land, the group went to that of another member, until all the lands were prepared.

House construction was also a group activity. When a man wished to build a house, he called on his friends and neighbors for assistance. All went to the forest, felled the

trees, deposited the trunks in the designated place, made
the roof of palm leaves or some other material. . . . Landa
notes that hunting and fishing were likewise collective enterprises.

After all of the above, it is scarcely necessary to state
that art was collective—a collective, magico-religious art.
The duties assigned to the architect, the sculptor, and the
painter were the construction of pyramids, temples or
other buildings destined for worship, the decoration of
these structures with paintings or reliefs, the fashioning of
statues of the gods, of sacrificial stones, incense burners,
masks for the cult of the gods and the dead, and other
objects necessary to religion, i.e., works of art intended for
the community. In all the works rescued by archeology
that express a higher spirituality, with the exception perhaps of the period generally called "preclassic," we must
seek the relationship with religion, and in nearly all cases
we will find it.

Much the same can be said of the decoration: of the
plastic decoration of the buildings and of the adornment
of persons and of the statues and statuettes of persons and
gods. It is not the invention of an artistic imagination, its
function is not embellishment. The noses of Chac, the rain
god, on Maya constructions (in the Puuc and Chenes
styles) testify that the building and its inhabitants are
under the deity's protection. On the relief friezes of the
so-called Pyramid of Quetzalcóatl in Teotihuacán are
found, within the curves of the plumed serpents that com-
pose the friezes, representations of ears of maize, shells,
and sea snails. They are fertility symbols; like the plumed
serpent, they characterize the pyramid as a sanctuary of
Quetzalcóatl and Tláloc, vegetation gods. Above the entrance to the temple of Huitzilopochtli in Tenochtitlan was
placed a panel, used by the Aztecs not to represent feats
in arms by which Huitzilopochtli caused his people to be
triumphant: as we see in a drawing by Durán, the large
surface was decorated with skulls (bas-reliefs painted
white over a red ground). These skulls, in a location so
important and sacred, were a symbolic glorification of the
warrior, who sacrificed his life to the great god and who,

as a reward, would become a member of the god's following. The relatively few figurative representations on the necklaces, breastplates, and rings from Tomb 7 of Monte Albán are all effigies of mythological beings: the corn god, the death god, the descending eagle, etc.

The dance was sacred, a ritual performed to venerate and divert the gods. There was no dancing in pairs or freedom of movement. It was a group dance that "consisted of a certain limited number of evolutions" (Guzmán), subject to a rhythm followed strictly by all the dancers. The dance was magic conjuration, part of the ritual, intended to stimulate a state of religious ecstasy in the dancers and in the spectators (Westheim, *Ideas fundamentales del arte prehispánico en México*, Chapter "La Expresión Escultórica").

The work of art is one of the media that the cult needs and uses. It is therefore a necessity—a social necessity of a community whose life is formed by faith in the gods, by the cult of the gods.

Our present-day civilization is based on the machine, without which modern man cannot exist. He cannot even conceive of a world without the machine: without automobiles, telephones, derricks, or screws; and should some superior power arise capable of eliminating at once all machines, we would find ourselves more forsaken than primitive man before the forces of nature. We would be in the same straits as someone in an oxygen tent who is choking because his supply of oxygen has been cut off. For pre-Hispanic man, a world without the gods would have been a world in which he could not breathe, in which he could not live.

The statue of the deity is the deity itself. Magic thinking identifies the image with the thing. The image seems more real than the thing itself because the image has been given form and shape, and the form is a manifestation of psychic energies. The man who believes in magic cannot conceive that interventions in human affairs, the object of his conjuration, can come from an invisible god. Without the god who has been given form, which he sees close at hand in his own community, he would feel "deserted by the hand of God." To whom would he offer sacrifices, if not to the statues of the gods?

Only once in the history of religion has a people—the Jews—been menaced by their leader: "Cursed be he who makes an image or likeness—an abomination to Jehovah." An astonishing order, a demand almost too severe—the Golden Calf—even for the profoundly believing Hebrew nation. This faith in the invisible god (adopted later by the Mohammedans), in the pure and absolute concept of the divine, presupposes a unique and singular moral and spiritual strength and imaginative power. It likewise presupposes that concept of an all-embracing God that Judaism developed on the base of monotheism. The polytheism of ancient Mexico created a pantheon that could not be a purely abstract concept or an incorporeal phenomenon, immaterial and timeless. Man needs the image of a god, a particular god and of each of the gods, in order to be able to adore and offer sacrifices to any one of them. It is the artist's task to create the image of the deity, not merely as an adornment of the temple or as a luxury, for this art is an applied, subordinate art at the service of an extra-artistic purpose: survival of the community.

This is what determines its form and makes its effect so profound. The image of the divinity is believed in. It is not found in the temple or in front of the temple as a decorative object to delight the eye in search of an esthetic emotion, or in search of the originality of the creative power and personal stamp of the artist. Its greatness, its meaning, and its value are not due to this, however heretical it may sound to the impassioned art lover, but to the intensity of the religious experience that the faithful bring to what the Bible calls "the craftsman's handiwork." Collective experience, collective emotion, of a religious community for whom the image becomes sublime, sacred, and worthy of adoration solely because it is transformed into an incarnation of the divine. The same can be stated of the religious art of every cult, of Giotto no less than Byzantine, Assyrian, or pre-Columbian art. The spiritual emotion that the work engenders in the spectator and which he in turn directs back to the work is what gives it such increased value over and above the purely artistic. It is what makes all great art and all genuinely religious art a collective art, and which the artist of our day will not be able to achieve so long as his production continues to be directed to an exclusive coterie of connoisseurs and intimates for whom the "esthetic emotion" represents an escape from the vulgarity of daily life.

We have little information about the practice of art in the pre-Columbian world, while the important sources provide detailed data about the decorative arts and the techniques of the different crafts. Production of the plastic arts was in the hands of the priests, as was true of literature, music, the dance, and the study of the sciences—mathematics, astronomy, interpretation of the calendar, and medicine. This was also the case in medieval Europe when monasteries such as Mount Athos, Reichenau, San Galo, etc., were art centers, and the monks were artists. In close collaboration with the political leaders, the priests drew up the plans for the ceremonial centers.

The execution of works of art in stone, clay, and wood was surrounded with mystery. The artists (to use a word with which we are familiar) remained isolated while they worked. According to Landa (*Relación de las cosas de Yucatán*), they were confined to huts built exclusively for this purpose, where no one was allowed to see them and where they underwent a peculiar ritual in which they burned copal, drew their own blood as an offering, fasted, and abstained from sexual intercourse. Like the other priests during services, they painted their faces with black paint "as a symbol of fast and abstinence." Any transgression of this ritual was considered a grave crime and a serious risk. While the work was in progress, writes Landa, the images of the gods were sprinkled with blood and incensed with copal. In the Maya month of Chen, the new idols were "blessed" (to borrow a term used by the Catholic Church) in the temple, after which they were handed over to their owners. In the statues of the deities there is a semicircular hole in the center of the chest for the gold or jade "heart" inserted during a solemn ceremony. Not

FIG. 8. Tláloc. *Vaticanus A Codex*

until the heart was in place did the "craftsman's handiwork" become an idol.

It is unnecessary to say that the form and content of the
works created under these circumstances were subjected
to rules no less categorical. Departure from what the cult
commanded and what was ritually traditional would have
been a sin. There was none of the "interesting artistic personality" that we find surrounded by an atmosphere of
romance since the times of Greek antiquity and the Renaissance. The identity of the creator vanished behind the
creation. Those artists were as anonymous as the priest,
who is not a person but a "servant of God," and the works
they created were symbols, not proofs of their personal
talent.

We do not know the name of a single artist of ancient
Mexico. We do not find reference to any designer who
was particularly distinguished or to any work that, like the
Zeus of Olympus, enjoyed an extraordinary esteem. The
artist was an agent of the community, individually unim-
portant.

As a member of the clergy, the community supported him together with the other priests. Consequently, there is not a single work that is "signed" by its maker. Furthermore, there exists scarcely anything that might be called an "artistic signature," that personal expression clearly recognizable in any artist's work, thanks to which it has been possible, in the field of European art, to attribute certain works to a particular master even though we know neither his name nor anything of his life, e.g., the Master of Flémalle, the Master of Moulins, Master of the *Housebook*, Master of the *Death of the Virgin*, and many others. Perhaps this is our fault to some extent, because investigation of the art of ancient Mexico is still in its infancy and we may yet achieve results in this field. But it may be assumed that a profound and penetrating study from the point of view of stylistic criticism would not give us any further information, precisely because the representative intention was not directed toward a personal or original artistic signature. Jacob Burckhardt imagined a "history of art without names." The whole history of pre-Columbian art is a history of art without names.

It also seems that what we term "evolution" was achieved through "strata," to use an archeological term, rather than from person to person (Mantegna>Raphael>Titian), or from work to work (Michelangelo>Rembrandt). We have been able to determine the dates of the construction of many Maya steles and other monuments after deciphering their inscriptions, but with these exceptions it has been necessary to turn to ceramics, where chronological classification is possible through the geological strata in which they are found as well as certain technical or formal details, in order to gain some idea, even though an inexact one, of the course of this evolution. The evolution was not a conscious one. It should more correctly be called a determined will to persevere.

Attachment to traditional form is an inherent feature of all monumental religious art. Whenever spiritual emotion loses its identity, and esthetic experience substitutes for it, as in the Classic Maya, a new and interesting formal configuration arises as one of the ends of artistic creation. God

is not new or interesting; God is old and eternal. To give
plastic expression to this old, traditional, and sacred representation of the divine is the mission of art. If our desire
for an individual artistic style, for an individual personality
and mode of expression, is satisfied only slightly if at all
by pre-Columbian art, it is precisely because the function
of this art was to give the masses of the faithful the form
that embodied age-old symbols which, as transformations
of their devotion, were above the individual, expressive,
visionary, valid for all and comprehensible to all.

The element of fantasy contained in this art is a formal
fantasy, not a narrative one. As its goal is to create symbols, it has to use formal elements that express the inex-
pressible, the ungraspable, that which is not understood
through the senses. It resorts to the formula, to the sign
of magic virtue, so that a form associated with reality or
with the nonsymbolic will not serve its purpose. Just as
iron ore, a natural product, must first be processed and
purified before it acquires the hardness and elasticity of
steel, so must that art, based on a constant and systematic
observation of nature, "process" and purify the natural
form so that it becomes pure, spiritual form. An example
of this is the two serpents that coil around the eyes, nose,
and mouth of Tláloc. There are some works in which these
serpents still retain their natural shape, but these have
not yet reached full expressivity; there remains far too
much association with reality and the mysterious, transcendental virtue of the symbol is still lacking. It must be
purified, refined, until it is converted into the abstract form
of the two circles around the eyes of the god, like the
goggles of a cyclist. These two circles around the eyes
become the symbol of Tláloc. The symbol suffices and is
the more eloquent because it stimulates the imagination.

The associative form transmitting natural elements does
not raise man above reality. On the contrary, it subjects
his fantasy to reality by establishing reality as the norm.
To destroy the representation of reality in order to penetrate to the meaning: this is the goal and magic force of
the symbol. Thanks to the symbol, the imagination becomes productive and capable of conceiving the incon-

ceivable, the divine. In the temple of the Athenian Nike in the Acropolis, there is a relief of a goddess fastening her sandal. A sculpture of charming grace, but—can a goddess stoop to fasten her own sandal and still remain a goddess? Humanization is carried to such an extent here that nothing is left of the divine. The world of ancient Mexico would not have been able to imagine that a god would be required to perform so menial a task as that of fastening his own sandal. It instinctively rejects such a close approach to reality and, in general, any expressive measure used to narrow the gap from the transcendental and the unearthly to the profane and the earthly. Alienation from naturalness is one of its axioms. To apply the norm of naturalness to the suprasensible and the divine would be to enfeeble the gods, as Preuss states in a different connection. "Any modification of the strictly geometric forms, any approximation to the animal or vegetable world, lessens and weakens the implacable clarity of the monumental tectonics, and forces that on which everything depends to submit to the conditions of growth and of life, i.e., of temporality," says Schmarsow (*Grundbegriffe der Kunstwissenschaft*). Judaism prohibited images because any representation can be only an approximation and the concept of God should preserve its infinity. Ancient Mexican art is the attempt to give plastic expression to the divine concept in so far as it is humanly possible. Therefore it arrives at pure, spiritualized form, an expression not of nature but of natural law, that natural law revealed to it by heaven, in which it sees the eternal and in which its theogonic system is anchored. Thus it attains stylization, an overcoming of materiality through its impregnation with form and spirit. And thus it arrives at symbolism, at the sign that substitutes for the object and through which it succeeds in freeing and conjuring the forces that are acting in the object. Its creating is an ordered one: a geometric-cubic unity, the mass of a block, clean outline, axial orientation, symmetry, rhythm. It employs its creative power to establish this order, whether for the construction of pyramids or the painting of a mural.

This art does not usually tell a story, or if it does, tells

it with indifference. What European art narrated and depicted down through the ages—memorable events, heroic
actions, Olympic champions, Roman Caesars and generals,
medieval scenes of martyrdom, Renaissance emotion in
the presence of nature, gallant rococo adventures: ephemeral happenings, ephemeral experience, a carved or
painted newspaper, so to speak—none of this is considered a worthy subject of art. Man's gaze is directed to
something higher. Myth, the gods, the law—these are the
subjects worthy of artistic creation. The codices (with the
exception of the Mixtec) speak of celestial bodies, of the
acts of the gods; they are an interpretation of the Tonalámatl. Seler calls them "books of prophecies." Pre-Columbian art does not seek to divert or to entertain. It speaks
of the old and the oldest, of the origin and meaning of all
being. That is what it relates over and over again, repeat-
ing it incessantly, engraving it on man's mind and conscience so that he will have it before him, be conscious of
it, and never forget it. That art is a hymn, an apocalyptic
vision—a sculptured, painted *Popol Vuh*—with the expressive rhythm of the hymn and the visionary force of the
Apocalypse.

It says what it has to say clearly, exactly, and concisely.
In the mural, in the codex, a clear line—black or white—
outlines the figure. This is important or it would not be
here. It is isolated, without spatial relationship, in imaginary space. There is no perspective, foreshortening, or
shadow. There is no illusion or any attempt at illusion.
What is mere appearance does not count. Julius Lange,
in a study on the art of the Egyptian reliefs, says: "They
do not yet know the laws of the purely phenomenal. . . .
Without any doubt they have noticed that the object as
phenomenon has a different appearance from that of the
object in itself; that in the phenomenon the dimensions
and proportions of the object itself change. But the importance of the phenomenal for man's artistic spirit is still
not clear. The phenomenon is judged only as something
negative, as a trick that deforms the truth and the reality
of things. . . . It would be considered unworthy of art to
let itself become mystified by an optical illusion and in-

duced to show the appearance of things. To represent
them in perspective, foreshortened, would in that epoch
have been deemed a childish and extremely ridiculous
error." Not only is this a distinct artistic attempt at optical
realism (and in no way a primitive one), it is a conscious
repudiation of illusion. The pre-Columbian statue of rigid
frontality is constructed symmetrically on an axis; it is a
clearly outlined block. Often it is a monolith with a relief
carved on its front, e.g., the Teotihuacán Chalchiuhtlicue,
and Stele 8 of Naranjo (Guatemala). There is only one
view, since the spectator's position is fixed. Sculpture of
the European baroque period invites the spectator to walk
around the work, and from each different angle he has a
new and surprising view. The intent is to turn the fixed
into the fluid, ambiguous, and untenable, an illusionistic
spectacle, an attraction in which baroque mentality delighted. A spectacle, an attraction—but how absurd for a
culture like that of Teotihuacán!

Just as the hymn, without explaining or rationalizing,
repeats untiringly this alone: God is great, God is holy,
God is all-powerful—so too, one of the decisive formal elements of pre-Columbian art is rhythm. It accents, under-
lines, instills only the fact that it wants to manifest. Let us
recall how religious emotion is expressed in the Psalms.
In Psalm 47 we read: "God is gone up with a shout, the
Lord with the sound of a trumpet. Sing praises to God,
sing praises: sing praises unto our King, sing praises. For
God is the King of all the earth: sing ye praises with understanding."

Georges Raynaud, who translated the *Popol Vuh* into
French, complains of such frequent use of the parallelism
"not only of ideas and phrases or parts of phrases, but also
of proper names (gods, heroes, chiefs, legendary places),
each one linked to another proper name, very often of
perfect uselessness, of equal or almost equal meaning." Of
perfect uselessness for the reader who sees the *Popol Vuh*
as no more than a document of exotic folklore, but essential as an expressive recourse for the Quiché priest (to
whom we owe its wording) in order to give to mythical
tradition the efficacy and vigor of the transcendental and

the sacred. Surrounding the pyramid of Quetzalcóatl in Teotihuacán we see the heads of the gods Quetzalcóatl and Tláloc, the same heads three hundred and sixty-four times without interruption. The jaguars and eagles of the Tula reliefs, adopted later at Chichén Itzá, that alternate in an invariable rhythm. The serpent heads, equidistant and equal in size, in the belt of serpents at the Tenayuca pyramid: the head of the same serpent, threatening, sinister, whose tongue appears between its half-open jaws. The niches at Tajín, the geometric, abstract ornament around the entire structure in a movement without pause, without beginning, without end, without a goal, like an Oriental ornamentation. That solemn order refuses to offer the spectator new impressions, new sensations, new emotions at every step (as does one of the most admired creations of Greek art—the Parthenon frieze), but it is not monotonous. Repetition is affirmation here, a way of engraving the message on the mind, emphasis, invocation, a yearning for conjuration, a prayer. It is a magic sign, as Eulalia Guzmán explains in her fundamental essay on the basic concepts of pre-Columbian art in Mexico. "This mystical or contemplative union, half terror and half love, makes him feel the rhythm of the cosmos and vibrate to the same measured beat, hieratical, majestic. . . . The rhythm has an effect not only religious, but magical. . . . The rhythm was a means of channeling psychic powers, of heightening them, and even of producing ecstasy."

## The Spirituality of Pre-Cortesian Art

Worringer (*Form in Gothic*) states that "Gothic has nothing to do with beauty." Actually, in the Gothic style, beauty is not the end of artistic creation. It mobilizes all its creative energies to give expression to metaphysical-religious experience. What we recognize as beauty we place there ourselves. Worringer goes even further: "The so-called beauty of Gothic is a modern misunderstanding."

It seems to me that all of this can be applied without reservation to the art of ancient Mexico, for neither does pre-Cortesian man create art for art's sake. In artistic creation, he too pursues the goal of translating his religious feeling into the language of plastic form. If the works of that artistic world do not confirm, or even if they offend, our concept of beauty, which is that of Western civilization, it is not because of any inadequacy in pre-Cortesian art, but inadequacy on the part of the spectator who, misled by prejudice, applies invalid standards to it.

Riegl has shown us the error of measuring a work of art from the past by a criterion that does not originate with the intentions behind its creation, whether these be a traditional formula such as the classic Greek or a contemporary standard, more suggestive and in many ways more dangerous. The National Museum of Anthropology, Mexico, possesses a parrot's head of basalt from Xochicalco, 22½ inches high (Plate 11). This is a strange work and its very strangeness is fascinating. The head is in the shape of a triangular prism whose front edge is the beak. The perfectly round eyes are not mere depressions, but holes open right through the mass of the head from one side to the other. The mouth is also a hole. Seen in profile, this bird's head resembles a cubist composition of Picasso, from his mature period.

The formal affinity is amazing; it is amazing how closely this Mesoamerican creation approaches Picasso, or vice versa. But despite this, we must not overlook the fact that the basic conditions—spiritual, artistic, psychic, metaphysical—are diametrically different, that Picasso's constructivism, which is esthetic and intellectual in nature, has its origin in a state of mind entirely different from that in which this psychogram of magic intuition was conceived.

The decisive qualities of this artistic activity are the terrible and the sublime. Under the influence of European concepts, there has been an attempt to establish one other quality in this art, that of beauty, alleging that the works of the late epochs and of the Maya baroque were approaching this. But the evolution manifested in these creations is not orientation toward new artistic ends, but the incipient decadence and weakening of the creative powers, resulting, in all probability, from a decline in religious feeling and a change in the social structure.

The psychomotive force of the Gothic is a passion for redemption, the upward impulse of the soul hungry for God, which is given form in the cathedral reaching toward Heaven. It is a personal redemption, the salvation of the individual soul from that perdition called original sin. This presupposes the individual. The man of ancient Mexico, who lacks personal individuality, similarly does not exist as an individual in the sphere of religion. He is submerged integrally into the collectivity. According to myth, the task of upholding the world falls to him. A work for giants, a tremendous burden that cannot be placed on the shoulders of a merciful savior because such does not and could not exist in the pantheon of ancient Mexico. If man should for a moment fail to perform his task, the community, the world, and he himself would come to an end.

The gods are severe, horrendous, and merciless, bloodthirsty gods who eat the hearts of men and drink their blood. It is a world at once terrible and sublime, and there is no possibility of escaping it. The Gothic could deny imperfect, fatal reality; it could lose itself in an ethereal dream of unearthly grace, clarity, and beatitude. Pre-Cortesian man cannot deny the world, since he must maintain it even though it is a "place of much work and torment," nor has he a beyond to which he can flee. And there is no such thing as grace; the individual has no personal privilege or hope of being able to escape his destiny.

An esthetic study of Mesoamerican art must start from the integral subjection to religion and the peculiar character of this religiosity, and it must be remembered that such subjection was not considered a restriction, but the true end of artistic goals. If within the orbit of European culture the function of art was very often to propagate new ideas and ideals, in ancient Mexican art this function, if it existed at all, must have been quite secondary. So-called "progress," the impulsive force of Western civilization, lacks meaning in the pre-Hispanic world as it does in Asia, the creator of great religious systems and great religious art. The mission of pre-Cortesian man is not to change the world or create a new world order, but to conserve the old, eternal order. This is why Alfonso Caso, referring to the Aztecs (*The Aztecs: People of the Sun*), attributes the blame for the "fatal limitation of their culture" to this conservative tenacity. This reference may apply more to the material aspect of the civilization, but it is also applicable to the artistic sphere. Because of the lack of desire for change or for technical and artistic progress, architecture used the same expressive elements for centuries, a unique phenomenon in the history of art. The evolution we see or think we see in the art of ancient Mexico is probably only an evolution in manual dexterity rather than a succession of phases differing from each other by a fundamental change in artistic goals. It is the same difference as between Byzantine art and that of the Hellenistic era, between Gothic and Romanesque, between baroque and Renaissance. Mesoamerican art, especially in its culminating points of Teotihuacán and Monte Albán, maintained the same formal conceptions over the centuries. The psychic-spiritual hypotheses of this art would not have permitted an evolution toward beauty, i.e., an abandonment of its religious character for a predominantly esthetic attitude. In certain artistic climes such as Raphael's Italy, the ideal of beauty is the standard, the point of departure, and the goal of artistic creation. The pre-Hispanic art of Mexico does not aspire to beauty but to expressivity, to vigor of expression. The head of the eagle warrior is beautiful even according to the standards of Western civilization, but it must be remembered that this work is no longer inspired by the visionary power that imparts a sacred note to the circle of jaguars and eagles in the cave of Malinalco. The visionary begins to be submerged in the visible. The "disinterested complacency," which according to Kant constitutes the experience of art, is a definition derived from a specific ambit of artistic creation: classic and classicist art. It is fitting in this context, and even more with respect to "art for art's sake," a consequence of classicism. But the formula of "art for art's sake," a product of bourgeois mentality that is only a refuge in the merely optical and in formal resources, a flight from the value and importance of content and which has no meaning at all, is senseless with respect to vast and important spheres of artistic creation. Goya's *Disasters of War* did not spring from, nor are they understandable from, the attitude of disinterested complacency (in the first place because what they try to arouse is not complacency but horror), and even less, great religious art— that which does not limit itself to the representation of religious themes, springing as it does from a psychic stratum whose only reality is subjection to the divine: the art of ancient Asia as well as Byzantine; likewise, as Worringer states, the Gothic, and, most decidedly, the art of ancient Mexico.

Religious art does not and cannot create works merely to be looked at complacently. Quite to the contrary, the statue of a god or the image of a saint are designed expressly to cause "interest," but religious interest. A work of art of religious inspiration is an incarnation of the divine. It is of no importance whether or not it pleases, whether or not it satisfies either an unconscious or a cultivated esthetic sensibility. The Great Coatlicue was certainly not "beautiful" to the Aztecs, whatever their concept of beauty may have been, nor did they wish it to be. Its mission was to convey a pathetic and terrifying idea of the all-powerful earth goddess from whose womb springs all life and who in turn devours her offspring.

The gods were an adornment of Greek life and were not taken very seriously (Lucian). They were very human gods even in their manners, passions, and journeyings, as, for example, the amorous adventures of Zeus, father of the gods. Longinus says that Homer tried to bring the gods down to the level of men. The Apollo Belvedere and the Venus de Milo are gods brought to this level, and that is all they are. What justification could there be for such creations, no longer filled with the imaginative force of religion? Only one, beauty. In all probability (sources tell us nothing in this respect, but it is a fairly convincing supposition), it was the Greeks who raised the concept of beauty to an artistic criterion after secularizing their religion with that bucolic paganism so admired by Nietzsche. Occidental civilization inherited this criterion from them, and with it, the identification—fatal to the experience of art—of natural beauty and artistic beauty. "Art may be called perfect when it seems to be nature" (Longinus). The Renaissance made beauty the object not only of a cult, but also of a science. "Nature is a cosmos, subject to what we have recognized as its law: beauty" (L. B. Alberti). Since then, the Western world has believed in beauty and sees in it the finality, the true and only legitimacy, of art. The esthetics of the nineteenth century supplied the scientific basis for this belief. Certainly the principal representatives of the art of the nineteenth and twentieth centuries—Goya, Courbet, Daumier, Picasso, the surrealists—did not subscribe to such an esthetic and even rebelled and continue to rebel against it. The repudiation of their works by their contemporaries is based precisely on the fact that their works are in conflict with the social and esthetic convention of beauty, a convention so widespread and with so many pretensions to universal validity that in effect it determines the esthetic judgment of the public, and that even the majority of artists have accepted and do accept as the standard of creation.

And what of the art of the great number of artistic cultures whose goal was not beauty? Parenthetically, *which* beauty? For after all, so-called classic beauty is not the only kind. That such cultures did and do exist should not surprise us; we cannot at all explain the works that they produced as proofs of their inability or backwardness. In a lecture given at the beginning of this century at the School of the Louvre, Salomon Reinach, a connoisseur of art esteemed in his day, said: "India had no art before the period of Alexander the Great, and as for Chinese art, it began to produce works of art during the European Middle Ages." Do these words not reveal a ridiculous presumption and a lack of artistic knowledge? A dangerous lack, as we have since learned.

We know nothing of the esthetics of ancient Mexico. "The Aztecs," observes Vaillant (*The Aztecs of Mexico*), "did not have a term for 'fine arts,' nor did they speculate about esthetics, nor make objects to be contemplated for their beauty alone. They had none of the socially sterile attitudes towards art which we adopt in our culture. Instead, they recognized the value of superior workmanship and used its products to honour the gods who were intermediaries between man and the infinite power of the universe."[1]

The artist, like all able craftsmen, was called *toltécatl* among the Nahua people. "*Tulteca* means 'Artisan Man' because the men of that Nation were great artisans" (Torquemada, *Los veinte i un libros rituales i monarquía indiana*).[2] There does not seem to have been a Mesoamerican Aristotle. At least, no maxims such as his have been preserved, nor do post-Cortesian sources give us any infor-

---

[1] Otto Kümmel, eminent Sinologist, states that the word "art" did not originally exist in China and that it entered China (via Japan) in the nineteenth century, as a translation of the English term *fine arts*, i.e., that it is an artificial creation.

[2] In the *Cantares méxicanos*, annotated after the Conquest, poetry was designated as "flower and song," a phrase of metaphorical meaning (León-Portilla: *La filosofía náhuatl*).

mation on this subject. We must derive the esthetics expressed in that art from the works of art that have been saved, surely not a bad procedure provided our search is unblurred by preconceived ideas.

We may presume that what we call "profane art" did not exist, except for the production of such indispensable objects as arms, household goods, clothing, etc. The symbol for a "conquered city" was a burning temple with the place-name alongside, from which we infer that a people considered itself subjugated when its sanctuary was destroyed. The adornment of the house was its hearth, i.e., the idol of the fire god with the vessel intended for offerings. Even objects of applied art such as arms, household goods, and clothing were decorated in the main, if not exclusively, with religious symbols. There have not been found any indications of a worldly imagination—natural forms, flowers, birds, or other animals, love scenes, etc.— similar to that which inspired European and even Asiatic metalwork. This was outside and beneath the sphere of this art. Not even man as an individual, as a personality, was worthy of being represented. "The portrait is not religious," says Eulalia Guzmán ("Caracteres esenciales del arte antiguo mexicano—su sentido fundamental," in the magazine, *Universidad de México*, 1933, Nos. 29 and 30). So far as I know, representation of figures that can be considered portraits have never been found, with the exception of a small piece of goldwork found in Texcoco, believed to be a present to the king of that region, which quite possibly is the portrait of the Aztec monarch Tízoc (1482–86). The seated figure wears a royal crown with a feather headdress. In the background is the symbol of a wounded or bleeding leg, the sign of Tízoc such as it appears in several codices and stone sculptures. The story is told that the courtiers of Montezuma II tried to persuade him to have a portrait of himself made in relief for his palace at Chapultepec, and that the superstitious and neurotic king, harassed constantly by evil presentiments, refused, stating that this would bring misfortune; but that finally he consented. Roman art reaches one of its highest points in the portrait busts of the Caesars and victorious generals. In ancient Mexico not even war, although deemed sacred and imposed by the gods, was used as a motive to glorify the victor with a portrait. In the National Museum of Anthropology, Mexico, is the Stone of Tízoc, a sort of "Aztec Trajan's Column," showing in relief the acts of war carried out by the Aztecs at the command of this sovereign, but this monument glorifies Huitzilopochtli, to whom the "people of the sun" owed their victories, and it was destined to be placed in the great temple of Tenochtitlan.

In the reliefs at Sakkara, the city of the dead, the Egyptians have left us a vivid and faithful picture of their daily life. "They sacrifice animals for offerings; they brew beer, bake bread, sow and reap . . . they build boats, throw bowls on the potter's wheel . . . the scribes in the chancery register the abundant offerings" (Rosa Schapire: "Aus der Totenstadt Sakkara," *Das Kunstblatt,* 1925, No. 8). What an instructive glimpse of the Egyptian world of the Old Empire! In the Temple of the Warriors at Chichén Itzá, there is (an exceptional case) a mural painting that represents life in a village. We see the women inside their huts, busy at their domestic tasks; merchants arriving with their products; fishermen hard at work. This mural is one of a pair showing the invasion of Yucatán by the Toltecs and the overthrow of the Maya. The two paintings complement each other. Both are a glorification of Kukulkán, the god who brought his warriors to the peninsula and led them to victory.

A contemplative conception of nature is lacking in pre-Columbian art. Landscape, when we find it, serves specific purposes: in the Temple of Agriculture at Teotihuacán, it frames the offering of the products of the earth; in the "Earthly Paradise," the mural in the Temple of Tláloc, it gives a suggestive impression of the arcadic existence enjoyed there by those protected by Tláloc. There was no such thing as lyric emotion, giving oneself over with delight to the beauty of silent nature, such as Corot brings us, for example, and for that reason it was not expressed in art. Landscape painting, satisfying the weekend nostalgia of the city dweller who has no roots in the land, did not exist for those people because their cultures were still very young. Even in European painting the pure landscape makes a relatively late appearance in the sixteenth century with Brueghel, born about six years after the Conquest. It is still the duty of Mexican art to arouse transcendental thoughts. It is epic creation, filled with action, with *ethos*. It speaks of myth and gives expression to the divine. What must be believed and what is believed is given plastic form. "The whole art is impregnated with a feeling of religion and magic. Its end is not imitation of the beautiful forms of nature, as in imitative art, but the representation of an idea, or of what surpasses the world of the senses, i.e., the religious" (Eulalia Guzmán).

To the Greeks (Plato), nature is idea become phenomenon, "a methodical arrangement such as human governments try to establish" (Erwin Rohde, *Psyche*). Their intellectualism blinds them "to all those forces in life that cannot be identified by the senses and weighed with the mind" (Sheldon Cheney, *A World History of Art*). In the Gothic Age (St. Thomas), nature is a reflection of divine wisdom and grace. The pre-Cortesian conception of nature is born of the dualism of its theogonic system that expresses itself as an unending struggle for extermination between the constructive and the destructive forces. Gay Mount Olympus, greedy for pleasure, was a "gallery of beauty." Christianity created the poetry of the cult of the Virgin, the *Mater Dolorosa* tenderly holding the body of the crucified. It created the Good Shepherd, the Redeemer who carried the cross to save mankind. The Mexican gods were incarnations of the forces of nature, at times kind to man, but more often hostile, destructive, demoniacal, and man had to pay with sacrifices for what they gave him: good harvests, sufficient rainfall, the warmth of the sun.

Wilhelm Wundt (*Mythus und Religion*) observes that "among the effects that myth everywhere attributes to demons, evil was predominant from the beginning, so that all people believe evil spirits to be older than good spirits." Fear turns into adoration. The German word *Ehrfurcht* (adoration) is a compound noun, with *Furcht* (fear) the principal element. The concept of terrible and terrifying becomes the concept of the divine.

Of course, man is not entirely a plaything of the demons. He has reason to be a fatalist but ought not despair, for he possesses the magic power of conjuration. Nevertheless, he is afflicted with uncertainty. Is his own power sufficient? Will it not be offset and nullified through some error in following the rules, through adverse influences or unfavorable circumstances? That struggle—the magic power of nature, of the gods and the spirits, against the magic power of man—is what introduces such tremendous tension into the life of pre-Cortesian man. For him there can never be harmony, harmonious equilibrium, but only an alleviated tension, and he attains this alleviation only through magic conjuration.

His conception of nature is impregnated with this tension. A straightforward experience of reality is impossible. Human life has forcibly to be continual struggle, continual defense. Reality is turned into abstraction. The all-powerful, demoniacal will to destruction acts as a principle and law behind the ephemeral phenomenon. This destructive force does not live in man's imagination as an abstract idea, but, in the dialectics of the pre-Columbian world, it adopts concrete form and is anthropomorphized, becoming human or animal. The elements of nature are gods and these in turn are personified. The plumed serpent is not only the symbol of Quetzalcóatl, it *is* Quetzalcóatl. There exist plastic likenesses of serpents, eagles, tigers, dogs, coyotes, toads, armadillos, lizards, but these are not what we call animal sculpture. These animals are symbols, personifications of gods, translated into the plastic forms that correspond to the conceptual world of ancient Mexico.

The terrible is transformed into the sublime. Let us take as an example the image of the Great Coatlicue. Active force, energy of destructiveness, subject to something higher, to the cosmic order, within which even what is terrible is a foreseen and necessary principle. An alleviation of tension. The Doric column can become purely abstract form, balanced harmony. In the art of ancient Mexico, the craving for abstraction, the tendency toward spiritualization, is in perennial conflict with the actual content of the representation.

To give shape to the sublimely terrible is the task of the pre-Columbian craftsman. This too implies a contradiction, since if the sublime is purified passion, then to provoke the feeling of the terrible is to provoke the passion, to expel man from the province of the serene and the pleasant. We know that Lessing greatly admired the Laocoön group because the anonymous creator of this work succeeded so marvelously in mitigating what is terrible and sorrowful in the expression of the Trojan priest overwhelmed by the serpents that the spectator has no reason to become very frightened. In this way, according to Lessing, is greatness achieved. Pre-Cortesian art does not mitigate the terrible, which would deprive the gods of their divinity. In spite of that, a truly sublime greatness is achieved.

For Lessing, who represents the Age of Enlightenment (which was wholly perplexed before the divine and determined to comprehend it, and everything else, through logic and reason), it is a difficult problem to represent the divine without sacrificing its essentials, i.e., its divine character, or, as he expresses it, the way to visibly represent the invisible. He arrives at the conclusion that painting is incapable of this, while sculpture has at its disposal an adequate resource, the colossal (*das Kolossalische*). He indicates as a concrete example the goddess Minerva who, in the work of Homer, throws an immense stone at Mars. "Well, now, I ask . . . how tall must the goddess be? If her stature is proportionate to the size of the stone, the miraculous disappears. A person three times taller than I should naturally be able to throw a stone three times larger. But if the height of the goddess is not proportionate to the size of the stone, then we should have a manifest improbability. . . ."

A manifest improbability! Here is the esthetic problem of artistic rationalism, convinced that the transcendent and metaphysical conception must be represented with realistic and illusionary means. Here is the difficulty encountered by classicistic art, determined that even the divine shall be familiar to those lacking imaginative capacity. Here is the dilemma for those of our own day who approach pre-Columbian art with the criterion "more naturalistic, less naturalistic," and who are disappointed not to find either naturalness or natural beauty.

It is as absurd to apply this criterion of verisimilitude to pre-Hispanic art as to any other visionary, nonrealistic art. The reality that the artist of ancient Mexico must express and that in many cases he has succeeded in expressing in grandiose form is the representation that the collectivity develops of the myths and the gods. And the expression of the divine, of what is the foundation and meaning of life, must be great and sublime. It is not a matter of giving it the appearance of reality, but of making it believable.

Therefore, the artist created the formal idiom of a visionary expressionism that discards associative elements because they limit and paralyze the imagination, a cubico-geometric language, a language of signs, objective, exact, and of universal validity.

The realism that Lessing had considered incapable of making visible the invisible can be sufficient and adequate when it tries to satisfy the esthetic exigencies of a refined sensibility, but not the necessity of metaphysical experience that fills the religious soul. And the humanization of the divine, the degradation of the divine to human proportions, would have seemed blasphemous to pre-Columbian man.

It is possible to understand the art of ancient Mexico, to penetrate its most profound essence, only if we take into account the powerful visionary force that impregnates and determines it.

In its search for a plastic idiom adequate to give expression to the visionary, that art arrives at a symbolic form to which it incorporates elements of reality in order to intensify the effect by means of contrast. It is able to shape the terrible, a dimension of decisive importance in a conception of the world based on dualism. It entrusts to Form the function of stimulating the religious fantasy. Subject to Law, to Order, to Rhythm, Form itself becomes an instrument of magic conjuration.

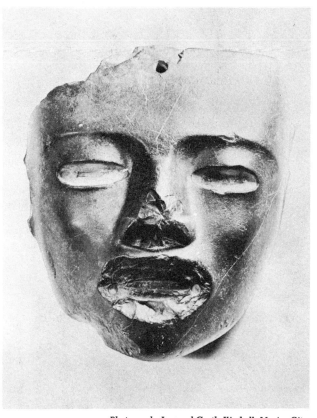

*Photograph: Irmgard Groth-Kimball, Mexico City.*

PLATE 30. Mask. Stone. Aztec. Kurt Stavenhagen Collection, Mexico City.

*Photograph: from the museum.*

PLATE 31. Mask of a prince-priest, from the tomb of the Pyramid of the Inscriptions, Palenque. Mosaic of different colored jade. Maya. National Museum of Anthropology, Mexico City.

*Photograph: National Museum of Anthropology, Mexico City.*

PLATE 32. Stucco mask. Palenque. Maya.

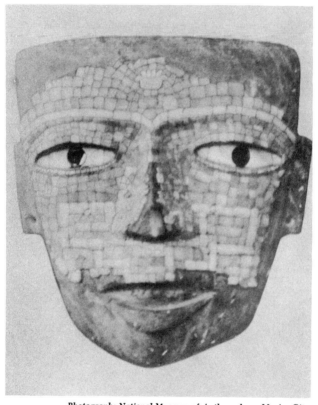

*Photograph: National Museum of Anthropology, Mexico City.*
PLATE 33. Mask. Mosaic. From Tlapa, Gro. Teotihuacán.

PLATE 34. Wall from the Salon of the Frets. Mitla. Zapotec.

*Photograph: National Institute of Anthropology and History, Mexico City.*

PLATE 35. Temple of the Tigers. Chichén. Itzá.

PLATE 36. Bottom of a bowl. Ceramic. Kin-Lishba. By Byron Cummings.

*Photograph: Irmgard Groth-Kimball, Mexico City.*

PLATE 37. Figure of a woman. Ceramic. Tlatilco. Kurt Stavenhagen Collection, Mexico City.

PLATE 38. Head. Ceramic. From Tlatilco. Preclassic. National Museum of Anthropology, Mexico City. Miguel Covarrubias Collection, Mexico City.

*Photograph: from the museum.*
PLATE 39. Feminine figure. Ceramic. Chupícuaro. National Museum of Anthropology, Mexico City.

PLATE 40. Mother. Ceramic. Remojadas inferior. Preclassic. National Museum of Anthropology, Mexico City.

PLATE 41. Three women. Ceramic. Tlatilco. Preclassic. Diego Rivera Collection, Mexico City.

*Photograph: from the museum.*

PLATE 42. Feminine figure with two heads. Ceramic. Tlatilco. Preclassic. National Museum of Anthropology, Mexico City.

*Photograph: from the museum.*

PLATE 43. Feminine figure with two faces. Ceramic. Tlatilco. Preclassic. National Museum of Anthropology, Mexico City.

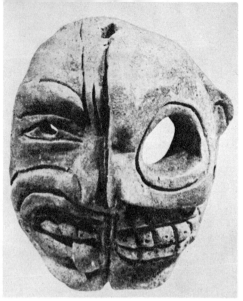

PLATE 44. Life and death. Ceramic. Tlatilco. Preclassic. National Museum of Anthropology, Mexico City. Miguel Covarrubias Collection, Mexico City.

*Photograph: from the museum.*

PLATE 45. Magician. Ceramic. Tlatilco. Preclassic. National Museum of Anthropology, Mexico City.

*Photograph: Irmgard Groth-Kimball, Mexico City.*
PLATE 46. Figure of a man. Jadeite, from Guerrero, Mezcala. Kurt Stavenhagen Collection, Mexico City.

*Photograph: National Institute of Anthropology and History, Mexico City.*
PLATE 47. Ceremonial knife. Stone. La Venta.

Photograph: *National Institute of Anthropology and History, Mexico City.*
PLATE 48. Jaguar. Stone. La Venta. Museo Parque de La Venta,
Villahermosa.

*Photograph: from the museum.*

PLATE 49. The old god or the god of fire (Huehuetéotl). Ceramic, from Tres Zapotes, Vera Cruz. Preclassic. National Museum of Anthropology, Mexico City.

*Photograph: National Institute of Anthropology and History, Mexico City.*
PLATE 50. Colossal head. Stone. La Venta. Museo Parque de La Venta.

Photograph: National Institute of Anthropology and History, Mexico City.

PLATE 51. Altar 4, La Venta. Museo Parque de La Venta.

*Photograph: Albrecht Victor Blum.*
PLATE 52. Stele I. Izapa. La Venta culture.

*Photograph: Walter Steinkopf, Berlin.*
PLATE 53. Chalchiuhtlicue. Stone.Teotihuacán.Völkerkundemuseum, Berlin.

PLATE 54. Xiuhtecuhtli. Stone. Teotihuacán. Kunsthistorisches Museum, Vienna.

PLATE 55. Armadillo. Ceramic. From San Rodrigo Aljojuca, Puebla, Teotihuacán. Völkerkundemuseum, Berlin.

*Photograph: National Institute of Anthropology and History, Mexico City.*
PLATE 56. Telemones. Tula.

PLATE 57. Pyramid of Quetzalcóatl (Building "B"). Tula

Photograph: National Institute of Anthropology and History, Mexico City.

*Photograph: National Institute of Anthropology and History, Mexico City.*
PLATE 58. Coatepantli (Wall of Serpents, detail). Tula.

PLATE 59. Toltec warrior. Relief on a pillar. Tula.

PLATE 60. Polichrome decoration of a vase, from Chamá. University Museum, Philadelphia.

*Photograph: National Institute of Anthropology and History, Mexico City.*

PLATE 61. Pyramid E-VII-sub. Uaxactun. Guatemala.

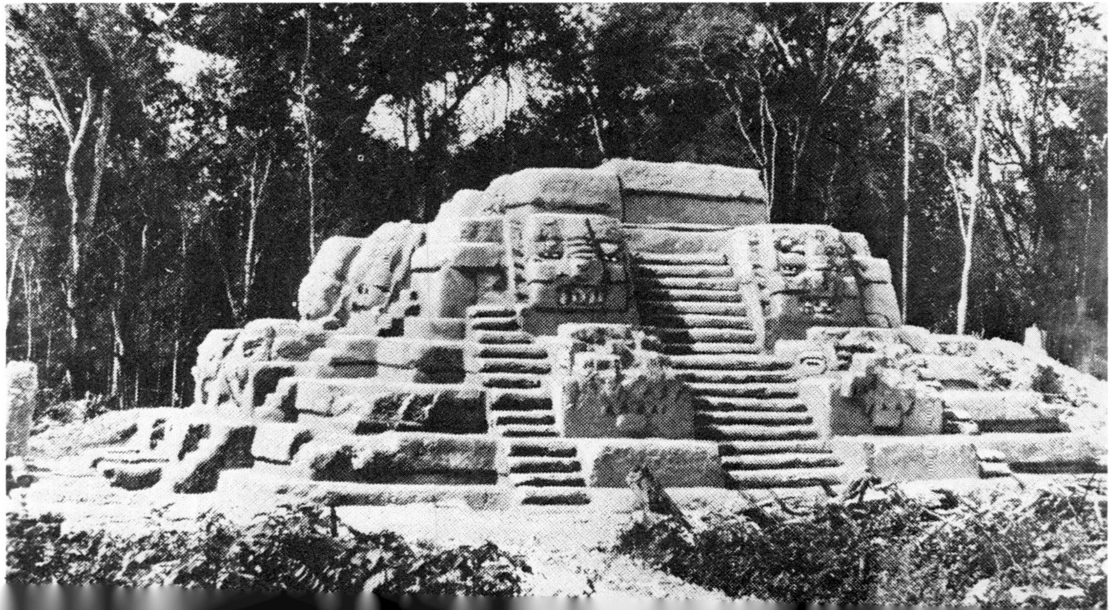

PLATE 62. Gateway. Puuc style, Labná, Yucatán.

PLATE 63. Palenque Chiapas. Maya.

Photograph: National Institute of Anthropology and History, Mexico City.
PLATE 64. Temple of the Sun. Palenque, Chiapas. Maya.

## The Conception of Nature

Knowledge of the heavenly bodies was a passion with the peoples of ancient Mexico. It was *the* science, the only one worth knowing, since it revealed to them the existence, actions, and reactions of the gods. Observation of astral phenomena and the frequency of their appearance and disappearance was a matter of vital transcendence, the first and most urgent social necessity. They thought it impossible to maintain the earth's normal operation without an exact and detailed knowledge of the celestial system. The most important duty of the priests was to read the status of the cosmos in the stars.

Almost every temple contained what we call "observatories," or at least an observation post from which celestial phenomena were noted.[1] The observers were constantly alert, day and night; nothing that happened in the heavens must escape their attention, and everything was interpreted by sages who understood the order and considered each sign of irregularity a gloomy presage. Thanks to this intense, minute, and perennial observation of the heavenly bodies, they acquired a knowledge of astronomy far beyond that of their European contemporaries.

Beyond revealing very great knowledge, the astronomical data in the three Maya codices that have been preserved, especially those in the Dresdensis Codex, are surprisingly exact in their calculations and predictions. This is the opinion, based on their investigations, of E. Förste-

[1] From the drawings in the Nuttall and Selden Codices (Fig. 9), we gather that the method was extremely simple—the eye of the observer is behind two crossed sticks, and the point of a stele or a corner of the temple was used as a sight.

FIG. 9. Representation of an observatory. *Selden Codex,* 5

mann, interpreter of the Dresdensis Codex, of John E.
Teeple of the Carnegie Institute ("Maya Astronomy," *op.
cit.*), and of H. Ludendorff, director of the Potsdam astronomical observatory. I cannot permit myself any critical
judgment in this respect. Ludendorff, who thinks that the
tables of the Dresdensis Codex constitute a recording of
ecliptic combinations for a period of thirty-three years,
re-established the calculations on which they are based
and arrived at the conclusion that they are absolutely correct; that the differences existing between the two computations are very slight, since they consist at most of
only one day. According to Alfonso Caso ("Nuevos datos
para la correlación de los años azteca y cristiano," *Estudios de Cultura Náhuatl,* Vol. I, 1959), the day was
calculated in ancient Mexico from noon of one day to noon
of the following day. It is not improbable that this explains
part of the differences discovered by Ludendorff. The fact
that the Mexican codices do not permit of such a simple
control is explained by Seler as follows: "In the Maya
codices we find detailed calculations, a scrupulous exactitude in fixing dates and intervals. In the Mexican codices,
there is only an insinuation of what is really arithmetic.
Arithmetic is relegated to second place; the images occupy the first. One has the impression that the Mexican
codices remind the initiate of what he already knows,
while the Maya codices establish or transmit knowledge."

Of course, the admiration we feel for the knowledge of

astronomy attained by pre-Columbian people should not blind us to the fact that its object was fundamentally different from that of our Keplerian astronomy. The one and only goal that guided them in studying the movements of the stars was to read in them, in the regularity and possible irregularities of their trajectories, the activity of the divine powers. If physics teaches us that one force, the attraction of the sun, causes the movement of the earth and the heavenly bodies, the ancient Mexican believed that this force was the action of the gods, and what he tried to explore was the nature of the gods and the intentions behind their actions. Even more important, that knowledge regulated his conduct toward those forces on whose benevolence or malevolence earthly existence depended. What he was investigating with the greatest zeal and with admirable diligence and care was not the "Law of Nature." Men of today—with or without scientific preparation, although actually we are all infiltrated from childhood with scientific and technical thought—find this absurd, and even more absurd, almost inconceivable, is that with such a mental attitude the Maya could assemble such precious knowledge. But the knowledge and exactitude of these facts gleaned by careful observation is one thing. To know that the facts obey what we call the laws of nature is something else again. Newton's law of gravity was discovered comparatively recently, in the seventeenth century, but the phenomenon of gravity and its effects were understood from very remote times. If a receptacle were filled with water, man knew from observation and practical experience that he had to place it with the opening on top or the water would spill out. And he also knew that if he dropped it, it would break.

What the starry skies revealed to pre-Cortesian man were the signs, presages, and revelations of divine plans. If the position of the stars warned him of poor harvests, drought, famine, he had to make supreme efforts to conciliate the rain god, the fertility gods, or any other spirits influential in the matter, so that they would not neglect to perform their functions.

The order manifested in the cyclical recurrence of phenomena took on a sacred and even divine character, thanks to its measurability. That order under which the gods and the spirits worked was, for man, the Law.[2] (When we use the word "astronomy" in the following, we do so with the understanding that it is a science essentially different from what the word means to us.) Just as we know that the decisive factor in artistic creation is the will to art, expressed differently by different peoples, temperaments, and epochs, so too can we speak of a will to science. And we must start from the fact that pre-Cortesian astronomy is governed by a different will to science than Keplerian. "There exist," says Spengler (*The Decline of the West*), "as many numerical worlds as there are superior cultures. . . . Number is not the same for all humanity, but in each case corresponds to a certain type of humanity."

"Primitives perceive nothing in the same way as we do," affirms Lévy-Bruhl (*How Natives Think*). "Whatever the object presented to their minds, it implies mystic properties which are inextricably bound up with it, and the primitive in perceiving it, never separates these from it. To him there is no phenomenon which is, strictly speaking, a physical one, in the sense in which we use the term." All this can be applied also to the peoples of ancient Mexico, who were not at all primitive but, on the contrary, highly civilized.

Pre-Cortesian man cannot imagine that a phenomenon necessary to his existence, such as the rising and setting of the sun, is a physical act caused by the revolution of a celestial body, the earth. To him, the earth, the sun, and all the other creations of nature such as mountains, rivers, clouds, etc., are manifestations of certain beings,

[2] In the same sense, Babylonian astronomy is a mythical interpretation of the Universe. Ernst Cassirer (*An Essay on Man*) writes: "What man really sought in the heavens was his own reflection and the order of his human universe. In order to organize the political, the social, and the moral life of man it proved to be necessary to turn to the heavens . . . The first and essential aim of astronomy was to win an insight into the nature and activity of these powers in order to foresee and to evade their dangerous influences."

spirits or gods, who live in them, govern their existence
and conduct, and induce them to actions identical to or
at least similar to those of man.[3]

The sun that man sees as it rises and sets is the sun
god traversing the firmament. When it sets, the god dies,
sinking into the earth's breast. The dog-headed Xólotl
conducts him to the lower world, just as a dead man is
guided there by the dog buried with him. The sun dies
in order to be reborn with new vigor and brilliance.
The jaguars and eagles, souls of the dead warriors, accompany him in his ascent, and when he arrives at the
zenith he is greeted by the souls of women who died in
childbirth, who care for him along his path toward rebirth. And just as at midday, the hour of rest, so to speak,
the souls of the dead warriors are transformed into hummingbirds and in this guise descend to earth to suck
honey from the flowers, so, too, the souls of the dead
mothers, after having accompanied the sun to the lower
world, wander in the night around the crossroads, be-
witching children and making them sick, frightening
women, and luring men to indecency, adultery, and other
sins. Since in the timeless and spaceless world of magic
thinking there is neither causality nor contradiction, it is
not unusual that that representation of the death of the
sun coexists with another conception, that the sun must
undertake a bitter combat in the nocturnal sky against
his adversaries, the army of the stars, which he must defeat with the help of his following, the warriors who
died in battle or on the sacrificial stone, so that he can

[3] According to Burgoa (*Geográfica descripción*), the Mixtec
legend of the founding of Tilatongo relates that one of their
chiefs set out to conquer land where they could settle. When
he reached the region of Tilatongo, he found it uninhabited.
The land was a desert scorched by the sun. As he could not
believe that the land did not belong to anyone, he presumed
that the lord of the region was the sun, and he challenged it to
battle. When in the evening the sun sank and the clouds were
tinted pink, he believed he had killed it, and when it had set
completely he declared himself the victor and founded the city.
The fact that the sun reappeared the next morning could not
shake his conviction that one of his arrows had killed it.

rise again, victorious and resplendent in the morning sky. "His victory means a new day of life for men," (Caso).[4] We repeat the question stated above: what would any physical explanation mean beside this mythical interpretation that governed men's conduct and placed upon them the obligation to offer human hearts and blood to the deity, so that he would not succumb in battle and would continue his function of lighting and heating the earth? The death of the sun, i.e., the setting of the sun, is at the same time the sacrifice, the man who offers his life to the gods; while the rising of the sun signifies his rebirth, his rejuvenation through the sacrifice.

The rising and setting of the sun, which thus find a plausible explanation in the mind of pre-Columbian man, are, however much they might have impressed him, a relatively simple phenomenon compared to that of the moon and the planet Venus, "who according to myth immediately sprang forth from her [the moon]" (Eduard Seler, *Códice Borgia*). With its constantly changing phases (new, full, crescent, waning), the moon is a cosmic spectacle that since time immemorial excites the fantasy of all people and lands. Not the least reason for this was the knowledge or suspicion, likewise from earliest times, of the deep influence that the moon exercises on the development of vegetation, on fertility, growth, maturation, even on the human organism, and according to a belief held even recently, especially on the feminine body— keeping in mind a certain coincidence of the cycle of the

---

[4] The Egyptian cult to the god Ra offers a surprising parallel. "Every night when the sun-god Ra sank down to his home in the glowing west he was assailed by hosts of demons under the leadership of the arch-fiend Apepi. . . . To aid the sun-god in this daily struggle . . . a figure of his foe Apepi, represented as a crocodile . . . or a serpent . . . was made of wax. . . . Wrapt in a papyrus case, on which another likeness of Apepi had been drawn in green ink, the figure was then tied up with black hair, spat upon, hacked with a stone knife, and cast on the ground. There the priest trod on it . . . The fiends . . . felt the injuries inflicted on their images as if they had been done to themselves; they passed away, at least for a time, and the beneficent sun-god shone out triumphant once more" (Frazer, *The Magic Art*).

lunar phases with the cycle of menstruation. When the sun is born again, it has the same shape as before, but the moon is subject to a continual change. We see it grow, become larger, reach its fullness, and gradually wane. Seler uses this to establish a relationship between the missing leg of Tezcatlipoca and the crescent quarter of the moon when the lower (i.e., leg) section is missing; and he maintains that the Great Coatlicue in the National Museum of Anthropology, Mexico, with two serpentine heads in place of her own, which had been cut off, symbolizes the waning moon when the upper part is missing.[5]

Since the phases of the moon succeed each other in periods of regular duration, the moon becomes the measure of time. In all probability the division of the pre-Cortesian month into twenty days characterized by particular signs is based on vigesimal calculation. By means of the moon myth, Seler tries to explain the fact—unusual, at first glance, in a world in which the concordance of the numbers and numeral series almost reaches the proportions of a phobia—that these same symbols were also enumerated from one to thirteen, a series totally unrelated to the vigesimal system. The revolution of the moon took twenty-seven and one third days, during half of which time it grew and the other half waned. According to Seler, the number twenty-six (twice thirteen) was chosen as an approximation, either because observation was not yet very exact in the primitive epoch in which the calendar was computed, or because it was most inconvenient to divide the number twenty-seven by two. It is also possible that they did not count that one day on which the moon is invisible. The day was not divided into twenty-four hours, but into twenty-two: thirteen hours of daytime, to correspond to the thirteen heavens, and nine of night, governed by the nine Lords of the Night.

One need not be "moonstruck," something quite fashionable among mythologists, to admit that among the cosmic ideas of pre-Cortesian man the lunar myths oc-

---

[5] This calls to mind the Chaldean account of Bel, the creator of men, who had his head cut off in order to mix his blood with the earth. From this bloody clay he made man.

cupied first place, and that their importance was much
greater than that of the sun and the earth myths, these
latter related to the moon myth. When the Spaniards
landed in the New World, they saw that the powerful
Aztec Empire sacrificed multitudes of human beings to
Huitzilopochtli, their tribal deity. And since this practice
made an intense impression on them, it is only natural
that the idea spread throughout Europe that the cult of
the sun predominated in the Aztec Empire. But what
probably happened is that here, too, the sun outshone
the moon.

The moon, represented by those people as feminine, is
the adversary of the sun and she can appear only when
the solar god has died and descended to the lower
world. Eternally transformed and renewed, the moon symbolizes the uncertainty of all life, the perennial change
to which everything earthly is exposed, which is the fundamental idea that inspires the conception of nature in
ancient Mexico. Further, she is, so to speak, a cosmic
confirmation of the belief in rejuvenation, a belief from
which the cult of Adonis is derived in the Hellenic world
and that of Osiris in the Egyptian. The moon, "the pro-
moter and even the cause of all genesis," is also connected with the idea of growth, essential in an agrarian
religion; one of her symbols is the sea snail, the sign of
birth. The gods of fertility are related to her: Xipe Tótec,
the god of tender maize; the gods of pulque; Tlazoltéotl,
goddess of the earth, of love, of sin, and of voluptuous-
ness, who symbolizes procreation by giving birth to the
young maize god; Xochiquétzal, goddess of flowers, of
the dance, and of love, patron of homemakers as well as
of courtesans. And finally the moon, being the night
traveler, "the eye of night," is related to Tezcatlipoca,
god of the setting sun, Tezcatlipoca the obscure, the all
powerful, who sees everything in his mirror and punishes
every sin.

How does the myth of those people reflect what we
have just stated abstractly? Perhaps the most convincing
example is the interpretation in the Borgia Codex of the
double appearance and disappearance of the planet

Venus, the evening star and the morning star. Seler's commentary on the corresponding plates of this manuscript (Nos. 29–46)—which are for him "the nucleus and doubtless the strangest part of the Codex"—is entitled, somewhat romantically, "The Voyage of the planet Venus across the Underworld." It deals with the transposition of the different phases the planet presents during its revolution to the legend of Quetzalcóatl, who went toward the East to meet the sun and sacrificed himself on a pyre, his heart being transformed into the morning star. The disappearance and reappearance of that star are represented as the journey and the sacrifice of the priest-god. We see the planet Venus evanesce amidst the solar rays, descend dying through the opening in the earth to the lower world, to be destroyed in the North, the region of "stone and cold." We see Xipe Tótec, i.e., the setting moon, raising in his right hand the head cut from a skeleton. We see Quetzalcóatl transformed into Venus, who comes out in the nocturnal sky and enters the temple of night, rendering homage to the lord of the night. Then we see a mortuary bundle wrapped in a mantle, around which coil figures similar to the wind god, symbolizing night and death. We accompany Quetzalcóatl when he leaves the womb of the earth goddess, descending from the region of light to that of darkness, from the sky where he was a star, to the lower world. There the star of night, now dead, appears as a skeleton. And now the miracle takes place. From the front chamber of the temple to the principal chamber lead two paths, along each of which walks a figure of the god. One represents a Quetzalcóatl living, or destined to live; the other a Quetzalcóatl dead, or destined to die, painted in the "color of bone," which is the color of death—white with red spots. "The god passing through the chambers," Seler explains, "appears, we may say, divided." Two Quetzalcóatls— again that dualism that we find symbolized in the name of Ometecuhtli, "two lord." The next plate shows the two Quetzalcóatls confronting each other in the ball game. The one painted the "color of bone" is conquered by the one destined to live. Another scene, above the ball game, pictures the immolation of the vanquished god. He lies on the sacrificial stone with his chest opened; his heart is being removed. The priest who celebrates the ceremony is the Quetzalcóatl who is living or who will live. Thus, as in the Teotihuacán legend the god Nana-huatzin, Quetzalcóatl's double, hurls himself into the flames to bring about the rebirth of the sun, so the Quet-zalcóatl destined to live again is cooked in a large vessel on top of the fire. In the center of the following plate is a human heart from which springs a flowering tree. Quet-zalcóatl, disguised as a hummingbird, is kneeling in the treetop. The god, i.e., the planet Venus, has been born again. He had to be sacrificed, he had to descend to the lower world, to be resuscitated and rejuvenated, as the moon is resuscitated and rejuvenated, so that he can rise again, in the form of a hummingbird. (Exactly like Quetzalcóatl, after his autosacrifice on the pyre, so too the maize god, after being buried in the earth, must traverse the lower world, in order to reappear in the East, the region of dawn, springtime, and youth. In the *Popol Vuh*, the book of legends of the Quiché Maya In-dians, the twins Hunahpú and Ixbalamqué must de-scend to the lower world. After passing through the various subterranean regions, after successfully complet-ing the magic trials and winning in the ball game against the demons of darkness, they come out into the firmament transformed into the sun and the moon. Rafael Girard [*Los mayas eternos*] considers Hunahpú as an elucida-tion of the maize god, who, having completed in dark-ness—beneath the surface of the earth—the spirit's par-ticular duty, "rises to heaven, changed into the solar god.") On the final plate, not to say the final apotheosis, Quetzalcóatl is shown in the moment of kindling the new fire on the heart of the earth goddess. The morning star, who "precedes the warrior," can reappear magnificent in the sky.

This is the mythological or, from the pre-Hispanic point of view, the scientific interpretation given by the Borgia Codex of the five phases of the planet Venus. What was observed and calculated with scientific exacti-

tude becomes a vivid and impressive representation of the
rebirth of Quetzalcóatl, the Mexican messiah. This is the
law that the man of ancient Mexico seeks: what we have
previously termed the cosmic order.

Here is one of the great epic poems of humanity, comparable in vigor and spontaneity of vision to the *Iliad,* the
*Song of the Nibelungs,* and the *Song of Roland,* with the
difference that its hero is not a warrior setting forth with
arms and shield to subdue and kill his enemies. It is a religious epic like that other great religious poem, the *Book
of Job.* While Job's heroism rests in his steadfast faith
which does not waver in the midst of the most cruel suf-
ferings and tribulations, the hero here is the priest-king
of the Toltecs, the benefactor of his people, who triumphantly joins the other deities that govern the destinies
of the world and of men.

This visionary poem is instructive for us from another
angle. Just as the conjunctions of the planet are a matter of phenomena explained entirely by physics and
astronomy, the images in the Borgia Codex enable us to
compare our conception of nature with that of pre-
Hispanic man, which in general we know only through
signs, although these are very clear and of a sufficiently
large number to permit us to draw precise conclusions.

Pre-Columbian man is an excellent observer of phenomena. Numerous works of art attest to the probability
that he has seen better and more intensely than we. Studying Förstemann's dissertation on the Dresdensis Codex,
we are impressed by the precision the Maya achieved in
the observation of celestial phenomena. They were able
to calculate to the day the periods of the planet Venus,
but that world was not and could not be interested in the
physical cause of this movement. "The real cause will always be sought in the invisible world, in metaphysics,
beyond what we call 'nature'" (Lévy-Bruhl). The visible,
which they explore with an unparalleled meticulousness,
is transformed in their imagination. The movements of the
planet Venus are the effects of the actions of Quetzalcóatl, or, rather, *are* the actions of Quetzalcóatl. For the
world that created the Tonalámatl, this is reality.

Examples are countless.

Just as they could not conceive of the planet Venus as a star appearing and disappearing in the sky in accordance with some as yet unknown physical law, neither could they think of lightning as a physical phenomenon: to them it was an animal sent or rushing headlong from the sky to earth, the fire serpent hurled by Tláloc, the god of rain and of the rain of fire, who caused the destruction of the third world. They also represented lightning in the form of a dog, since it is "that which bites and devours." This is how we see it in the Dresdensis Codex (Fig. 10), as a dog hurling itself from the sky. "As lightning is the animal that sinks into the earth, that cleaves the earth," (Seler) the dog is also the companion of the dead, who opens the paths to the lower world. Xólotl, the god with the head of a dog, is frequently represented together with the fire serpent, which symbolizes lightning.

FIG. 10. Lightning. *Dresdensis Codex,* 58

Earthquake is explained as a movement of the deities charged with upholding the earth, who, wearied by their heavy task, pass it from shoulder to shoulder. Man must hurry to replenish their strength by offering sacrifices to them. "The Tlaxcaltecans attributed tremors and earthquakes to the fact that the gods who upheld the world became tired and were then replaced, which caused the tremors" (Muñoz Camargo, *Historia de la República y de la ciudad de Tlaxcala*).

The representations of Chalchiuhtlicue in the codices show a stream of water that gushes from the goddess and carries off men and objects. The interpreter explains that the water is a symbol of the vanity and inconstancy of earthly matters, an idea expressed in the saying, "Water carries away everything." In the Telleriano-Remensis Codex, a man with a shield and a bundle of lances and a woman with a wicker chest are dragged along by the water. According to Pedro de Ríos, the man represents the loss of possessions and death in war; the woman symbolizes a person sold as a slave.

The man of ancient Mexico could not conceive of movement as a mechanical force. It was represented as a spirit who took hold of men, animals, stars, and so forth, in order to drive them on. The twenty day signs are representations of concrete beings or things, like serpent, rabbit, water, dog, house, obsidian knife, flower, etc. There is only one exception, the seventeenth sign, which corresponds to Ollin, movement (Plate 13). This means that "movement" was as concrete to them as a serpent or a house.

According to the belief held in ancient Mexico, the blowing of the wind produces the movement of the sun across the firmament. Ehécatl, the wind god, pushes the solar globe. The bearers of the sun were two red serpents called Xixiuhcoa. The Xixiuhcoa were also the two coiled snakes on the altars of the north and south sides of the Tenayuca pyramid, whose crests were pointed to indicate the direction of the setting sun on the days of the solstices.

The hummingbird was a symbol of resurrection. It was believed that during the dry season this bird hung from a tree, dead, dry, and without feathers, and that it revived when the rainy season began. Sahagún says: "They come back to life each year; in winter they hang by their beaks from the trees: hanging there, they dry out and moult. When the tree becomes green again, the bird returns to life and his feathers reappear, and when thunder announces the approaching rains, the hummingbird awakes, revives, and flies." Therefore the souls of the dead warriors appear as hummingbirds when they descend from the sky. And since Huitzilopochtli is the patron of those who die in war and since he himself revives each morning, the hummingbird is his attribute. His name says as much: *huitzitzilin* means hummingbird. His head-dress is made of hummingbird feathers and he is usually shown with his head appearing through this bird's beak.

The butterfly, symbol of the planet Venus and of the dead warrior, is likewise the symbol of fire and of the fire god. In Plate 13 of the Borgia Codex, the act of kindling a

FIG. 11. The sign Ollin. *Borgia Codex.*

fire is characterized by a butterflylike figure, which flies from beneath one of the sticks. Why does not a flaming torch symbolize fire, as it does in almost all other parts of the world? What is the relationship between a butterfly and fire? Eulalia Guzmán ("Caracteres esenciales del arte antiguo mexicano," *op. cit.*) says: "The quivering of a bright flame reminded them of the agitation of a butter-fly's wings."

In addition to steel armor, spades, and bombards, the Spaniards also introduced the horse to the New World. The Aztecs, who had never seen this animal, found it a monstrous, inconceivable being that filled them with ter-ror. What did they think of this animal, to which the pre-Cortesian peoples attributed the superiority of the Span-iards? In what form did they incorporate it into their own cosmos? Bernal Díaz, one of Cortes' captains, relates that when Cortes undertook a punitive expedition to Honduras in 1524, he passed through Tayasal (today Flores) on the Island of Cosumel, where Canek, the chief, received him cordially. One of the horses had fallen ill and Cortes was obliged to leave it there in the care of Canek. After the Spaniards had marched off, the Indians installed the horse in one of their temples. To them, it was a powerful Spanish god, the creator of thunder and lightning. They brought it the usual offerings of fruit, animals, flowers, honey. Naturally, it died of hunger. The horrified Indians carved a stone image of the horse and placed it in the temple, where they adored it as they had previously adored the god it represented. When two missionaries, Fuensalida and Órbita, arrived in Tayasal in 1618, they found there the statue of the horse.

FIG. 12. Annihilation of the mountain. *Bologna Codex*, 10

The morning star (Tlahuizcalpantecuhtli) is the warrior who precedes the rising sun. With his weapon (his rays) he clears a path through the firmament for the solar god. The *Anales de Cuauhtitlán* tell how on set dates the morning star kills different kinds of beings: old men and women, great lords, rain (so that rain cannot fall), water (so that drought will ensue). In the Bologna Codex (Fig. 12) is represented the death of the mountain, which is also a living being. From its wound gushes a broad river of blood which flows around a heart also perforated by the morning star's lance.

When the artist of ancient Mexico draws a tree,

he shows the trunk, the flowers, and the root. The root almost always takes the form of serpentine jaws or an eagle's beak, by which the trunk anchors itself, so to speak, into the earth. The root is never omitted, because it is the characteristic, decisive element. To the man of ancient Mexico, the image of the tree would not be complete without the root; it would be only a stick decorated with flowers. The Western artist shows the trunk, the treetop, the branches, and the foliage in which there occasionally are flowers. He limits himself to what is visible. The root lies beneath the surface of the earth and therefore is not included. When Dürer or Leonardo do occasionally draw roots, these are roots that rise above the ground or are an anatomical study, let us say, of an excavated root. Dürer's realism is a capturing of the optic phenomenon; the realism of pre-Cortesian man is his knowledge of things, making visible the forces that work in them and thanks to which they actually exist. Beyond the exterior aspect, he tries to penetrate to the depths, in this instance literally to the depths of the earth, beneath the surface of the ground, until he reaches what is to him the essential.

Therefore, there does not exist that limitation that results in accepting as "reality" only what is perceived by the senses, considering everything inaccessible to them, everything suprasensible and metaphysical, as occult, fantastic, and so only relatively true. Pre-Columbian man does not distinguish between perception and imagination except in the sense that the perceptible and the perceived inspire in him a degree of distrust, not through any incapacity to understand the "real," but through an intimate necessity for appraisal. He does not care what something is, but what it means. His appraisal of something depends on its representation, which never begins with a material basis. It begins with his idea, developed through psychic experience and magic intuition, dream and subconsciousness, and, not least, the tradition of the clan. Therefore, man believes in his representation. And as in all parts of the world where causal thinking has not yet substituted for magic thinking, he believes in it so intensely that rational knowledge enjoys no esteem whatever as a constituent factor or a determinant of worth. The famous debate of the Middle Ages between realists and nominalists, in which the former believed in the real existence of ideas while the latter maintained that these were only creations of the intellect, is here resolved intuitively through the magic conception of the world: in the sense that the reality our senses present to us is only fiction, that the only reality lies in supernatural forces apprehended not by the senses, but only by the imagination.

The life of a man of magic thinking is an eternal day-dream to which not even death puts an end, since death does not properly exist in magic thinking: it is only a passing to another state of being.[6]

This is why the world of ancient Mexico is more complex than the world of determinism: it touches the spheres of both the visible and the invisible. The metaphysical is not an added dimension with its own measurement and law; it is an integral part of his cosmos, resulting in the peculiar unity of that conception of the world.

From such a conception of the world and of nature there arises, naturally, the conception of art. To represent a specific natural phenomenon, e.g., the serpent, eagle, jaguar, hummingbird, snail, i.e., whenever Aristotle recommends that the artist "copy nature," no attempt whatever is made to capture and transmit what is optically apprehensible. It is always definitely emphasized that the object depicted—the serpent or the eagle—and the form in which it is depicted are a substitution; that not the animal itself but the spirit or deity embodied in the animal is represented. A substitution myth, the mystery of metamorphosis: elements found in varied forms and in many religions. Just as the Maya knowledge of the stars could not become astronomy in our sense of the word, neither could pre-Cortesian observation of nature lead to naturalistic realism (as we understand it). It is an ex-

[6] With this, primitive man made one of humanity's great discoveries—that of the soul, i.e., of the being or spirit that abandons the body during sleep and after death, leaving it motionless.

pressive art, a reflection of the psychic-religious experience of reality and suprareality.

This raises the question as to whether the categories "abstract" and "concrete" can be applied to this art. In magic thinking, as we have already stated, this contradiction does not exist. The boundaries between the abstract and the concrete are blurred, as reflected in the artistic creation. One of the numerous examples of this is the statue of the Great Coatlicue in the National Museum of Anthropology, Mexico, in which abstract and realistic elements are blended. That mixture occurs so often that it can be considered one of the most characteristic features of that art. When the word "abstract" is used here, it is only for want of a better, as a technical recourse and with the realization that it is a notion foreign to the art of ancient Mexico.

Terms like "faithful to nature" or "unlike nature" also lack meaning here. They are wholly artificial concepts invented by the modern science of art merely as convenient classifications. All artistic creation, from whatever age, reflects the conception of nature held in its own time, and especially the social level that determines such creation. In this way, the work of art is understood by those for whom it is intended and attains social value and validity. If we today do not yet understand it, it is because our art, or at least the greater part of our artistic production, is still in the realm of wall decoration or of ephemeral, expository subject matter. El Greco's painting reveals his conception of nature as much as the work of Rembrandt reflects his, with the difference that in the art of El Greco, impregnated as it is with Toledan mysticism, all corporeity is dematerialized, filled with the passion of the soul that yearns to approach God and to be united with Him. El Greco imparted that transcendental character to form and color because his vision of the world was transcendental.

Furthermore, what our theory of art calls "faithful to nature" refers only to a mode of creating suitable for the optic convention of our times, and all artistic creation that more or less obeys this norm appears to us to be "faithful to nature." But there is no doubt that the intention of the

Byzantine, Romanesque, or Gothic artist aspires no less nor with less energy to establish his conception of nature in his work. If we feel that this work is "unlike nature," it is because he did not see in a worldly, rational manner, but in accordance with his religious, visionary, and spiritual conception of the world and of nature.

When the pre-Cortesian craftsman represented in expressive form those occult, mystical forces that act mysteriously within and behind phenomena, he was representing his own reality. His magic thinking did not prevent him from observing discerningly and using the results of such observation. We should remember the great number of plastic representations of serpents whose realistic fidelity to nature cannot be excelled by any European sculptor. But what does this mean? Does it mean an approach to what we call "realism"? Is it not rather that the plastic idiom of ancient Mexico, which takes advantage of so many and such diverse resources, also assimilates these elements in order to give expression to its spiritual, psychic, and religious conceptions?

# PART TWO
# The Expression

## 5

## The Esthetics of the Pyramid

The pre-Columbian and the Egyptian pyramids have only one thing in common: the name "pyramid." The Mesoamerican pyramid is a stepped pyramid divided into various sections. On the platform at the top, in front of a temple that is primitive both in structure and in the distribution of its chambers, were placed one or two statues of the gods (this last feature a peculiarity of the Aztec pyramid: Tenochtitlan, Tenayuca, Teopanzolco). Stairways, one of the most characteristic features of the pre-Cortesian pyramid, lead to the platform and the sanctuary. The Egyptian pyramid is a stereometric body. Above the square ground plan the walls rise without interruption to the vertex, a mathematical point, where there is no image, no temple, no stairway that connects it with the ground. There was an epoch when Egypt built stepped pyramids, stepped but without a stairway, but this form was abandoned in remote times. The pyramid of King Zozer at Sakkara (Third Dynasty, circa 2950 B.C.) was composed of five zones; that of King Seneferu (Fourth Dynasty, circa 2600 B.C.) of seven, of which only three remain. Seneferu ordered a second pyramid built in Dahshur, which fixed the type of the Egyptian pyramid, and the stepped pyramid disappeared completely from Egypt. It did not suit the temperament of that world.

The Egyptian pyramid is a funeral monument, designed to preserve the Pharaoh's body for centuries, together with the offerings that accompanied him to the tomb so that the great lord would not lack in the next world any of the luxuries and conveniences that had brightened his life in this. It testifies to a personality cult carried to its ultimate extreme, to the passion for immortality of a mighty man who raises a cyclopean monument so that his memory will be stamped forever on the minds of men. The decisive factor in this architectonic creation, the motive and purpose of its construction, is the mortuary chambers. "A hole in the ground," Worringer calls them [*Egyptian Art*], adding that the ground plan seems "an exhibition of the intestines of a constructive mass." "The different chambers are hollow, like caverns in the solid mortar of the walls" (U. Hoelscher, *Grabdenkmal des Koenigs Chephren*). The man of ancient Mexico did not practice this cult of the dead or the cult to personal vanity. Further, his architectonic sensibility, fundamentally unlike that of the Egyptians, was expressed not in an architecture of caverns, but in an architecture of open spaces.

The Mesoamerican pyramid is not a superstructure over a subterranean construction, although at times it enclosed the sepulcher of a prominent person, as in the Temple of the Inscriptions at Palenque; neither do we consider the cathedrals as superstructures over the sepulchers of the prelates and priests whose remains rest in them. The Mesoamerican pyramid is a socle, a base for a temple that was located on its upper platform.

No foreign model was necessary for the construction of the pre-Cortesian pyramid. It grew out of the religious conceptions of those people, out of the "worship of height," and out of the technical-constructive principles of an architectonic activity that over the centuries had scarcely overcome the primitive conditions imposed by the force of gravity.

Of course, the purpose of the pyramid is to raise the image of the divinity high above the human, but despite the vertical tendency inherent in its form, pre-Cortesian architecture manifests a marked will not only to counteract this upward impulse of the constructive mass, but also to deflect it, with astonishing dialectics, toward the horizontal. Notwithstanding its enormous height of over two hundred feet, the Pyramid of the Sun at Teotihuacán (Plate 15) gives the impression of a wide, spacious building extended along the plain. That horizontal orientation expresses a determined and very energetic will to form that reveals a great deal to one who can interpret the forms in terms of their *Wesenswert* (value of the essence). With a real obsession, all possible resources are used to impose a horizontal tendency upon the vertical disposition. The stairway of the pyramid, which interrupts the upward movement again and again at short intervals, divides the structure into different sections that are wider than they are high. At Calixtlahuaca (Plate 19), the walls of the pyramid are broken up into three strongly accented parts. For technical reasons, i.e., to give greater stability to the construction, they used sloping faces, one of the few elements of constructive evolution in the Mesoamerican pyramid. But this introduction of vertical movement is immediately neutralized by the insertion of wide surfaces bordered by stone fasciae, the so-called panels (*tableros*). The decoration of these panels, whether it be reliefs or paintings, develops a definitely horizontal rhythm. Examples: the plastic decoration of the pyramid of Quetzalcóatl at Teotihuacán (Plate 7), where the heads of Quetzalcóatl and Tláloc alternate in rhythmic succession and where, beneath the panels, the plumed serpent stretches out in undulations around the entire perimeter of the structure; Xochicalco (Plate 16), the meander formed by the twisting of the plumed serpent. At Tajín (a peculiarity of this culture), the entire body of the pyramid from top to bottom is decorated by horizontal rows of rectangular niches hollowed out in the walls, which greatly strengthens the horizontal effect (Plate 10).

Such a decided will to form, which certainly cannot be explained by technical necessities and only in part by the religious requirements, reveals an astonishingly clear and diaphanous conception of the world.

The Greek temple, such as the Temple of Poseidon in Paestum, has a definite horizontal effect. The force of the upward impulse of the columns is optically annulled by the wide, massive band of the architrave. The Medici Palace in Florence, broad and heavy, is horizontally disposed. The Greek and the man of the Renaissance be-

lieved that through their knowledge of nature and of the
forces of nature they had become lords and masters of
the Universe, and that all the cosmic enigmas had therefore been solved. The stepped pyramid, with its horizontal portions placed one above the other, represents the
heavens, the thirteen zones of heaven.

To pre-Cortesian man, heaven is the image of harmony, unchangeability, eternal order above the instability,
the struggle of the opposing forces to which everything
earthly is subject. There is none of the ecstasy, none of
the Faustian anxiety of Gothic man who, seeking the
supra-earthly in the earthly, wanders without respite, and
who is raised by metaphysical longing toward the inconceivable and divine with a magnificent gesture. A gesture, a yearning, a longing, to which he gives form and
expression in the miraculous magic of the cathedral. Worringer speaks of an "intoxication of the senses" and characterizes Gothic *pathos* as "sublime hysteria." The world
of ancient Mexico does not know such ecstasy, longing,
or upward impulse because it does not find the supra-
earthly to be enigmatic. "The concept of limitless, empty
space does not exist; the Universe is divided into regions
inhabited by gods and souls in an established hierarchy"
(Eulalia Guzmán, "Caracteres esenciales del arte antiguo
mexicano," *op. cit.*)

The pre-Columbian pyramid, however primitive its
structure may be, reflects a cosmic knowledge sufficiently
vigorous to sublimate the will to monumental expression
and to channel it toward pure, abstract, geometric form,
to impregnate the architectonic with a powerful spiritual
feeling. Perhaps this rising above the fortuitous and in-
finitely changing sensory phenomenon to the abstract con-
ceptuality was the great, dominant experience of those
so mistakenly called "peoples in a state of nature." Finding
themselves confronted with a nature that seemed to them
chaotic, blind, formless, and incomprehensible, they must
have considered it a miracle to be able to oppose the
threatening darkness with a human and spiritual order
crystallized in elemental forms, a clear and monumental
world; to be able to link that world created by them—a

religious creation—with the primordial element of their religious conceptions: the movement of the heavenly bodies that revealed the wonders of a perfect, mathematical regularity. "The Universe is written in the language of mathematics" (Galileo).

Cuicuilco (Plate 14), the preclassic pyramid in the Valley of Mexico, is an artificial hill. A path winds up and around its inclined walls. This type of construction would have been rejected at Teotihuacán because it was the reproduction of a hill, a copy of nature, of gross materiality and spiritual poverty. True to its artistic will, Teotihuacán tries to separate itself from nature. Reality (and association with reality) is profane, not sacred; it is below the sphere toward which its religious temper aspires. Teotihuacán architecture, based on functional values of form, develops the panel as the most characteristic of its formal features, that panel so typically its own: a wall rising at a right angle (Plate 20). Such a smooth, vertical wall is rarely if ever found in nature itself. Further, the panel, surrounded by a projecting frame, expressly accentuates its character of something artificial.

The Aztecs adopted, or tried to adopt, various elements from Teotihuacán, but not this panel. In their pyramids —Tenayuca, Teopanzolco (Plate 22)—the slope rises at an acute angle with a bold, vigorous, and magnificent impetus. Perhaps it was necessary to use the slope of the ground as a foundation to give a more solid support to those enormous piles, but surely it was not only this. Being a young nation, consciously overflowing with youthful vigor and filled with impulses bursting violently at every moment, the Aztecs could not attain the mature serenity and purity of Teotihuacán art or the spirituality of its pyramids. Teotihuacán is internal monumentality. The drive of Aztec art toward a monumental effect cannot dispense with exterior measures.

The orientation of the pyramid obeys geometric and astronomical principles. Following the movement of the sun, it is aligned in an east-west direction. Furthermore, the temples of the Toltec civilization—Tenayuca, Teotihuacán, Cholula, some of those at Chichén Itzá—all show a deflection of 16 degrees to 17 degrees from the east-west axis (Ignacio Marquina and Luis R. Ruiz, "La orientación de las pirámides prehistóricas," *Universidad de México,* 1932, Nos. 25 and 26).

Montezuma II wanted to rebuild the great Temple of Tenochtitlan because it was "slightly crooked," i.e., it did not completely coincide with this astronomical orientation (Ignacio Marquina, *Tenayuca*). The statue of the divinity in front of the temple was not supposed to cast any shadow on those days when the sun passed through the zenith (May 16 and July 26). Among the Maya, the new year began on July 26; they called that day "the descent of the sun god" (Fray Diego de Landa, *Relación de las cosas de Yucatán*). When, in 1577, Philip II, referring to that tradition, inquired about the days when the sun passed through the zenith in the different towns, one of the answers was couched in the following words: "On such and such a day, the sun visits our city" (Zelia Nuttall in *El México antiguo,* September 1931).

The band of serpents of the Tenayuca pyramid was composed of fifty-two serpent heads, in accordance with the fifty-two years of the native century (Enrique Juan Palacios, *Arqueología de México*). The Pyramid of Kukulkán (The Castle) in Chichén Itzá has nine terraces, divided into two halves by the great stairway: twice nine is the number of months in the solar calendar. There are 364 steps in the stairway, the topmost platform being the 365th, the number of days in the solar year. Each of the two stairways of the Pyramid of the Sun at Teotihuacán has 182 steps, for a total of 364. The Pyramid of Quetzalcóatl, also at Teotihuacán, was decorated with 364 heads. Within the strict symmetry of these hieratic-religious creations, an uneven number like 365 was impossible. During the most recent excavations at Tajín, it was discovered that one of the niches of the upper part, in the sixth section, had been almost hidden behind a stairway. This means that what was important and decisive was not the exterior appearance, but the fact that there be exactly 365 niches. In European architecture this problem would have been solved by narrowing some or all of the niches of the upper section so that there would be the desired number on each side of the stairs. Here no such expedient was resorted to. And why not? Because modifying the shape of the niches would have destroyed the unity of the construction, that in its clarity, rigor, and dignity has great affinity to the plastic conception of the Toltecs. They did not wish to violate the uniform rhythm of that decoration of niches that the entire constructive body of the pyramid obeys. It was less disturbing to allow the stairway to pass over one of the niches.

The nineteenth century—sentimental, romantic, addicted to the picturesque—which invented so-called "landscape gardening," an imitation of all nature within the confines of a garden, rejected French baroque gardening as artificial: formal flower beds marked off by rows of trees and shrubs planted equidistant from each other, pruned to the same height and shape; water contained in geometrically shaped pools. The Frenchman of the era of Louis XIV called this "humanizing nature." Humanizing nature, incorporating it in and subordinating it to the human spirit. The creative spirit of man imposes his will even on nature, ordains where and how a tree shall grow and what form its foliage shall display. It may be that something akin to this "humanizing" moved the pre-Cortesian peoples to give to their constructions the austerity and purity of abstract geometric forms, to adapt the buildings to the terrain, or else—contrariwise, as happens frequently—to adapt the terrain to the architectonic plan. The hills chosen for the sacred places were leveled off carefully and with tremendous effort in order to create plane surfaces of vast dimensions, suitable for terraces, patios, plazas, etc. Holmes (*Archeological Studies Among the Ancient Cities of Mexico*) says of Monte Albán: ". . . the whole mountain had been remodeled by the hand of man until not a trace of natural contour remained."

Defenseless before a demoniacal and hostile nature, before what we today would call "destiny," pre-Columbian man, thanks to his creative power, could for once overcome such disorder and such destiny, for the earthly is diffuse and incomprehensible, while the divine is clarity.

Worringer, who sees formalism in Egyptian art, and a sort of "Americanism" in its tendency toward the colossal, interprets its "abstract rectilinearity" as a "cold stylization without inspiration and absolutely inexpressive," completely lacking in a "sensual feeling for nature," which, according to him, the Egyptian lacks in general. Without here going into the details of this Egyptian problem, it should be said that none of this can be applied to the "abstract rectilinearity" of the Mesoamerican pyramid. While it is true that this pyramid evinces a strong will to overcome the instability of the phenomenon by a process of spiritualization that can be expressed only in abstract form, it is also true that there is here manifested an equally strong will to interweave the abstract form with a plastic or pictorial decoration, in the panels, that gives proof of an exact observation of nature.

The pillar—developed by Greek rationalism until it attained the functional form of the Doric column—assumes in Chichén Itzá the shape of an erect serpent that hisses in a menacing fashion, its tongue darting out. The pyramid at Tenayuca is circled by a band of serpents that imparts to the geometric body a breath of organic life, of something sprouting from the earth. These serpents at the base of the pyramid give the impression (and certainly this was the intention of its builders) of having just left the bosom of the earth. The entrance to the cave of Malinalco is the jaws of a serpent. Remember too the serpent decoration at Xochicalco. All of this reveals, together with the greatest sensitivity for the decorative value of the surface, what Worringer misses in Egyptian art: a sensual feeling for nature, of rare spontaneity and captivating expressive strength. Both the stele and the statue show that same mixture of abstract form and organic details.

As I have said, the pre-Columbian pyramid is an architecture of open spaces. This is equally true of the Greek temple with its peristyle, meant to impress whoever looked at it from without. Behind the columns was the *cella* containing the statue of the god, but "only the archeologist is interested in the interior of the Parthenon" (Charles Rufus Morey, *Medieval Art*). Christianity gathered the faithful into enclosed spaces in order to merge them into one community. It built the basilica and the cathedral. Although it is true that in the Mesoamerican pyramid there was an image of the deity inside the temple (generally composed of two or three chambers), it is no less true that in most cases a statue of the god was also placed in front of the temple, together with the sacrificial stone. Worship was celebrated in the open air. The masses congregated in front of the pyramid and performed their dances in the patio or on the platform. The necessary interior rooms for the priests' cells, the buildings intended for purposes related to the cult, are small, narrow, insignificant, and without direct light.

Since spacious interiors were not desired, construction techniques remained at a rudimentary level, limited to the building of massive and compact walls. Construction of the arch, the element that supports the walls, that permits rooms of greater size and height, and that really initiates the development of "spatial awareness," was unknown. A "false arch" did exist, especially among the Maya, and it is also a fact that a true arch was built at least one time. Seven arches span the chamber in Tomb 4 at Monte Albán, a Zapotec creation. They are not segmental arches, but between the two inclined ceiling slabs another is introduced as a keystone. This is not the keystone of the Roman arch, which lends solidity and resistance to the construction, but a support based on the principle of the arch. There existed among the Zapotecs, therefore, an architect who knew how to use the arch construction. This could have been of great importance in the development of architecture, as it was in Europe, but in Mexico this discovery did not attract attention. Evidently its importance was not recognized. Why was this so? Not only because progress, and especially "technical progress," was not appreciated, but also doubtless because construction of interiors was of secondary concern to those builders.

Despite the care exercised in excavating many of the pyramids and the caution employed in the restoration of some of them, what we see of the pyramids today is no more than a torso. In saying this I am thinking not only of the temples, which were built of perishable materials and therefore fell victims to the action of time and man. The pyramid was the dominant factor in a great ensemble of structures and empty spaces within a "master plan," as we would call it. With the small pyramids placed in front, as they were in front of the Pyramid of the Sun at Teotihuacán, with the wide plazas for worship, with the patios and platforms bounded by the walls of the buildings, these sacred sites were ensembles of a uniform structure, of intentional uniformity, conceived consciously and according to a plan. Empty spaces for the religious ceremonies, for the congregation of the faithful, great axes with the sanctuary as the visual center and goal. Something of the organization and grandiose homogeneity of such an ensemble can still be glimpsed at Teotihuacán, where the wall of the so-called Citadel, the patio of the Temple of Tláloc, and the axis absurdly named "The Street of the Dead," have been preserved.

A work by the architect Ignacio Marquina, *Estudio arquitectónico comparativo,* contains the plans of all the Mexican pyramids discovered to date, reconstructed by the author—a notable effort of Mexican archeology. There it is made clear that abstract-geometric thinking is not limited to the individual edifice, but that every constructive body is incorporated into a global ensemble subject in turn to a severe and perfect mathematical order. And the decisive factor, which even the most careful preservation of the individual building is incapable of transmitting, is the admirable sensitivity revealed in the free play and exact relationship between buildings and plazas. The most impressive example of that unity of conception is Monte Albán.

Those ensembles of buildings and empty spaces attest to a sensitive intuition of space that in itself is sufficient to ensure to pre-Hispanic architecture, notwithstanding its primitive technique, a predominant place in the history of world art. And in them we see once again that the plastic value is enriched by the dialectic tension between the total, abstract conception and the experience of reality manifested in details.

The pre-Cortesian pyramid, like the Egyptian pyramid and the Chinese pagoda, was erected in all its splendor by men who lived in miserable huts or caves. The individual and his housing did not mean anything. What was built, and built in such gigantic dimensions, was built for the community. "The surplus energies of the peoples of America were absorbed by the religious requirements, as soon as they had taken care of the bare necessities of life" (Vaillant). The Pyramid of the Sun in Teotihuacán has a volume of 45,000,000 cubic feet; the weight of its stones has been calculated at four million tons (Palacios). Weights had to be transported and moved without machines, without iron, without vehicles (not even the wheel was known), without draft animals. For the construction of such pyramids, only one force was available—human labor. Without taking into account its artistic value, the pyramid of ancient Mexico is one of the most impressive testimonials to the collective spirit and the collective will of man.

## 6

## The Mask

A common art form even in archaic times, the mask is one of the most characteristic elements of all the cultures of ancient Mexico. Judging by the abundant discoveries that have been made, it occupied an important place in the imaginative world of those men. Part of the ritual, and intimately linked to the cult of the dead, it has a magico-religious significance. With its help man is transformed into the being it represents, and all the physical and magical qualities of the being pass to him. The warriors disguise themselves as eagles or jaguars. The mask is their uniform; it transmits to them the strength, audacity, and agility of these beasts, not only in their own imaginations, but also in that of their enemies, who tremble before the superiority of the mythical beings. In certain Maya regions, masks of Chac, the rain god, were placed on the façade to show that the building and its occupants were recommended to the protection of that most powerful deity (Plate 77).

The mask is one's other self. Pre-Cortesian man has two names; besides the one he uses in daily life, he has a ritual name, which is the sign of the day of his birth. Two names, two distinct personalities: one corresponds to the corporeal and the real, the other to the ritual—or, so to speak, psychic—and the suprareal. The mask is the expression of his suprareal personality.

The mask was worn as a pectoral or as part of a pectoral, on a headdress or belt, as well as over the face. Where the mask was worn was of no importance. Whenever he wore it, man was subject to its emanation. This accounts for the many small masks that have been found, which served as talismans for defense and protection. The smoking mirror of Tezcatlipoca is a species of mask, by which the god sees everything and discovers all crimes and which he wears in place of his missing foot or as a pectoral. In Santa Rita, a mural (belonging to Maya-Toltec culture) has been preserved that represents a sort of office of the dead. Two priests are dancing around a drum to which is attached a mask of the death god. The significance of the scene is that the god is in the drum and the drumroll is the voice of the god. Sahagún says that these drums were considered "like gods."

Just as the crown represents and gives effect to the sovereignty of a monarch, the magic power of the deity is represented by his characteristic adornment, one of the principal elements of which is the mask or masks he wears.

This magic process of transubstantiation, by virtue of which the deity is impregnated with the nature of the being represented by the mask, also acts conversely: the spirit, the power of the deity, is transmitted to this being just as it can be transmitted to any creature of nature, to any man or animal chosen by the deity. Thus the mask elevates its wearer above others of his species and indicates that he is invested with supernatural gifts. The dog, who has the duty of conducting the dead to the lower world, like his model the god Xólotl, is transformed into Xólotl, thanks to the mask. The disguise performs a magic transformation: the common domestic animal becomes a being endowed with divine powers.

The "Olmec mouth"—which also appears in the form of a mask—a sign of power and dignity among the Olmecs, is a transformation of the jaguar, their tribal god. Among the attributes of the Toltec and Aztec sovereigns is the mask of Quetzalcóatl, whose name the Toltec sovereigns bear. This means that each of them not only possesses the power, the goodness, the wisdom, and even the sense of justice that characterize this god, but also that he *is* Quetzalcóatl.

When Cortes landed at Vera Cruz in a year *Ce Ácatl*, one of the years in which Quetzalcóatl was expected to return, Montezuma really believed that the great god had

come back to his people and that a messianic promise was
thus being fulfilled, according to which his return would
initiate a new era of prosperity and peace. As Quetzalcóatl's "lieutenant," he felt obliged to send the returning
one the four "suits of the god." In Chapter IV of Book
XII of Sahagún's work, those four outfits are described
with all their details and accessories the necklaces, earplugs, shields, bucklers, mirrors, and sandals—and four
masks are also mentioned. Cortes sent these "presents" to
Emperor Charles V. It is believed that the mask of Xiuhtecuhtli, owned for centuries by the Medici and today
in the Ethnological Museum, Rome, is one of those masks
presented to Cortes by the Aztec sovereign. The head of
Xiuhtecuhtli, with a nose ring in the form of a stepped
fret, appears through the jaws of a serpent, and at each
side of the face appear coiled Xixiuhcoa (the plural of
Xiuhcóatl), i.e., fire serpents (of which only one remains).
It is a mask of "fine turquoise" mosaic mounted on a
wood base. The high esteem that these rare stones enjoyed
is shown by the Náhuatl word, *teoxíhuitl*, "turquoise of
the god," or, "divine turquoise." Use of this "fine turquoise"
was prohibited in any masks but those of the gods or of
the kings. In many ceremonies the priest who played the
role of the god's representative dressed himself in the vest-
ment and mask of the god, e.g., in the feasts of the "de-

FIG. 13. Representation of a mortuary bundle. *Magliabechiano
Codex*, 72

scent of the deity," in which the god visited the community. In the feast Xochíhuitl, in honor of Macuilxóchitl, the god of music, dance, and pleasure, one of the priests, "decked himself out in the finery of this god as if he were his image or person, which meant the god himself" (Sahagún). It was a ritual obligation to invite Macuilxóchitl to the merchants' banquet. Wearing the mask of Macuilxóchitl, the priest representing the god appeared at the house of the host. If he were not invited, the god became angry and punished with serious venereal disease those who participated in the banquet. Twice during the feast Izcalli ("growth") they took out of the temple an image of the deity to whom it was consecrated: once adorned with a turquoise mask and with quetzal feathers, and once with a mask of red coral and black obsidian, and with macaw feathers. In his commentary to the Borgia Codex, Seler explains that this double adornment "symbolized the sprouting and maturing of the maize."

The most critical moment in the lives of the peoples of ancient Mexico took place at the end of each fifty-two-year period, when the calculation of the ritual year coincided with that of the solar year. During those special days, men were gripped by apocalyptic anguish. The night was peopled by dangerous demons. Masks of paper or maguey leaves were placed on the weakest members of the community—pregnant women and children—for it was feared that pregnant women could be changed into monsters and kill their relatives and that the children would turn into rats, especially if they were allowed to fall asleep. On Plate 34 of the Borbonicus Codex, where the renewal of the fire is represented, we see women taking refuge in the interior of a house, awaiting the signal that the danger has passed. Near their heads appear the masks. In this case, the mask served as protection, i.e., magic protection. Because of the mask, the demons, misled by the disguise, did not recognize the victim they sought and the course of misfortune was averted.

The mask formed part of the trappings of the dead. When a body was cremated, as was customary with the Toltecs and Aztecs, the so-called "mortuary bundle" was made of cloth—a bundle shaped like a seated person, covered with the vestments of the deceased—that was placed on the wood or stone box or the ceramic urn that contained the ashes; a mask was tied on in the place of the head. Where cremation of the dead was not practiced, a mask covered the face of the deceased. In the tomb of a Maya prince-priest discovered by Alberto Ruz Lhuillier in the Pyramid of the Inscriptions at Palenque, a pile of green stones was found beside the skeleton: parts of a mask, which was reconstructed with most admirable care. Also a mortuary mask is the splendid and singular work in the National Museum of Anthropology, Mexico, of Teotihuacán style. It was found in a tomb in Tlapa (State of Guerrero) beneath the remains of a skeleton (Plate 33). The face consists of small pieces of pale-green jadeite. On this green background are incrusted tiny pieces of reddish shell, which represent—once again—a lip ornament in the form of a stepped fret and, on the forehead, an ornament, or, better, a symbol: a "precious vessel," i.e., a vessel intended to receive the sacrificial blood. As this extraordinary work attests without any doubt, the masks were in no way portraits. They were symbolic images, concept images. "Impenetrable," says Laurette Séjourné in speaking of the Teotihuacán masks (*Pensamiento y religión en el México antiguo*).

Since the pre-Cortesian mask in general, not only the mortuary mask, is an image concept, the image in which man saw himself just as he was, or, rather, just as he wished to see himself, it is logical that each of the different cultures of ancient Mexico developed its own peculiar type of mask, which lets us distinguish clearly its specific creative will. Therefore, a comparison of the masks of different origin—Teotihuacán, Aztec, Olmec, Totonac, Maya —gives us in each case very important information about the idiosyncrasy of the formal language of the respective cultures.

The legend of Quetzalcóatl relates that in order to disconcert and ruin him, his enemy Tezcatlipoca made him a present of a mirror. When Quetzalcóatl saw his image in the mirror, his ugliness terrified him and he ordered a mask made for himself, without which he would not show himself to the people. It is the first flight of Quetzalcóatl, *the flight from himself,* the flight toward another personality, higher, and more sublime.

## 7

## The Stepped Fret

Together with the plumed serpent, the stepped fret (Xicalcoliuhqui) is the most typical ornamental form of the Valley of Mexico, territory of the Nahua tribes. It is as characteristic of Nahua culture as the stylized lotus flower is of Egyptian art, the rosette of Assyrian art, the palmette and the meander of Greek art, and the ornament of lacery or plaits, an ornament steeped in exaltation, of the Celto-Irish. We find the stepped fret as far north as Arizona (Pueblo Indians, Casas Grandes), passing through Yucatán, to as far south as Peru, where it is of predominant importance in ornaments. In Yucatán, it is introduced by the Toltec invaders. It also appears in the Classic Maya stage, imported perhaps from the Central Plateau, but it can in no way be considered a typically Maya ornament.

Within the compass of the Nahua tribes, the stepped fret figures in innumerable variations and on every sort of object, religious and profane: in architecture, sculpture, painting, fabrics, and ceramics. The Aztecs called it the "volute of the calabashes" because it was the favorite ornament of the potters. In Mitla it is the representative decoration in the palaces of the high priest and of the king. In Tajín, the different types of stepped fret are impressive because of their monumental form, so different from the cursive elegance of the frets at Mitla. It is often found in the stone or feather mosaic that covers the shields of the warriors, but it never appears in connection with the god or the cult of the dead. For example, it is never found on Zapotec funerary urns but is frequently related in some manner to the gods of water, wind, and fire.

In a documented study of the stepped fret illustrated with approximately 250 examples, Hermann Beyer (*"El origen, desarrollo y significado de la greca escalonada"* in *El México Antiguo,* Book II, Nos. 3 and 4) distinguishes in its basic form three elements (Fig. 14): 1) the steps, 2) the center, and 3) the hook; but this does not affect the differences in graphics and composition that exist between the nearly spiral form and the geometrically stylized meander. What is the meaning of this form, which is a combination of dissimilar and even contradictory elements?

FIG. 14. Stepped fret. Basic form.

For Beyer, to whom we are indebted for his numerous and important contributions in the field of Mexican and Maya archeology, the stepped fret is a purely decorative formal element, "an artistic creation that serves to ornament monotonous surfaces whatever their form, size, or material." Regarding the form to which his investigation refers, he admits that either serpents or waves may have been imitated, but the available data, he says, "does not permit us to decide on one or another of the many possibilities." It must be admitted that in this case we have no documental proof supported by written or other sources and it may be that there is no possibility of proof because there cannot be any; because the stepped fret appeared in such remote times that its meaning and significance are beyond elucidation, at least with the present resources of Mexican archeology, and perhaps not even in the future. But although we must for now renounce irrefutable proof, we shall not for that reason relinquish the search for its meaning and significance.

The following consideration faces us especially: the art of ancient Mexico is markedly religious art, an art of suprasensible contents of knowledge. What determines the creative will is not the esthetic experience but the religious. That this, the most intimate and powerful among transcendental experiences, intensifies to the highest degree the artistic expressivity in all cultures—Assyrian, Byzantine, Gothic, Mexican—is seen clearly when we investigate from which psychic stratum spring the impulses of artistic creation. It cannot be doubted that the religious experience gives the soul an impetus incomparably more intense than the esthetic experience of "art for art's sake."

Pre-Cortesian art shows a great determination to completely fill all surfaces. Just as there is no vacuum in the cosmic structure, there cannot be one in the work of art. But, as always in great art of a religious character, it is not just a matter of covering surfaces. What is created always "signifies" something, reveals something about the myths or the gods, no matter how slight or remote the relationship may be. One example from many: the flower (*xóchitl*), a decorative element pleasing to nearly all artistic cultures, was for the Mexicans a symbol of blood, especially the blood of sacrifice and of autosacrifice. In the codices, a bowl adorned with flowers represents a vessel for the blood of sacrificial victims. Seler, whose investigations begin with the exterior aspect of the object represented in order to penetrate to its meaning, says: "In Mexican antiquity there is nowhere found anything arbitrary, capricious, or merely fantastic. Every creation has a definite meaning and significance" (*Las llamadas vasijas sacrales de los zapotecas*).

If we abide by this experience, it is difficult for us to believe that one of the essential ornaments of the world of ancient Mexico was no more than a decorative element. In the first place, the great frequency of the stepped fret and the fact that it was used for centuries oppose this thesis. As we can observe from some of the "dying" European styles, any exclusively ornamental form would have spent itself in the course of time, lost its attraction, and been superseded by new formal creations with new fascination and suggestive force. The stepped fret was not replaced by new ornaments, because the Nahua people saw in it a psychic or magic value beyond that of the esthetic. The stepped fret is no more a purely decorative form than is the cross. Manuel Gamio (*The Population*

*of the Valley of Teotihuacán*) says: "The aesthetic value
of decoration of those [pre-Columbian] times differs from
that of today in the sense that the former not only en-
deavored to incarnate the beautiful for its beauty but that
it was at the same time symbolical . . . it synthesized the
deepest and most emotional problems of existence . . . the
purely decorative value of the conventional design is re-
markable and it produces a deep esthetic emotion; but,
we repeat, its originators associated with it such transcendental ideas that their emotions were far more complex and deeper."

The stepped fret has its origin in an era when man
cannot yet permit himself the luxury of a purely ornamental art. He is still disturbed and threatened by the
enigmatic and unfathomable world that confronts him, and
must still ask himself before every phenomenon what it
contains, what mysterious forces it harbors. What he creates from such psychic attitude expresses his instinct for
self-preservation and his will to defend himself. Without a
doubt, the stepped fret is a sign, a kind of talisman. It is
conjuration and protection. Since it is never associated with
death or with the death god, it may be assumed that it
constitutes a sign of magic protection against death, perhaps a fetish or totem, transmitted from remote times
through innumerable generations until the arrival of the
Spanish conquerors.

Gordon interprets the stepped fret as a stylization of the
serpent, an interpretation that as far as I can determine
has been adopted by many Mexicanists. Seler believes
that the stepped fret is a representation of the waves and
"of the wind that makes eddies in the water" and to a certain degree this opinion reinforces Gordon's. In the imagination of pre-Cortesian man, the snake, living by choice in
humid places, is closely associated with water. In the
Pyramid of Quetzalcóatl at Teotihuacán, marine shells and
sea snails are the ornaments that accompany the serpent.
In the mural of the Temple of Agriculture, the waves have
almost the same form as the undulating lines of the serpent's body.

It appears that the stepped fret is the fire serpent, light-

ning, the attribute of Tláloc, who in the conception of the
priests is first of all the god of the rain of fire that causes
the third destruction of the world. The zigzag form can
be interpreted as a bolt of lightning, the so-called hook
as clouds of fire or smoke, possibly also the tip of the tail.
Plate 33 of the Borgia Codex represents a black god who
"holds up in each hand the undulate object [of double
curvature], bristling with fangs, that symbolizes lightning."
Figs. 15 and 16 show two fire serpents from the Borgia

FIG. 15. Fire serpent. *Borgia Codex,* 33

Codex whose bodies, composed of trapeziums fitted one
within the other, have a stepped contour, "a peculiarity
that generally characterizes the fire serpent, or Xiuhcóatl." From the jaws and body of one of them (Fig. 16),

FIG. 16. Fire serpent emitting flames in the form of hooks. *Borgia
Codex,* 46

spit twisting flames—volutes in the form of a hook—"the
object similar to *cuítlatl,* from which issue tongues of fire
and smoke, the symbol of fire." It is very probable, then,
that we have here, drawn with great clarity and in a

simplification typical of a sign, the form that led to the
steps and the hook of the stepped fret. Seler identifies
that serpent with lightning, and the deity who hurls the
lightning with Xólotl, "the natural companion of Tláloc,
god of the mountains, clouds, rain, and lightning"; with
that same "dog-headed Xólotl who in his own being
represents the fire that falls from the sky, i.e., lightning."
In this connection, a drawing on Plate 23 of the Vaticanus
B Codex is very interesting. Near the four upholders of
the sky and under the sign Ollin, movement, we see the
fifth region of the world, the center, symbolized by a
figure falling—and falling down a stairway!—into the jaws
of the earth (toward the center of the world, Fig. 17).
The interior of the earth is characterized by transverse
stripes parallel to the slope of the stairway, and, with great
exactitude and clarity, the triangle beneath the stairway
constitutes the "center" of the stepped fret. This representation recalls again the dog Xólotl, who, "being the
animal of lightning, the fire that sinks into the earth, the
animal who cleaves the earth," is also "he who opens the
roads to the lower world." In my opinion, these two drawings reveal without any doubt that the stepped fret
originates in the sign of the fire serpent, the sign of lightning. And the zigzag form of the stairway is at the same
time that of the stepped pyramid.

Obviously, a purely formal investigation limited to a
study of such isolated elements as the spiral, the broken
line, etc., is insufficient here. We must seek the value of
the essence of such form and abide by what is consciously
or unconsciously manifested as creative will in an ensemble of formal elements. An undulating line can be reduced as in the Greek meander to an exclusively decorative form, to a rhythmic ornament intended to cover the
surface and which in the minds of the spectator and the
artist is related only very vaguely if at all with the natural
model that inspired it. But an undulating line can also sug-
gest to the spectator and to the artist very definite ideas,
although it be stylized to such a degree that a person
alien to that imaginative world and to its psychic and spiritual hypotheses sees in it nothing more than an ornament.

It proves nothing that our eyes cannot at first glance distinguish in the stepped fret the serpentine form from which it probably is derived. Rather, it shows that since time immemorial the Nahua people were so familiar with this sign that the stylization could be limited to a mnemotech-

FIG. 17. Xólotl, falling to Earth. *Vaticanus B Codex*, 23

nical insinuation. In those days everyone knew what was meant by this symbol, which in the course of long tradition had gradually adopted the form of the stepped fret. A similar case and typical example of the modifications that a sign can undergo without ceasing to be a sign is that of the two rings around the eyes of Tláloc. Originally these were two serpents, so closely associated with the rain god in the pre-Cortesian imagination that they became his sign, and in the representations of this deity they were frequently a substitute for his head. We know this because these two serpents are still clearly to be distinguished in the many images of Tláloc that have come down to us. That transformation of common signs, gradual but so radical that at the end of the process the original form can scarcely be detected, is in no way a Mexican peculiarity, but a very general occurrence. The Roman capital "M" is a modification of the Phoenician "m." In all Mediterranean countries "m" is the first letter of the word *"mar"* (sea). It appears in the Phoenician alphabet as a stylization of the ocean wave. In the Roman alphabet the movement of the wave becomes a "V" suspended between two symmetrical strokes having the same angle of inclination. The primordial form, i.e., the undulating wave, is now glimpsed only dimly, but the origin is unmistakable. In this case we know some of the intermediate links; in the stepped fret, they have not been preserved.

The stepped fret differs from the majority of ornamental forms familiar to us—the palmette, rosette, Egyptian lotus, etc.—by its totally asymmetrical structure. One can attempt to draw an axis through it in any direction, but symmetry never results, another indication that it originated as a sign. But this method of studying the stepped fret is misleading. It is wrong to study it as an isolated form since it really does not exist as such. Beyer mentions two exceptions: one, that of the warrior's shield, where it is adapted to the circular form of the shield; the other, that of a seal of Tlatelolco. The seal was a kind of type face by which the drawing was stamped on the skin, probably as a substitute for tattooing, making it unnecessary to paint the same drawing several times. The combination of steps, center, and hook, the basic form, to abide by Beyer's definition, is merely one link in a chain. Actually, the stepped fret arises only through the combination and repetition of a number of basic forms. In some cases, e.g., the Labná "Arch," the basic form is repeated inversely like an image reflected in a mirror so that it produces a symmetrical ornament, like the palmette. In general, several frets are united in rhythmic succession, almost always horizontal. In Mitla, where the walls are decorated with three rows of frets one above the other, the horizontal orientation is strongly emphasized by the intermediate bands that separate them. Not even in the Salon of Frets does the vertical direction predominate. The asymmetrical form is inseparable from and carries forward the rhythm of the whole. It might well be said that the stepped fret derives meaning and plastic value from absorption in multiplicity. From this we deduce that the decisive factor in the morphogenesis of the fret is dynamic rhythm.

Comparing the stepped fret with the Greek meander,

an essential difference must be pointed out. Whether square or spiral in form, the Greek meander is a line that develops uniformly and in perfect harmony, without interruption or contrasts. It is an abstract geometric form, in which the original model is so refined and dematerialized that it is difficult to identify. Eurhythmy of line that reaches equally toward all sides of the squared surface and divides the surface uniformly. A restrained ornament, so well ordered that each movement gives rise to the next, logically calculable and calling to mind Euclidian geometry. Objectivity, absolute neutrality in the presence of the phenomenon, the formal configuration of a world confident that it has overcome chaos. "An ideal play of organic tendencies," says Worringer of the Greek meander (*Form in Gothic*). "Freed from all dualistic memories, man celebrates, in art as in religion, the realization of a felicitous state of spiritual equilibrium." It is, so to speak, the projection, into the plastic domain, of the unities of time, place, and action, categories established for the drama by Aristotle. A Greek sculptor could say: "A successful work of art is the result of scrupulous exactitude in the application of multiple arithmetical proportions." "The divine proportion." We might also say: divinization of proportion. Sensuality is absorbed by logic; life becomes abstract idea. That ideal form is the highest aspiration of the Greek will to art. Absolute harmony, as achieved with peerless perfection in the meander, is what won the admiration of the world to Greek art through the centuries.

The stepped fret contains no trace of such harmony, nor does it seek to. The destructive logic of sensuality is definitely not the ideal of ancient Mexico. In that world there is no Archimedean point beyond life where the powers that regulate the universe maintain themselves in "happy stability." To pre-Cortesian man, the powers that built the cosmos are dynamic, and what sustains it is the tension by which they are mutually held in check and the intensity of this tension that can never relax at any point. He is not able to arrive at serene contemplation. He must act to offset the danger; he must be alert, he must struggle and offer his own life on the sacrificial stone. From another point of view, it could be said that what prevents the man of ancient Mexico from achieving that dignified harmony is his strong psychic impulse, whose constantly renewed energies beg for release. Antagonistic tendencies, bound by rhythm, by form, i.e., by a spiritual order.

The dynamic rhythm of the stepped fret springs from the clash of antagonistic formal elements and from the violent interruptions that are produced again and again in its drawing. The stairway is a vehement ascent; the hook breaks this movement, twists it, destroys it with identical vehemence. It is as though a demoniacal force had committed itself to annihilating all the energy inherent in the stairway. In the next figure we see the same ascent, the same interruption. Each time that the stairway breaks away, it is prevented from achieving a free, unhampered development; its destiny is always to come upon the counterforce that destroys it, pushes it back down to the level it started from. There is never a harmonious flow. There is a struggle of elements, an interruption of the course of the movement, a brusque change of direction, a new advance, a new defeat, birth and death. A rhythm that rests in the constant repetition of the motif and in an energetic contrast among the different elements. Eulalia Guzmán compares it to the rhythm of pre-Cortesian music, which does not have any melody, and with the dance, whose esthetic goal "ought not to be realized in each individual separately but in the group as a whole." Sahagún mentions a dance that was celebrated in the "month of autumn" in honor of the goddess Teteo, in the great "feast of the sweeping." This dance, which lasted several days, was called "moving the hands from one side to the other." "The uniformity of the motion, i.e., the collectively unified rhythm, does not have pleasure as its object but is a religious function, magical above all," writes Eulalia Guzmán. She correctly compares this dance with a "fret in motion."

To this contrast between movement and countermovement, to the constant production of this contrast, the stepped fret owes its very powerful intensity, which is at the same time the expression of a strong vital feeling. We should be able to establish a comparison with the Celtic ornament of lacery or plaits, interweaving spasmodically and finally coiling in upon itself. But the tension inherent in the stepped fret is different. The Celtic ornament, the forerunner of Gothic ornamentation, reveals a longing for God, a yearning for redemption by God, Who is sensed but cannot be grasped. Ecstasy, the burning of the soul expelled from Paradise, condemned to suffer by its subjection to the body, being forced everywhere and in every way to seek "reunion" with God. An exalted *pathos,* an excessive longing that flies all limits and obstacles, explosive in every gesture. A feverish excitation. And in effect that ornament of laceries, the turbulence of its zigzag, resembles a curve of fever. That obsession with God does not acknowledge the earthly. It wishes to overcome it, and, overcoming it, destroy it. The stepped fret produces tension within an established order. There is not that disturbance, that tangle of forms displacing each other, seeming to devour each other. The various formal elements are isolated, cleanly outlined, separated from their environment by a strong contour. Its trajectory lies between two fictitious horizontals, but occasionally these are real. Never does the ornament overstep this limitation; there is absolute surrender to order. The *pathos* that prevails is disciplined, free of exaltation. The hook, often dentate—as though it were desired to interrupt even the tranquil flow of this line—breaks the vertical movement of the steps, true, but the detour toward the horizontal always follows the given order. The hook does not develop arbitrarily even when it is a spiral. Within the defined irregularity and asymmetry of the whole, a homogeneous rhythm is strictly and rigorously observed.

The expressivity of a creation lies in the intensity of the stresses produced by its formal elements. To illustrate this fact we refer to a phenomenon in the field of electricity: current increases when it encounters resistance. This is applicable to all expressive and imaginative art. On the other hand, classicist art aspires to an organization of forms in which all divergent forces are harmoniously reconciled in a sphere of formal equilibrium far above all anguish, even metaphysical anguish.

This elevation above the real world—the world of caprice, of irregularity—considered impure, represents for classicist art the ideal of beauty. The Greek meander is graphic expression of a radical absence of tensions. It is perfection and at the same time total inexpressivity, which, in accordance with the Greek mentality, is an asset rather than a defect. It has been said that "Greek art is beyond all becoming." It is realized in the contemplation of existence. This is its greatness and from the viewpoint of the expressionist will to art, its lack of vitality. It is the European that the Greek balanced against the Oriental, that could not resign itself to the merely real and whose spirituality is an ascent toward the suprareal, the only sphere in his judgment that reveals the supreme truth, the real reality. The stepped fret is the plastic precipitate of an internal, vehement excitation, of an impulse to act; in its rhythm is projected a vital feeling of incessant conflict, advance and regression; the advance, and the check imposed on it again and again by the antagonistic forces. Surely it is not by chance that the art of ancient Mexico, like Celtic and Early Germanic art, shows a strong preference for the animal motif: serpent, eagle, tiger, hummingbird, butterfly, turtle, dog, coyote, etc.—the animal, whose characteristic peculiarity is motion, mobility. Neither is it by chance that the static cultures—Egypt (the lotus), Greece (the palmette) —demonstrate an equally strong preference for the vegetal motif.

The Greek meander can be read forward or backward. It unfolds toward both sides in a uniform rhythm. Mechanized movement, perfectly unified in its drawing, accent, spacing. One more among the many perfections that Greek art boasts. It is movement and especially the idea of movement, but movement not subject to any one direction. The stepped fret moves in a definite direction, indicates its direction emphatically, and that emphasis passes to the spectator, like a spell that fascinates him and subjects him to the influence of its magico-religious function.

Pre-Columbian art also developed the meander, a meander formed by the undulations of the plumed serpent. We see it at Xochicalco and in the Pyramid of Quetzalcóatl at Teotihuacán. The meanders on the façade of the Temple of the Tigers at Chichén Itzá are composed of two entwined serpents whose undulating bodies terminate, one at each side, in serpentine heads. The animal has become ornament. But the abstraction is never so radical that the natural model is forgotten. And it cannot be otherwise. This meander is more than a play of form, more than ornament; it is an ornament with a meaning. And, like the stepped fret, it does not lack direction. It always has a direction, a goal, and an end. In the Temple of the Tigers, the meanders wind toward the four corners of the building, oriented in accordance with the cardinal points and representing the four corners of the universe. In other cases, such as the frieze of tigers between the frets in the same temple at Chichén Itzá, in the friezes at Tula, in the serpentine meanders at Xochicalco, the movement is directed toward the center, toward the entrance of the sanctuary, where the idol and the sacrificial altar are found. Movement with a pre-established trajectory and goal.

There is neither prescribed trajectory nor previously established goal in the ornament of ancient Asia. It expands on the surface toward all sides. The favorite form is the rosette or star that emits its rays uniformly in all directions from a center. The rosette is an expression of absolute symmetry; drawing a diagonal through any one of its points results in two symmetrical halves. The rosette is the form without beginning or end, in which motion and rest are superposed. In it is achieved the fictitious point at which zero and the infinite coincide. What develops is a tapestry of ornaments of perennial rhythm, dematerialized, unrelated to the material and to the material phenomenon, an artistic image of the starry sky with its myriad shining points, a cosmic order that man may experience, but into which he may not enter; Oriental wisdom that arrives at perfect passivity.

The essential element of the Celtic ornament of lacery or plaits is the double spiral that shoots off, gyrates, twists around itself, and is ruptured continually in an exalted motion, entangled in itself and imprisoned in its own entanglement, from which it finds no exit—the Faustian yearning of the North. Motion without rest, whose plan, goal, and meaning are only the dynamics of the motion. In the spatial miracle of the Gothic cathedral that delirious exaltation will end by achieving its supreme goal: God.

Charles Rufus Morey (*Medieval Art*), discussing the Celtic spiral, cites an Irish legend about a man who leaves his home and sets out on a walk. He does not know where he is going. He leaves the place where he is, to go somewhere else, to go from his own world to some unknown, mysterious world that he dreams of, whose vision disturbs him, and that he never reaches because at the end of his journey he finds himself again at the place that he started from. This, translated into the language of form, is the Celtic spiral, which unravels in order to coil up on itself anew. The rational Greek, whose ornament is the meander and the palmette, would determine his destination before starting, select the shortest road between the two points, and set out directly toward his goal. The Oriental does not travel; immobile and absorbed in thought, he remains seated in front of his tent. He does not have to travel because he has the world within himself and he lives life in his vision. And the man of ancient Mexico? For him, all roads lead to the gods, the shapers and builders of the universe. He has no other goal. His thoughts, knowledge, and belief are directed only toward them. This is his clarity, his certitude. He cannot give himself over to passivity, to Oriental quietism. He is pressed by the cosmic mission that has been entrusted to him: to maintain the world, to prevent the catastrophe. But all the roads are peopled by spirits, demons, the sacred and threatening animal—the serpent—whose destructive power he must divert and conjure through adoration and magic.

The spiral form exists in all cultures. It has one almost identical basic form with many variations, but the value of the essence (*Wesenswert*) is, in each case, entirely different. The Celtic spiral is ecstatic longing for redemption; the Greek meander is neutrality, euphony, esthetic harmony; the Oriental tapestry of ornaments is a passive submersal in the consciousness of the infinite. And the stepped fret expresses the vital tension of forces subject to a rhythm.

In his explorations at Kin-Lishba, a settlement of the Pueblo Indians in Arizona, Byron Cummings found a great number of exceptionally beautiful and interesting ceramic vessels, many of them decorated with the stepped fret. In his book *Kin-Lishba,* Cummings dates these vases between 1050 and 1350 A.D. Fig. 25 shows a characteristic example. In the center of the vessel is a circular band surrounded by an area decorated with a striped ornament. The exterior contour line rises in a curve, is brusquely interrupted, descends vehemently as a straight line toward the center circle, and rises again as a curve only to be pulled down again with the same violence. The same system of curves and straight lines is repeated near and in respect to the circular edge of the vessel. In order to unite the different levels of the drawing that result from this organization of the stripes, there are four quadrangles joined to each other by other rising curves whose ascent begins, in each case, at the lower line of the quadrangle. An expressive tension, produced by the repeated introduction of resistance, as we said in connection with the stepped fret. Summing up the rhythmical disposition of that vessel from Kin-Lishba: ascent of the line, interruption, and again ascent; limitation of the motion by the circumference of the circles, which are what regulate the dynamic ensemble.

In the world of the meander and the palmette, the part of the surface delimited by the rising curve would have been joined to another part oriented in the opposite direction by a descending curve, thereby obtaining a symmetrical form, a perfect neutralization of the motion. But this is precisely avoided. A creative will is in operation here whose goal is not to compensate for the antagonism of the lines of motion, or have them regain a static equilibrium, but, on the contrary, to underline and accentuate that antagonism in the strongest way, through rhythmic repetition.

The ceramics of Casas Grandes have a characteristic decoration: within a rectangle and oblique to its axes is another, smaller rectangle whose sides extend to the perimeter of the larger. This forms four triangles that enclose other, smaller triangles. A strong decoration, in which each part of the surface stands out vigorously from the rest. Why, we ask, is this rectangle not subdivided evenly into other quadrangular forms? We may assume that the formal sensibility of those Indians would have rejected such disposition as inexpressive. Formal sensibility that had to be expressed in the violent play of unleashed antagonistic forces subject to a superior order: the rectangular outline. That same type of expressive decoration, that same prolongation of the sides of a square or rectangle beyond the perimeter of the figure, is also found in the Central Plateau, e.g., in the seal from the Valley of Mexico (Fig. 18). In some cases the extended lines form

FIG. 18. Seal. *Drawing by Jorge Enciso.*

an extraordinarily decorative scroll. There are many Mixtec vessels in which a large spiral, occupying the space in the center, is continued into another, smaller spiral. Egyptian and Assyrian art shows a preference for a similar formal motif: four spirals, one in each corner, joined by a convex, curved line, producing perfect symmetry. The trajectory of the line returns without any interruption to its point of departure, whereas the Mexican spiral or volute decidedly projects beyond its limits and erupts in the free space toward all sides.

If we examine the ornamentation of pre-Cortesian art

with respect to its manner of using the spiral, we arrive
at a surprising result. We cannot expect to find a similarity
to the Oriental variant—infinite motion within a finite,
limited form as we have just characterized it—or with the
Greek meander or the capital of the Ionic column, which
is something like a sterilization of the rhythm, as it were,
that governs the movement of the spiral. In pre-Hispanic
ornament we frequently find a form similar to the sign
§, in which the middle spiral is unwound, or a wider
spiral, whose upper finial is a spiral like a volute of smoke.
Such combination of two spirals, that without being or-
ganically united are placed one above the other, is enigmatic. Quite common as a ceramic decoration is a combination of spiral and circle, a spiral that unfolds in various
turns whose exterior outline is decorated with small, approximately quadrangular areas with outer sides rounded
off, almost forming a circumference (Fig. 19). What is

FIG. 19. Seal. *Drawing by Jorge Enciso.*

this? The stylized shell of a marine snail with its typical
protuberances following one after the other in a spiral
line. And we ask ourselves if the two spiral forms just
mentioned are not also a primitive representation of the
snail shell. Hermann Strebel ("*Zur Deutung eines altmexi-
kanischen Ornamentmotivs,*" *Globus,* 1897) and K. Th.
Preuss ("Hieroglyphen der Mexicaner," *Zeitschrift für
Ethnologie,* 1901) insinuated as much, but until now
their suggestions have had little acceptance. Both sup-
pose that the snail is even the prototype of the stepped
fret. Of considerable interest is an ornament (Fig. 20)
consisting of a combination of sea snail and stepped fret,
taken from the work of Jorge Enciso (*Design Motifs of*

FIG. 20. Seal. *Drawing by Jorge Enciso.*

*Ancient Mexico*) with the gracious permission of the author. There is no doubt that in the ornamentation of ancient Mexico the snail constitutes with astounding frequency the principal element of the formal repertory. And
I dare say that here is the explanation of multiple pecu-
liarities that we, the heirs of other artistic cultures, find
strange.

But it is not as important to show that the snail was
used with great frequency as a decorative motif as it is to
discover how far this form determined the structure of
the ornament, to what extent this rare formation—an
extraordinary effort of nature—dominated the fantasy of
pre-Cortesian man. This is a case of a spiral form that
develops around an axis in an incessant movement toward
one goal: the point. Strange dialectics of a formal structure
that unites symmetry with asymmetry. Are not these the
same elements that, beginning with the stepped fret, we
have been able to establish as a peculiarity of pre-
Hispanic ornamental form?

The snail symbolizes fecundity, i.e., it is a sign of good
omen. In the codices, the marine snail (*tecciztli*) always
appears in combination with the deities that represent
fecundity, growth, etc., e.g., the gods of the moon and of
pulque. It is one of the signs of Quetzalcóatl, who as
Ehécatl, the wind god, clears the way for the clouds laden
with fertilizing rain. Quetzalcóatl wears a collar of marine
snails; these also form his pectoral and his earplugs. In
the plastic frieze of the Pyramid of Quetzalcóatl, we see
snails and ears of maize at the side of the plumed serpent.
The Maya glyph for zero, the foundation of their numerical
system, is the snail.

The snail is likewise the symbol of birth. In the descrip-
tion given in the Borgia Codex of the resurrection of
Quetzalcóatl as the morning star, we read of the birth of
Xólotl: the god born of water rises from a snail shell (Fig.

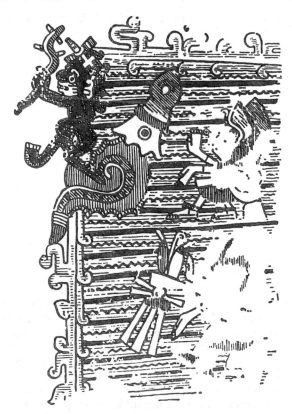

FIG. 21. Birth of Xólotl. *Borgia Codex, 42*

21); in one hand he holds a serpent, the sign of lightning.
Pedro de Ríos, interpreter of the Telleriano-Remensis
Codex, says: "Just as the snail comes out of its shell, so
too, man comes out of the womb of his mother." He adds
that this is why it is also alleged that the star of the night
—which is alternatively hidden in its "shell" or comes out
of it, shining brightly—brings about the birth of men.

"Even more clear is another relationship the interpreters
[of the codices] stress, the relationship between the moon
and women, the power that the moon exercises over the

female body and that is manifested in menstruation"
(Seler). The snail is therefore also a symbol of confine-
ment and, in general, of the female sexual organs. K. Th.
Preuss ("Kosmische Hieroglyphen der Mexikaner," *Zeit-*

FIG. 22. Tecciztli. The snail, symbol of birth. *Bologna Codex, 4*

*schrift für Ethnologie,* 1901) calls attention to the fact
that the spiral "always alludes to the navels of the goddesses," while it does not appear in the masculine figures
"on those rare occasions when they are shown nude." This
could explain why a utensil as specifically feminine as the
spinning whorl is so frequently decorated with the snail.[1]

The question arises as to why this form provoked such
interest, for while it is certainly fascinating, the Greeks
and Orientals would undoubtedly have rejected it because
of its lack of harmony. Why were not the Mexicans, like
others, inspired by a natural model of simpler structure?

---

[1] Among the little Tarascan statues are occasionally found
nude masculine figures with a snail over the genital organs,
which projects so greatly that the unity of the otherwise rather
flat bodily silhouette is materially destroyed. This leads us to
believe that this symbol was considered very important. It probably suggested great sexual potency, but it is also possible that
this is one of the symptoms of decadence so frequently manifested in late Tarascan sculpture. Ethnographers affirm that
homosexuality was quite common among the Tarascans. Paul
Kirchhoff points out that masculine bodies with strongly feminine characteristics, breasts, etc., as well as masculine figures in
feminine dress, are not rare in Tarascan sculpture. There is a
group of two figures grinding maize on a *metate,* a feminine
occupation par excellence. One of the figures represents a man.

After all, they stylized the flower into a form of perfect symmetry in the Nahua sign for the day of this name. Is not the preference for the snail due, to a certain degree, to an elective affinity, just as the palmette corresponded to the Greek will to form, the dentate thistle leaf to the Gothic, and the shell to rococo caprice? That dynamism manifested in the structure of the snail shell, the energy with which it is charged, the ordered asymmetry, the form that can only become Form in an incessant "becoming" by means of a discharge and struggle of forces held in an extremely complicated state of equilibrium; does not all of this correspond perfectly to the vital feeling of the pre-Cortesian world?

Studying the plans of the ceremonial cities, we see that they are all disposed geometrically along axes, that the patios and plazas have a quadrangular or rectangular form, and that the pyramid is placed in front of them at a right angle. But at the same time we are aware that within this truly grandiose unity the axial disposition is not strictly observed. There is a tendency to deflect the axis to one side, conserving the geometric organization of the whole.[2] The axis developed by a group of pyramids does not start from the center of the middle pyramid but from one of the lateral pyramids, or, as in Monte Albán, from a side wall of the most important pyramid, giving rise to a second axis, around which the different structures are equally grouped in strict geometric order. This is true of Mitla, too, except that there we must mentally add the plazas that joined the structures and which have not been restored. Identical phenomena can be observed in Cempoala, Xochicalco, and Ixkún (Guatemala). As an exception we cite Ranas, Queretaro, the fortress and ceremonial city where, because of very special topographi-

[2] A graphic representation of such axial deflection is to be found in a drawing of the Borgia Codex (Fig. 23), in the "quadrate of strips or ribbons," as Seler calls it (*Das Tonalamatl der Aubin'schen Sammlung*). He believes there is here an association with a game "that, like the ball game, seems to have been related to a series of mythical or cosmic conceptions and about which, unfortunately, the sources known to date do not give us any information."

FIG. 23. Quadrate of strips or ribbons. *Borgia Codex,* 62

cal conditions—two deep and narrow valleys surrounded
by great rock formations—it was possible to build only
along the two axes that are joined in a right angle. The
most convincing example is probably Nakum, Guatemala,
where such deflection from the axis occurred not once,
but twice consecutively. In Teotihuacán, the masterwork
of pre-Hispanic planning, with a rigorously premeditated
distribution of space and masses and with a disposition of
marvelous homogeneity, there exists the imposing line of
the axis that begins at the center of the Pyramid of the
Moon and leads to the so-called Citadel. But this axis
does not pass through the Temple of Quetzalcóatl, which
could have been the grandiose goal of the axis—an effect
that the European baroque would never have renounced
—but to one side, forming a right angle to it. One of the
walls surrounding the patio, parallel to the axis, touches
it. The Pyramid of the Sun, placed farther back, also
forms a right angle to the central axis and its patios touch
this axis. The deity who was venerated first and foremost
at Teotihuacán was Tláloc. The murals in which the
image of the rain god appears repeatedly and insistently
attest to this. Therefore, it is natural that the sanctuary
of Tláloc be found in the center of the sacred city, on the
axis between the Pyramid of the Moon and the Citadel.
But that sanctuary of Tláloc is not at all a dominant structure standing in the center or at the end of the axis. It

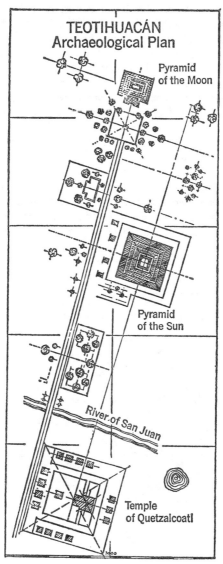

FIG. 24. Teotihuacán. Plan. *According to Marquina.*

is a plaza with an altar for sacrifices, on a level much lower than the rest of the terrain. The eye and the axis pass above it. The temple and the priests' quarters flank the axis. Why this strange distribution? By placing the structures farther back, but in such manner that their façades parallel the axis so that their relationship to it is maintained and emphasized, plazas are formed, perspectives opened, and spatial movement gained. Strong accents are imposed on the spatial ensemble. Elements are introduced into it that create animation by means of contrasts. An architectonic unity closed in upon itself is opened to one side and at the same time opens up another closed spatial quadrate, also closed in upon itself. This is not a mere juxtaposition or succession of buildings and plazas, but a system of related spaces of rich diversity of aspects. Despite its strictly geometric organization, this system has no trace of schematization. All is complication, powerful tensions, dynamic animation of the spatial life.

In summary of what we have just explained, a classic example of all this is the decoration on one of the vessels found in Kin-Lishba (Fig. 25). Here we have the

FIG. 25. Decorated vessel. Ceramic. Kin-Lishba. *According to Byron Cummings.*

stepped fret, the spiral, the acute-angled triangle, and here too we find the characteristic structural composition: asymmetrical distribution of the surfaces within the geometric form of the circle, vigorous motion, dynamic advance that again and again encounters another motion. The vital impetus of an art whose creative impulse is development—a perennial development.

# The Creative Will

*Building a Continent*

The men who populated the American continent came from Asia by way of the Bering Strait, which they crossed in various waves.[1] But the art of this continent, both Mesoamerican and Peruvian, was born as a creation of the pre-Columbian Indian, independently of other artistic worlds.

For some time now, a certain similarity between forms that exist in the Maya area and those of India and southeast Asia, e.g., a supposed lotus-flower motif in the Temple of the Tigers at Chichén Itzá, has given rise to the conjecture that an artistic influence was exercised by those Asiatic peoples over ancient Mexico. (In support of this thesis is the alleged similarity between the Mexican game called *patolli* and the Indian and southeast Asian game *pachisi*, as well as the fact that the *volador* is also found in many Asiatic countries.) Well, now—the Maya, as well as the other Mesoamerican peoples, did not have iron or the potter's wheel or certain food plants quite common in Asia, like rice, wheat, barley, and rye. The presumed contact with the continent of Asia would have brought a knowledge of all this. There were no draft animals. The wheel was not completely unknown: some small objects found in the State of Vera Cruz and in the Mexican highlands did have wheels. But it did not serve as a means of transport; it was used exclusively for toys. It is difficult to believe that those Buddhist missionaries who, it is maintained, arrived in the New World between 100 B.C. and A.D. 600, would have limited themselves to

[1] According to Paul Rivet, *Les Origines de l'Homme Américain,* immigration of Australians and Melanesians occurred later.

bringing only a few artistic forms . . . Rivet (*op. cit.*) rightfully says that the ignorance of all those objects in common use "eliminates, in a definitive manner, all the hypotheses that presuppose intervention, in the populating of America, by civilized races in possession of these diverse cultural elements."

Migration through the Bering Strait probably occurred around 20,000 B.C. In Sandia Cave, New Mexico, arrow points have been found that date from about 18,000 B.C., according to Carbon 14 tests. Those first immigrants were bands of nomads in search of new hunting grounds. The large animals—the mastodon, bison, elephant, camel, giant sloth—abounded in Alaska in the first glacial epoch. As a result of a change of climate on the American continent—an increase in temperature and a decrease of humidity—the pasturelands disappeared and with them the pleistocene animals they had supplied with food. The groups of hunters dispersed in successive waves over the entire continent. In Tepexpan, in the Valley of Mexico, eighteen miles northwest of Mexico City, there were discovered, along with the remains of an elephant, an obsidian point and a human cranium. Circumstances revealed by the excavation lead us to believe that the man drowned during the hunt or in flight. Further, there was the mark of a wound on the upper part of his thighbone, probably caused on an earlier occasion by an obsidian point. The site of the discovery was covered by a layer of limestone that was intact until the moment of exploration, which means that the Tepexpan man lived in an epoch before the formation of the limestone, which in the opinion of geologists took place eight or ten thousand years ago.

Those first inhabitants of America had a rudimentary civilization. The artifacts that attest to their existence are, besides hunting equipment, projectile points, dart throwers, flint or obsidian knives, as well as crudely worked stone tools, hatchets, chisels, files, gravers, sharpened bones, and a few others: whatever was indispensable to lead a totally primitive life. In places where they could supplement their diet with products of the soil, some groups in the course of time adopted a life that was sedentary or semisedentary to a certain degree.

These were the antecedents of the man who in the course of the last three or four thousand years before Christ changed the American continent into a habitable place; who, after long evolution, built a civilization that reflects his way of life.

His masterwork is the "invention" of maize, because in reality it was an invention to convert teosinte, an herbaceous plant of little nutritive value found only in the New World, into one of the most productive food plants, maize, which even today after several thousand years continues to be the staple food of the Mesoamerican peoples. What "archaic" man of pre-Columbian America achieved when he created maize is one of humanity's great feats, which history has more or less slighted. "It is the most important event in the economy and the civilization of America" (Enrique Juan Palacios, *Arqueología de México*). With the cultivation of maize, which the other continents would receive from America, a new world truly arose. And the transformation of nomadic tribes of hunters into a sedentary population of farmers dependent upon the land gave rise to a new conception of the world, which, as we shall see, would be expressed in the art, in the religion, and—what in this case becomes the same thing—in the philosophical thought of those peoples. According to Mangelsdorf, maize appears in the territory of ancient Mexico between 4000 and 3000 B.C. The specialists do not agree as to where that transformation of teosinte first took place: South America (i.e., Peru, the country of origin of another equally important food plant —the potato), Guatemala, Chiapas, or the Huasteca. In the ambit of ancient Mexico, the cultivation of maize began at the Gulf Coast, where the Huastecs subsequently settled, a fertile tropical region abundant in water. This explains the attraction that this area had for the northern tribes who advanced toward the sun, toward warmth, toward the cornfields. With the cultivation of maize, the peoples of the Central Plateau adopted a whole series of vegetation deities: Quetzalcóatl, Tlazoltéotl—who among

the Aztecs became Teteo innan—and Xochiquétzal. The
conception of Tláloc, the rain god, also came from the
Gulf area. Ceramics, the first manifestation of the artistic
sensibility, appears together with the cultivation of maize.

In the period of the so-called "pre-classic culture"
(1500 B.C. until approximately A.D. 200) we can show in
the two regions richest in discoveries—the Valley of Mexico (El Arbolillo, Zacatenco, Tlatilco, Cuicuilco) and the
zone south of the State of Vera Cruz (El Trapiche,
Remojadas, and the various sites of the culture of La
Venta)—a constant effort to perfect the still-primitive
techniques. The three stages into which this culture is
divided reveal how transcendental conceptions gradually
penetrate thinking.

The clay figurines manufactured by the ceramists of
the early and middle preclassic period are representations
of nude women. The so-called "lozenge" technique is
still crude. The pupil is represented by placing a little
ball of clay in front of the eye (Plate 37). A few incisions
made with a small stick indicate the lashes. The arms are
small rolls of clay, wide at the shoulder and narrowing
toward the opposite end. Actually this is only a forearm,
very characteristic in its curve and with the movement
well caught. The hands are omitted. At times a little red
paint at the bottom of the stump indicates them vaguely
and at other times we find that a few incisions signify the
fingers. The same applies to the feet. On the other hand,
great care is taken with the reproduction of the hairdo
and ornaments, since both are characteristic features of
the person. The highest artistic perfection is reached at
Tlatilco. The hypothesis that those nude women were
fertility fetishes has already been abandoned (Westheim,
*Ideas fundamentales del arte prehispánico en México,*
Chapter, "Tlatilco").

It is obvious that they were born out of the joy of creating and the admiration for the beauty of the female body.
Covarrubias says, referring to the excavations at Tlatilco:
"Evidently religious symbolism did not exist for the people
of Tlatilco." The zoomorphic vessels in the form of ducks,
fish, and birds lead to the conclusion that magic rites of

the hunt existed. Occasionally two-headed figures are found or figures with only one head and two faces. In this latter case there are three eyes, the center one shared by both faces. A sculptural type that has been found in Tlatilco and in some other regions is a kind of mask with two entirely different halves (Plate 43); one half has characteristically represented human features: the eye, the nose, the tongue that appears between the lips, and wrinkles above the eye and mouth. The other part is half a skull, with an empty eye socket. It is not at all unlikely that this is a symbol—the first—of the dualism that governs the Mexican theogony.

In the late preclassic period appear, for the first time, a monumental architecture—the Cuicuilco pyramid—and a monumental plastics—the colossal heads and altars of La Venta. Religious conceptions have now been formed. A cult and a ritual system directed by priests is already developing. Besides the family and the clan, the people come together in religious communities. For the exercise of the cult they need buildings, altars, and statues of the gods. The man who has come to realize that he—his person and his existence—depends on superhuman forces and beings cannot use the traditional artistic forms to express his metaphysical representations. The anthropomorphic sculptures of the Culture of La Venta (found in La Venta, Tres Zapotes, Cerro de las Mesas, Izapa) confirm this evolutionary process. In addition to small works of jade of rare technical and artistic perfection appear monoliths of gigantic dimensions. Some investigators try to explain the sudden appearance of this monumental plastics, whose antecedents are still unknown, as manifestations of an urban culture distinct from the rural culture of the villages. However, La Venta was not a city but a religious center, erected by a farming population who lived under a theocratic regime, like all the peoples of ancient Mexico until the overthrow of the Aztec Empire. There were no Mesoamerican cities in the strictest sense of the word until the "historical period," after the end of the Toltec kingdom. Ignacio Bernal (*Mexico Before Cortez: Art, History, Legend*) believes that there were only two:

Teotihuacán and Tenochtitlan. Mayapán too might be considered a city.

The plastics of La Venta appeared because of a new orientation in the religious sphere. Among the colossal heads were found Monuments 1 (reproduced in West-heim, *Ideas fundamentales del arte prehispánico en México,* Plate 54) and 4, whose helmetlike headdress reminds us of a relationship with the moon: incised in it is a band in the form of a U, from which stylized jaguar claws hang over the forehead. Among the Olmecs, as well as various Maya tribes, the hieroglyph in the form of a U—an allusion to the shape of the half moon—designates the moon. The jaguar is the animal of the nocturnal sky and of the lunar gods; the aged moon goddess is often represented with jaguar claws. The headdress refers, therefore, to fertility, which is the work of the moon. So, we may interpret the colossal heads of La Venta as representations of the vegetation god. Stirling found six altars at La Venta, sixteen at Izapa. Altars 4 and 5, approximately 8 feet 2½ inches long and 5 feet 3 inches high, are evidence of the incipient maize cult. Within a niche on the front face is seated a masculine figure, evidently the vegetation god, who holds in his hands a child, the new-born god of maize, whom he brought from the lower world to the light of day. The open jaws of a jaguar, tribal deity of the Olmecs, frame the group. The central plaza of La Venta, in which a pyramid was built earlier, is covered with a mosaic that also takes the form of jaguar jaws. In the relief that adorns one of the Izapa steles, a priest dressed with a jaguar mask clasps a vessel for hearts. The priest in the performance of his duties: this characterizes an art rooted in religious conceptions.

The sanctuary of Cuicuilco, situated in the Pedregal of San Ángel near Mexico City, is the oldest Mesoamerican pyramid (Plate 14). Its good state of preservation is due to the eruption of the volcano Xitle, probably around 600 B.C., when it was covered with a layer of lava. The excavations completed by the University of Southern California in 1957 show that the pyramid, constructed over three earlier edifices, with a round (or, rather, oval) plan, is already of the type that will be characteristic of the Mesoamerican world: the stepped pyramid.

It is a hill of adobe divided into five sections and covered with unworked stone joined without mortar, so cleverly that the walls have a smooth surface. Evidently they did not yet know how to work stone for a construction of such dimensions (a diameter of 410 feet and a height of 50 feet). We already find at Cuicuilco, although only placed in front of the constructive body, the stairways that lead to the place of sacrifices, and on the upper platform there had been a temple and an altar. And we find there another essential and typical feature of Mesoamerican architecture: the construction of buildings upon bases.

It is not possible to ascertain what kind of cult erected the Cuicuilco pyramid, but it has been possible to prove that that cult contained elements subsistent in the later high cultures. Among the idols discovered there (and also in other centers belonging to the same period: in Ticomán and in Tres Zapotes) was the image of an aged, seated god with a vessel on his head for burning copal. He is the fire god, "the old god," Huehuetéotl, the Xiuhtecuhtli of the Teotihuacán and Nahua civilizations. Clay representations of dogs have often been found in graves at the side of the skeletons. The dog as companion and protector of the dead in his perilous journey beyond the grave already existed, therefore, in the mythical conscience of the epoch.

The name Cuicuilco means "Place for singing and dancing." We should remember the pyramid of the "Dancers" from Monte Albán I, prior to the Zapotecs, which proves that at that time and place a cult was already established and the ritual of the sacred dance sufficiently advanced.

However divergent may have been the evolution that led to the different high cultures—Olmec, Teotihuacán, Maya, Zapotec—we cannot deny the existence of a whole series of elements that they have in common, elements essential to a world based on a structure of metaphysical-religious conceptions: the stepped pyramid; the erection of buildings upon bases; the duality of the theogonic system that was the governing principle of all the Meso-

american religions; the idea that it was man's duty to
maintain the gods by his own sacrifice; the Tonalámatl,
called *Tzolkin* by the Maya, a compendium and interpretation of the calendar and an integral part of the religious
system. These elements are the constant in all pre-
Cortesian cultures, by which they are unmistakably distinguished from all other cultures in the world. Such a
striking coincidence cannot be chance, is not chance. The
implication of a common origin is unavoidable, and this
origin must be sought in remotest times, in the epoch
termed "primitive" or "prehistoric."

It is not possible for the ritual calendar to have appeared
independently in different places.[1] Devised in view of the
religious necessities, it was so little subject to actuality
that it had to be combined with another calculation, a
calendrical one based on a more exact observation of nature, i.e., the solar year of 365 days. It is more than likely
that the calendar, together with the ritual which is based
on it, originated in the Gulf region, like the cultivation of
maize and the conception of the deities Quetzalcóatl,
Tlazoltéotl, Xochiquétzal, and Tláloc. That this is not
arbitrary supposition is demonstrated by some of the day
signs such as "alligator" and "monkey," names of animals
of the tropical jungle that do not exist on the Central

[1] In his account of the Aztec migration, Sahagún gives the
legendary interpretation of the vital importance of the Tonalámatl. He says that the Aztecs came to settle in Tamoanchan
("We seek our land."). "There the wise men and the sooth-
sayers, those who understand the books, set forth anew, taking
with them the black painting and the red painting, i.e., writing,
music, and the figurative arts. And of these wise men there remained only four, who, after the other wise men had left, consulted with each other on the following, saying, 'There will
come a time when there will be light . . . but, in what way
will the people be governed properly? What order will there
be in everything? Since the wise men took the paintings by
which they governed and by which they invented Astrology
and the art of interpreting dreams, they formulated the count
of the days and the nights, and the differences of time . . .'
Then they created the Tonalámatl and the count of the year
and the books of dreams. They arranged everything the way it
has been maintained until our own days. . . ."

Plateau. It is impossible that highland people invented these signs; it is obvious that they adopted them together with the whole calendar.

According to one current theory, the ritual calendar was an invention of the Maya. Well, there is no doubt whatever that the Maya, with their extraordinary astronomical knowledge, their brilliant arithmetical system, and their astonishing sense a sixth sense—of abstraction, amplified and developed the Tonalámatl and gave it a marvelous homogeneity and perfection. But neither is there the slightest doubt that it existed before their time. All traditions agree in naming Quetzalcóatl, the priest-god, as the inventor of the calendar and, as we have said, the conception of Quetzalcóatl comes from the Gulf region. The peoples established in the Central Plateau received it from the Gulf and made it their own. In the reliefs of the "Dancers" at Monte Albán, created by one of the Olmec peoples, Alfonso Caso found some hieroglyphics that testify that the Olmecs had already developed writing (as well as a numerical arithmetic, according to a date carved on Stele C at Tres Zapotes). From the glyphs, Caso infers that the ritual calendar "is very ancient in Monte Albán, probably anterior to the Maya *Tzolkin*" (*Exploraciones en Monte Albán*, 1936–37 Season). In La Venta, two sculptures have been found that are now in the Villahermosa Museum. One represents a priest. The other (reproduced in Westheim: *Ideas fundamentales del arte prehispánico en México*, Fig. 90) represents a jaguar wearing a mask, i.e., a priest of the jaguar-god. In both the head is thrown back and the gaze directed upward. Evidently this searching gaze is fixed on the firmament, i.e., the two priests are undoubtedly studying the course of heavenly bodies.

From all of this we can deduce that the origin of the calendrical system must be sought where the fundamental features of Mesoamerican religion and culture were formed, in the region designated in the old chronicles as "the oldest and most civilized," i.e., the region of the Olmecs, from which, within the Mesoamerican sphere, cultivation of maize also comes. And there can be no doubt that the calendrical system was the work of an agricultural people.

The nomadic hunter lives by day, by chance, by luck, and by the adventure of the hunt. If the catch is meager today, tomorrow may bring rejoicing and a sumptuous feast. The community of hunters cannot grow too large, for if it does, there is the danger that each one's share of the catch may be very small. Therefore, when the family or clan becomes too large, it divides into smaller groups, each going its own way. Isolation is a necessity to the hunter. His method of securing food explains and implies that his mentality is more individual than collective. He must be a faithful observer of reality, perspicacious, intelligent, and keen of eye. Tracking game and immediately grasping a situation are what he lives by. His metaphysical experiences are rooted in the totemic cult and in magic (as Frazer defines it, that is to say, as a vigilance that certain individuals gifted with magic power exercise over the forces of nature, contrasted to the suprapersonal omnipotence attributed to the deity in a true religious system). It is said in the *Crónica de Tezozómoc* about the Otomís and Chichimecs, nomadic tribes of ancient Mexico: "They did not adore any gods, nor did they have rites of any kind, they only went hunting. . . ."

The farmer cultivating his maize lives within collectivity and thanks to collectivity. Colonization of a particular region, clearing, irrigating, and cultivating the land, protecting the crops against assaults and robberies perpetrated by other tribes: these are collective tasks, almost always subject to collective rule. The farmer's thinking transcends today: from planting to harvest; from the present crop, which must suffice until the earth has produced new fruits, to the next crop. His thinking covers wider periods of time; he must plan, formulate long-range projects. If the hunter returns empty-handed, it is bad luck, but tomorrow his luck may change for the better. If the farmer's crop is destroyed, if the labor and effort of many months are in vain, it is a catastrophe that threatens everyone with hunger and death. The hunter does not have economic security, but the economic security of the farmer is exposed to great risks. "It is but natural for the psyche, under such circumstances, to take refuge in compensation of fantasies" (Paul Radin, *Primitive Religion*). The channeling of these fears and anxieties leads to the systematization of magic conjuration, which "has to be socialized" (Paul Radin, *op. cit.*). The farmer is dependent on the earth, but he is also dependent on the sun, heat, rain, on the vicissitudes and caprice of nature, on the position of the heavenly bodies, which can be favorable or unfavorable for him and his toil. He looks to the soil, but he also looks to heaven, to the celestial powers that are stronger than human will. He sees the individual, but he must also try to see the relationship between phenomena, the meaning that lies in them and behind them. In the rotation of day and night, in the cycle of the seasons, in the rhythm of birth and death is revealed an order and a law, established by the gods, maintained by the gods, and to fix this order, this law, to give it concrete form, he invents the calendar.

The religion of the pre-Cortesian peoples is an agrarian religion, or, rather, a maize religion. All the deities, which are the deified forces of nature, must concur so that the miracle of miracles can take place: the resurrection of the maize god in the lower world, the germination of the maize seed, the sprouting of the new plant. And the effigies of these gods are symbols, created by the imagination from its representation of the divine force, and created expressively, as the expression of something higher that is not tangible, that cannot be known by the senses or seen by the eye.

In his book *Die Malerei der Eiszeit,* Herbert Kühn explains, by this diversity of the social structure—in which the diversity of the conception of the world, the vision, and the thinking originates—the strange phenomenon that in primitive artistic production the imaginative-expressionist attitude is found alongside an imitative-impressionist one. He sees the cause of the split in the evolutionary course in the coexistence of hunting and agricultural tribes who, with their different forms of religious thinking, had to arrive at different modes of artistic expression.

What we observe in the archaic cultures of Mesoamerica confirms this opinion, however incomplete may be the material given us to date by archeology, especially with respect to the primitive stages. An imitative type of realism is transformed into an imaginative art; it is transformed gradually, in proportion to the generalization of agriculture and a sedentary way of life, in proportion to the formation of that collective system of religion.

Thus, that primitive epoch creates the foundation upon which the art of the high cultures that we call Classic will unfold most splendorously.

## 9

*Teotihuacán Culture*

The artistic will of Teotihuacán culture is outlined very clearly in the statue of Chalchiuhtlicue, "goddess of the living water" (Plate 53), a work of the fourth century, A.D., that was found in front of the Pyramid of the Moon at Teotihuacán. Chalchiuhtlicue, a monument approximately ten feet high, is more a work of architecture than of sculpture. It is an enormous block whose silhouette outlines the body of the goddess. The front face, the only plastically articulated one, as a matter of fact, is, so to speak, a relief sculptured in a block of rounded form. The hands, the garment, the face—all barely indicated—are flattened, approaching the bidimensional. Only the face projects slightly. A comparison of this representation of Chalchiuhtlicue with a round sculpture of La Venta or of the Zapotecs leads us to believe that the Teotihuacán sculptor wanted to counterpoint or even eliminate the monolithic, cubic character of the work, reducing it to a relief.

In the Medici Chapel figure of "Day," Michelangelo resorts to movement in order to model vigor, might, grandiosity—unbridled movement, vehement explosion, mastered only by the excess of strength. Each tense muscle struggles to escape from the mass of the flesh. The limbs push forward and upward, intersecting the mass of the body. The head is thrown back in a violent curve and the right foot juts out from the (curved) line of the base, destroying the contour, in order to burst with impetus into space. All of this is the exact opposite of what the Teotihuacán sculptor sought as his artistic goal and achieved in his work: instead of movement, supreme calm; instead of vehemence, disciplined strength; instead of the broken silhouette, a clear, firmly delimited contour subject to an architectonic structure. There are no interesting intersections. Even the details are shown frontally, in a clear, ordered, objective disposition. With his *pathos*, Michelangelo produces very strong psychic tension. For this baroque master the indecisive, the intangible, the pictorial —in outline, composition, organization of the planes—is an added charm, whereas in the Chalchiuhtlicue, anything that might endow it with charm is renounced. Chalchiuhtlicue does not impress through strength of gesture. It is silent, a concept. It does not represent, it signifies. It signifies divinity, greatness, omnipotence.

Michelangelo gives exalted expression in his figure to the ideas of reality that govern Western man, lending them powerful force, intense passion, ineffable emotion. The statue of Chalchiuhtlicue expresses in monumental form the idea of mythical reality that lives in the imagination of pre-Cortesian man. Through the exclusive use of pure, nonassociative, cubico-geometric Form, it attains the status of a symbol.

A common type of Teotihuacán sculpture later adopted by Aztec art is the image of Xiuhtecuhtli, the fire god— a figure seated in the oriental manner with crossed legs and a brazier on his head. The relatively low figure of the god seems to be a base for the brazier, in which there was always a fire to burn the offerings presented to Xiuhtecuhtli. Such idols, generally sixteen to twenty inches high, were used as household altars.

Prometheus, who stole fire from heaven and gave it to man, is almost always shown in full action, in dynamic motion. The Mexican gods, whom the myths describe as fighting, creating, destroying, dedicated to multiple activities, appear "in passive attitudes, more often seated than erect . . . the soft emotionalism of European art is almost totally absent" (George C. Vaillant, *The Aztecs of Mexico*). Samuel Ramos speaks of "a will to or toward the immutable."

How does Teotihuacán art represent this seated ancient? The work (Plate 54) has the structure of a block of rectangular, almost square form, and gives the impression of a figure encased in the block, divided into four horizontal sections, one above the other and so markedly architectural in character that they might almost be called floors. Above, the wide edge of the brazier with its abstract ornamentation—rectangles incised in the surface—creates a horizontal rhythm. Below, the crossed legs form another rectangle with a base wider than it is high, whose upper edge recedes slightly toward the center. Between the brazier and the legs is the head: the eyes and the mouth, elongated ovals. Although the artisan did not round the forehead in front, he nevertheless achieved plasticity by the "hole" and by the contrast of aerial mass and stone mass. The head, developed in free space, thereby gains in vigor and its symbolic significance is also stressed. Despite a selection of forms that prevent the cubic development of the mass, contrast alone produces a strong tension here, which prevents a feeling of flatness. All the elements are disposed within a plane of relief, but plastic corporeity is aspired to rather than the effect of a relief. Astonishing dialectics, produced by a consciously and eminently ingenious mastery of the formal elements. It is the dialectics of the stepped pyramid: a vertically constructed mass, whose verticality is "horizontalized" again and again. It is the same dialectics that we find in the structure of Chalchiuhtlicue, a cubic block carved in the style of a relief. It is the dialectics inherent in the theogonic system: the omnipotence of the deities and of the natural forces in their relationship with man, and, on the other hand, the spiritual capacity of man to weaken such omnipotence or to avoid its effects.

The body of Xiuhtecuhtli is eliminated. The Teotihuacán artist disdains "naturalness." Why? Shaping a religious symbol with expressive means, he limits himself in his creation to the essential, to the characteristic, to those elements that the believer associates with the concept of Xiuhtecuhtli: the brazier, the head of an old man, the seated position, and the crossed legs. All else is suppressed as unnecessary. A taller body would have introduced into the structure a vertical movement that the Teotihuacán

artist thought undesirable. Further, such vertical movement would have hurt its vital feeling, which is a pro-
pensity to a wide and calm horizontality. Surely it is not
arbitrary to say that the elimination of the body gave him
the desired opportunity to place the god's face, as the essential feature, in the center of the composition, i.e., at
the center of interest. And if we measure it, we find that
the exact center is the tip of the nose, that part that projects farthest from the plane of the relief. So balanced is
the organization of the forms and so strong the determination to inhibit all dynamic movement that a circle drawn
around the nose would almost touch the statue's four extremes.

The Egyptian scribe in the Louvre is also a seated figure of monumental character, but if we compare it with
Xiuhtecuhtli a decisive difference in the conception of
the two creations is immediately evident. The Egyptian
and the Teotihuacán sculptors achieve monumentality by
different paths and by entirely different tactics. The block
structure of the scribe confronts the space it occupies.
The mass of his body bulges toward all sides—the mass of
stone against the mass of air. The arms are held close to
the body, confine it like a frame; the hair surrounds the
face like a wig. The work has the form of a pyramid.
The crossed legs are a sort of base that is extended and
reinforced by the pedestal on which the figure squats.
The trunk rises above that base, stretching upward, as
does the head. The crown of the head would be the vertex. If imaginary lines were drawn from the vertex to the
most salient points, a triangle would result, a structure
that, as we have said, the Teotihuacán artist would find
undesirable. The brazier on the head of Xiuhtecuhtli al-
lows the sculptor to give the outline of his work the form
of an almost square rectangle. This is not because a vessel
on top of the head of the statue demands such rectangular disposition; on the contrary, since it elongates the head
toward the top, it tends to accentuate the verticality of
the figure, as in another piece of Egyptian sculpture from
the Middle Empire, the little statue of the "maid" or "water carrier" in the Louvre. She carries on her head a box

whose rectangular base is as wide as her head and widens
further toward its upper edge. That box, which adds
height to the slim little figure, is the top of a vertical
line rising from the tips of the feet and passing through
the legs, thighs, and trunk.

Very enlightening in this respect are the masks, where
the artist must limit himself to the representation of the
head. How does the Teotihuacán sculptor proceed? The
Teotihuacán mask has two characteristic traits that distinguish it from other types of Mesoamerican masks. First
is the tendency to widen the head, all resources being
used for this purpose. In the mask reproduced on Plate
25 the relationship with nature is modified to such a degree that the verticality is totally eliminated. The height
and the width of the mass of the head are approximately
equal, but the surfaces of the ears transform it into a
horizontally stretched rectangle. The head of Chalchiuhtlicue lends itself to the same observations. "Her face does
not form an oval, but a rigid frame," says Toscano (*Arte
precolombino de México y de la América Central*). The
second tendency, demonstrable in the mask mentioned,
is to flatten the cubic mass, giving it almost a bidimensional effect, but not to the extent that it resembles a
sculpture in relief. There is cubic development, but the
cubic is repressed and modified toward the plane. The
artist aspires to both plasticity and to the plane, and with
an unparalleled sensibility that is revealed in each of those
masks and in each of them astounds us anew, he achieves
the exact point where the two opposing tendencies seem
reconciled in a happy balance. A shade the more, and we
would have flatness. A slightly stronger accentuation of
the corporeal structure, and the result would be decorative stylization. Why that transformation, which at first
glance seems to have something artificial about it? It is
as if the artist drew back from the full corporeity of the
rounded form; as if he feared to lose himself in the merely
earthly; as if he wished to withdraw consciously and en-
ergetically from the heaviness, the nonspirituality of the
merely earthly. In the mask, of course, it is not possible
completely to renounce the relationship with the human

without sacrificing its special meaning, but it is possible to refine this human element, to reduce it to a minimum by means of form, to deprive it of its materiality, to spiritualize it. This is what happens in the masks, what gives them their nobility, their intimate monumentality. And there is no doubt that the Teotihuacán masks are among the works in which the art of ancient Mexico reaches one of its culminating points. In the morphogenesis of these creations, the question of good taste does not enter into play—although in the field of universal art there is little that surpasses or even attains their perfect taste—nor is it a matter of "stylization." In that conciliation of antagonistic elements is manifest the definite will to art. It is the plastic expression of a conception of the world governed by dualism.

At the end of the last century, a great mural was discovered in the Temple of Agriculture at Teotihuacán. A painted hymn, a plea to the deity not to withhold rain or an expression of gratitude for his having sent it. In the center of the composition are the offerings of the faithful —fruit and sea snails. On both sides, wide bands, one above the other: water, waves, and among them aquatic plants and all kinds of marine life, such as conches, snails, etc. What is represented here? Symmetry and rhythm. The objects portrayed, the painting, and all the details have as plastic values one goal: that of creating symmetry and rhythm. The "Earthly Paradise" of Tláloc, the important mural discovered at Teotihuacán-Tepantitla in 1942, shows the same composition and disposition. In the center a hill, beneath it a lake from which rivers wind toward the left and the right. Above, following the same rhythm, horizontal bands, in this case made up of people and trees (Westheim, *Ideas fundamentales del arte prehispánico en México*). In the reliefs of the Tula pyramid we see the same motifs in the rhythmic succession of endless rows: the jaws of a serpent devouring a man, the friezes of eagles and jaguars, the friezes of marching warriors (Plate 8).

A style of religious objectivity, a maximum of reserve and clarity. Limitation to the essential. Taciturnity, a retreat to the internal sources. No rhetoric, only the great *pathos* inherent in the solemn invocation of God. It is not prose, it is word made music. It is spirit manifested in the grand Form; Form subject to spirit, faith in the Form and in its divinity. Parallelism, constant reiteration of the same motif, of equal shape and at equal distance. The devotion of the worshiper who confesses, begs, implores.

Rhythm—in architecture, sculpture, painting, the ornamentation of pottery—that always unfolds on the horizontal. The horizontal, seen psychographically, expresses a vital feeling for which the conflict between reality and idea does not exist. It expresses the sentiment of men standing firmly on earth, however much they lift themselves up. It expresses the security in the earthly and the supraearthly. It expresses what it has found, not the search, not the torment of the soul before the enigma. Serenity, instead of anxiety. In the concept of the Mesoamerican world, reality and irreality do not oppose each other; they complete each other and are mutually absorbed.

As indications of a classic stylistic attitude, Wölfflin (*Principles of Art History*) enumerates frontality, closed form, evidence of the proportions of the mass, a cubically constructed mass, a precisely established form, symmetry, rhythmic repetition of the same proportions, axial orientation, detail developed as a closed, isolated, and isolable unity, linear structure (but not the broken line or the curve), color kept within the outline and used to illuminate (not to disintegrate by transforming it in effects of light, movement, space), being (not becoming, not change). If we accept these categories, the conclusion is that Teotihuacán art is *a classic art.*

A classic art, not *"the* classic art" of the Italian Renaissance that served as Wölfflin's example. Although the art of Teotihuacán and the classicist art of the Italian Renaissance spring from the same creative principle—we would like to say from the same method of achieving the refinement of form—we must not overlook all that separates them. The difference between them, which leads them to such completely different results, lies in their conceptions of the world, in their diametrically opposed attitudes before the cosmos.

Renaissance art, like its spiritual model Greek antiquity, is worldly in its essence even when it models religious themes. Anatomy, psychology, standards of beauty, rules of beauty. The seeing and the creating are "scientized." Leonardo writes his *Treatise on Painting;* the German Dürer, his book *On Measurement.* Great artists both, they are also great scholars obsessed by an eagerness to fix scientifically the canons of the beautiful. The goal is the beautiful or, expressed in a different way, the sensuous experience as form and content of the artistic creation. And that beauty is attained through observation, knowledge, capturing those elements of reality that seem to confirm such a feeling of beauty. The Renaissance accepts as reality what deceives the senses, e.g., perspective. For it, the earthly is sacred, the source of life and the fountain of energy. Nature, the form of the cosmic, substitutes for the cosmic. Teotihuacán art is directed toward the cosmic. What is important is the meaning of things, their cosmic value. And this is not a physical phenomenon but a spiritual one. It means that that art is visionary. The Océlotl-cuauhxicalli of the British Museum (Plate 114), a vessel for hearts in the form of a jaguar, is a symbol, the sign of the terrible and frightening Tezcatlipoca. The animal-god is represented as cruel and sanguinary, in the act of assaulting a man. The head is only the threateningly open jaws that, forming an extended rectangle, surround three sides of the face as far as the ears. It is not nature, but the representation in fantasy of a demoniacal force of nature. The spiritual-psychic fact, which is the only one that matters, is expressed through Form, through the elements that afford the possibility of knowing the spiritual by means of the senses. That discipline, to which Teotihuacán art submits each creation, gives evidence of its superiority, of a spiritual attitude that tends toward the grand, the definitive, the eternal. Teotihuacán culture ignores the agreeable, which belongs to a sphere that it has left far behind in its aspiration to the sublime. Its art is monumental art. Walter Lehmann (*Aus den Pyramiden-*

*städten in Alt-Mexiko*), in the paragraph devoted to Teotihuacán, speaks of a "noble simplicity and a serene grandeur," the formula by which Winckelmann characterized
the art of the Greeks.

Archeological explorations show that the Teotihuacán
culture, which covers approximately the epoch from the
fourth to the tenth centuries, A.D., is based on an archaic
civilization that, in the course of a slow organic process, is
assimilated and transformed by it and to which it joins its
religious content, metaphysical speculation, and lucid spirituality. Epochs II and III, in which it reaches its maturity,
contemporaneously with the classic Maya and the Zapotec
Monte Albán II epoch, constitute the highest summit of
culture in the Valley of Mexico, and, it may be said, in all
America. In the years 1955–58, Laurette Séjourné excavated a palace in Teotihuacán-Zacuala. During the exploration, she found various graves that contained offerings, the first graves discovered at Teotihuacán. The walls
of the palace were covered with murals, which the dis-
coverer interprets as representations of the Quetzalcóatl
myth (Laurette Séjourné: *Un palacio en la ciudad de los
dioses* "They [the Teotihuacán creations] undoubtedly
must be counted among the elite of art productions
achieved by the people of ancient America" [S. Linné,
*Archeological Researches at Teotihuacán, Mexico*]). In its
monumentality and reserved expressivity comparable only
to the religious art of Asia, Teotihuacán represents one of
the few great cultures of humanity.

## 10

## Toltec Culture

Until quite recently it was believed that Tollan, so often mentioned in the chronicles and legends as the capital of the Toltec Empire, was only a mythical name for Teotihuacán. True, in Sahagún's work there is a passage that fixes exactly the geographical location of the city that was the capital of the Toltecs: he says that they "populated the bank of a river that now bears the name of Tulla." But not even this precise information could shake the conviction that Tula was the great religious center, Teotihuacán. In 1939 a discussion was stirred up in the Sociedad Mexicana de Antropología, in the course of which Wigberto Jiménez Moreno affirmed categorically that Tollan and Teotihuacán are not identical, that Tollan belongs to a later epoch and that, according to an eighteenth-century map, it should lie in the vicinity of the present city of Tula, State of Hidalgo. Under the direction of Jorge R. Acosta and at the site indicated, work was begun and, as a matter of fact, the ancient Tollan arose from the ground, designated by Jiménez Moreno as "the city of Quetzalcóatl."

In the tenth century, the Valley of Anáhuac was invaded by bellicose Chichimec hordes that had come from the north. Led by Mixcóatl ("Cloud Serpent"), they established themselves in Culhuacán; their incursions started from there. Mixcóatl was assassinated. His son, born on a day *Ce Ácatl*—the calendrical name of Quetzalcóatl—added to his name Ce Ácatl Topiltzin that of this god. Around 980 he made Tollan—"Place of Reeds"—the capital of his kingdom. The reign of Ce Ácatl Topiltzin was a paradisiacal era for Tula. Arts and crafts flourished. Such was the abundance, prosperity, and riches that Ce Ácatl Topiltzin Quetzalcóatl came to be identified with Quetzal-cóatl, the priest-god. At that time an indissoluble con-glomeration of history, legend, and myth began to take shape in Tula.

Tula was conquered in the twelfth century by another group of Chichimecs led by Xólotl, builder of the Tena-yuca pyramid. With the destruction of Tula, the most im-portant happening in the history of Mesoamerica, and the exodus of its population (in 1224), there begins in ancient Mexico the transmigration of the peoples: the tribes set out on marches, kingdoms are overthrown, towns and cities are abandoned, one nation displaces another in a search for new ways of life.

Covarrubias (*Indian Art of Mexico and Central Amer-ica*) says that when the Chichimec hordes had founded Tula, "they became civilized, gave themselves the name 'Toltecs.'" The denominations "Chichimec" and "Toltec" were applied originally, in accordance with the respective level of civilization, to various groups, tribes, or peoples. In the *Anales de Cuauhtitlán*, the "nomads who lived by the arrow, without home, without land . . ." are desig-nated as "Chichimecs." They lived "still in darkness; and the reason why it is said still in darkness is that their repu-tation was still nonexistent while they continued to wander and still nonexistent the name of well-being." Alva Ixtli-xóchitl explains that the ". . .'Tultecas' were great arti-sans of all the mechanical arts: they built very large and famous cities, like Tollan, Teotihuacán, Cholula, Tolan-tzinco, and many others. . . ." Thus, the builders of Teo-tihuacán, whose ethnic affiliation has not yet been deter-mined, were considered "Toltecs," although not identical to the "historical" Toltecs who did not appear before the tenth century, A.D. After the discovery of Tula in 1941, archeologists, to distinguish both civilizations, adopted the terms "Teotihuacán culture" and "Toltec culture" (with respect to Tula).

Tula, the heir of Teotihuacán culture (although it also assimilated elements from Xochicalco, e.g., the structure of ball courts), developed an art of its own in an astonish-

ingly short time. A stylistic investigation based on the
formal language can prove various essential features that
reveal a great affinity with Teotihuacán.[1]

But the art of Tula does not reach that purification of
form, the spirituality, the "noble simplicity and serene
grandeur" that impregnates Teotihuacán art. It aspires
rather to sumptuosity, a sumptuosity that is at times decorative. Tula is, after Teotihuacán, a new and distinct
epoch, whose character—new and distinct—manifests itself
especially in architecture: in the introduction of new constructive elements.

The principal structure (called Edifice "B") is a pyramid of Quetzalcóatl, or, better, a pyramid consecrated to
one of the aspects of Quetzalcóatl: that of deity of the
planet Venus, of the morning star, into which his heart
was transformed. The whole construction was covered
with friezes in bas-relief. In those that have been preserved we see the sacred animals—the jaguar, the eagle,
and the carrion crow, these last two devouring a heart
—that alternate with a human head that emerges from the
jaws of a plumed serpent. Splendid decoration, that surrounded the entire pyramidal body, as we see in the frieze
composed of the heads of Tláloc and Quetzalcóatl on the
Pyramid of Quetzalcóatl in Teotihuacán and in the serpentine meander at Xochicalco. There are relief friezes
covered with painting everywhere in Tula: on the walks, in
the hall of the pyramid, in a room of the so-called "Burned
Palace," and in the *coatepantli* behind the pyramid.

Only four fifteen-foot telemones and four pillars of equal
height have been preserved from the Temple of the Morning Star. Aligned in equal rows within the palace enclo-
sure, they held up the roof beams. The telemones symbolize Quetzalcóatl in his aspect as morning star, i.e., as
the warrior who precedes the sun in the dawn and puts
the stars, representing darkness, to flight. As a pectoral he
wears a stylized butterfly. It is a symbol of the planet
Venus and of the soul of the dead warrior. His headdress,

[1] The affinity with Teotihuacán is likewise obvious in Aztec
art. The Great Coatlicue corresponds in its tectonic structure
and organization to the Teotihuacán Chalchiuhtlicue.

the headdress of the valiant warrior, is composed of precious stones and feathers. On the rear face of the telemones appears the symbol of the sun: above a buckler, a human face surrounded by four fire serpents. The four pillars have bas-reliefs that represent warriors with their typical dress, their arms, their plumes, etc.

The transcendental importance of the Tula telemones lies in the fact that beginning with them there is a new level of architecture in ancient Mexico, a new architecture moored for centuries to its primitive constructive methods, that was basically limited to piling stony mass on stony mass.[2] Because of this technical progress, the Tulanites could create in the Temple of the Morning Star a square interior space ninety-one feet long. In the "Burned Palace," at the west end of the pyramid, the square room measures seventy-eight feet. Placed in front of the façade of the pyramid is a large platform, in whose concrete floor, which has been preserved, we may still see the depressions where the fifty-four pillars were placed, which indicates that there was an enormous room. The stairway of the pyramid ends in this room.

Tula, which was able to solve a fundamental architectonic problem, can also be credited with having invented —within the Mesoamerican world—the atlantes: dwarflike supports for the altar table and the sacrificial stone, an invention that reveals, like the telemones and the pillars, the tendency to lighten the heavy structure by supports or bases.

Thanks to the creative power manifest in the architecture of Tula, this could be converted later, in a more grandiose, more fascinating way, into that of the new Chichén Itzá. When the Toltecs arrived at Chichén Itzá, they did not have to develop an architectonic style and structure. They brought these with them.

[2] At Monte Albán, six rubblework columns formed the entrance to the principal temple; in Mitla, too, is a "Salon of the Columns." According to Torquemada, groups of Toltecs from Cholula were established in Mitla. The six columns in El Tajín Chico also show a relation with the Tula Toltecs (Westheim: *Ideas fundamentales del arte prehispánico en México*).

## 11

## The Feudal Art of the Maya

Within the world of pre-Cortesian art, or more correctly, on its periphery, Maya art is a world apart, strange and fascinating. Related because it derives from the same hypotheses, but very different nevertheless as to evolution and development, just as Italian Gothic is very different from the Northern Gothic of France, England, and Germany. Comparing the Church of Santa Maria in Florence with the Cathedral of Amiens, we would scarcely venture to speak of the same conception of art. Imbued with Mediterranean spirit, with southern sensibility, with a subconscious Hellenic tradition, and anticipating the artistic will of the Renaissance, the Florentine cathedral takes no part in Nordic irrationalism and opposes to it its own personality. It may be said that the same relationship exists between Maya art and the characteristic creations of the Central Plateau, except that in this case it is the north, Teotihuacán, that represents the classic, while the south, the Maya region, produces a tropical rococo, anticlassic, capricious, and exuberant. If further proof be necessary to show the dissimilar character of Maya art, it is presented by the works of the so-called New Maya Empire— architecture, sculpture, the ornamentation at Chichén Itzá —where the spirit of the Toltecs of Tula infiltrated the Maya conception, transforming it, adapting it to the traditions that the new masters brought from the north.

The two oldest pyramids found in Mesoamerica to date are those of Cuicuilco near Mexico City and the one designated as E VII-sub in Uaxactún, Guatemala (Plate 61). This latter dates from the fourth century A.D. (The first stele of Uaxactún bears the date A.D. 328.) Covered by another pyramid at a later epoch and therefore very well preserved, it represents a more mature stage of evolution than Cuicuilco. Here an astonishingly high level of technical and artistic perfection was reached. The upper sections stand out from each other because of their cornices. Each of the stairways superimposed on the four sides of the structure is adorned with large stucco masks, those of the god Chac alternating with those of a serpent. The entire pyramid is faced with stucco. Perfection and esthetic charm are the obvious goals. Salvador Toscano (*Arte precolombino de México y de la América Central*) speaks of "the tendency to elegance and decoration, expressions of the baroque refinement of the Maya architect."

That very old Maya construction already contains almost all the features that would later integrate the peculiar character of Maya art: enjoyment of decoration and of play, fantasy, predilection for agitated forms, refinement displayed in the composition of the whole, delicacy of the individual forms, elegance, subtlety, esthetic perfection. What happens henceforth is only a higher perfection, a greater refinement, a more subtle elegance until at last decadence sets in. The sanctuary at Uaxactún, which introduces the Maya into the history of art and architecture, already serves as evidence of an elevated and mature culture. It is already baroque, to use a word that many apply to Maya art.

The baroque is, of course, an end rather than a beginning. Never, anywhere in the world, did an artistic evolution begin with the baroque. Is it possible to imagine a history of European art that begins with St. Paul's, with the Dôme des Invalides, with El Greco? Neither could Maya art begin with a baroque. To arrive at such a high level of artistic and technical perfection, it had unavoidably to follow a long evolutionary road. William Gates ("The Mayance Nations," *Maya Society Quarterly*, Vol. I, No. 3, June 1932), resisting the fantastic tales of certain Mayists, writes: "To say . . . that they passed from nonagricultural barbarians to high civilization, knowledge of astronomy and the development of their calendar within some five hundred years, is sheer absurdity." The year 3113 B.C., when the calendrical count of the Maya begins, is a legendary date, but it reveals that they had a vague knowledge of a past that encompassed thousands of years.

How did Maya art develop? Through what stages did it pass? We know nothing of this or of Maya prehistory either, which is still surrounded by impenetrable darkness despite the active work of investigation currently taking place.[1] There are no archeological discoveries that can

[1] For a history of the Maya Territory, called Mayab, the reader is referred to specialized works, e.g., Sylvanus G. Morley: *The Ancient Maya,* and J. Eric S. Thompson: *The Rise and Fall of Maya Civilization.*

For a better understanding of the artistic development, here is a brief résumé: It is probable that the Maya, in their route toward the south and west, arrived between the first and second centuries, A.D., in the region of Petén (Guatemala), where they founded Uaxactún as the first settlement of any importance. (Formative Period.)

The (so-called) Old Maya Empire, which comprised the territories of Chiapas, Guatemala, Honduras, northern El Salvador, with the principal centers being Uaxactún, Tikal (Guatemala), Copán (Honduras), and Palenque (Chiapas), is distinguished from the (so-called) New Maya Empire in the Peninsula of Yucatán, with its cities of Mayapán, Chichén Itzá, and Uxmal.

The Old Maya Empire was not a centralized state but an ensemble of many city-states, independent of each other and governed autocratically. Tiny states that, unlike the autonomous European cities—Greece, Italy, the Hanseatic League—did not consider it their noblest task to fight and conquer each other. The Old Empire (Classic Period), flourishing during the eighth century, lasted until the ninth or tenth century, when it suddenly abandoned the great religious centers.

The so-called transition period (889–1224) followed, after the migration of some of the Maya tribes toward the southwest and the majority of them toward the north, to Yucatán, whose principal religious center was Chichén Itzá, founded in A.D. 534, by the Itzas, who had to abandon it in 692.

The New Maya Empire (Mexican Period) began with the reoccupation of Chichén Itzá by the Itzas circa 975 and the foundation of Uxmal by the Xiúes circa 1000. The *Chilam Balam of Chumayel* speaks of two Toltec invasions in Yucatán: the first around 987, captained by Kukulkán, the second toward the end of the twelfth century. As a reward for the military aid lent to the Cocomes against the insurgent Itzas, Kukulkán received certain political rights in Chichén Itzá. The foundation of Maya-

clear up this problem. It is to be supposed that Maya culture, like that of Teotihuacán, has its origin in Olmec culture, particularly that of La Venta. But, what were the intermediate links? For a knowledge and evaluation of Maya art, especially for the interpretation of its plastic idiom, manifestations from the dawn of the Maya epoch should have been very instructive. The genesis of the styles, the adoption or abandonment of certain formal elements from that particular will to art, are of enormous interest from the psychographic viewpoint.

Teotihuacán is austerity, sublime quietude. Everything that was sensuality, life, or movement is refined, has become cubico-geometric form, a static equilibrium sought and found in the horizontal. The characteristic form of expression of Maya art is the undulating line. Constant movement, up and down, restless and playful, ruled by a nervous and overflowing fancy. The tropical counterpart of the rococo, the *rocaille*. We feel tempted to speak of a "tropical night's dream." A restlessness manifested not only on the exterior, in decoration, in the exuberance of the adornment that covers every surface with a frosting of figures, clever thoughts of a spirit that never tires of ca-

---

pán, which became the residence of the Cocomes, is attributed to Kukulkán.

In 1201, the "League of Mayapán" was formed, a not entirely voluntary union of the various Maya princes, who elected as their common chief Hunac Ceel, of the family of the Cocomes. By the Treaty of Mayapán the other Maya princes lost their sovereignty. They had to agree to live in Mayapán, where their situation was similar to that of the French nobility at court during the reign of Louis XIV. Under the Cocomes, commerce continued to develop. An aristocracy of merchants was formed, who exercised great influence even in the political sphere, and together with this merchant group an aristocracy of warriors, the result of the insurrections against the tyranny of the Cocomes.

Chichén Itzá was the religious center; Mayapán (destroyed by the Xiñes in 1451), the political center of the New Empire. The Toltecs, established in Chichén Itzá, introduced a new cult, that of Quetzalcóatl, called Kukulkán by the Maya (and Gukumatz by the Quichés). The much admired structures and works of art in Yucatán—Chichén Itzá, Mayapán, Uxmal—are creations of this period, which ended with the conquest of Yucatán by the Spaniards.

price: a restlessness that is expressed also in the tendency to modify the structural body, to introduce into architecture itself new features, sensational and very often straining for effect. To Teotihuacán, the old and traditional was the sacred; to stray from it would have been a crime. It appears that respect for the sacred tradition did not exist in Maya art, or, if it did, it was easy to bypass it. There is obsession with the new. The old is the antiquated and they try to overcome it with new inventions, with a new repertory of forms, in a word, with the modern. This is due, obviously, to the fact that the religious is not the exclusive goal and meaning of the artistic production; that along with the religious, relegating it to second place and at times substituting for it completely, rises the esthetic, the fascinating experience of the esthetic. What is especially appreciated is the artistic configuration, the talent and originality of the formal invention, the artistic script. Estheticism that is directed to the cultivated senses (which in the case of the Maya were supercultivated) of an exacting public of connoisseurs, who above all demand artistic progress, artistic emotion, artistic delicacy. This also explains that restlessness. What is already achieved, however subtle and original it may be, is but one stage on the road, a point of departure toward something more subtle and more original. All of this is evident in the architecture. The architects constantly introduce the most varied innovations. Of course, this zeal for experimentation stops short of the decisive, i.e., the construction itself. Nor do the Maya pass beyond the primitive constructive characteristic of Mesoamerica: the erection of enormous stone masses, uniformly rectangular blocks, rectilinear walls without convexities or concavities, built upon pyramidal bases. "There is probably no region in Middle America where architecture is more strongly rectangular than the Maya region," says H. D. E. Pollock (*Round Structures of Aboriginal Middle America*). In Xlabpak, John L. Stephens (*Incidents of Travel in Yucatan*) found a three-story construction with a twenty-five-foot-long frontage. The first-floor plan has a solid, cruciform core, from 115 square feet to 130 square feet in area, if I have

not erred in my calculations, that supports the upper
floors. The twenty-one interiors of the first floor surround
that core in the form of niches. At Naranjo, in the "Palace
of the Stairway of the Tiger Heads," Teobert Maler (*Peabody Museum Memoirs,* Vol. IV) ascertained that "in
later epochs reinforcements had been inserted in the rooms
on the east and west sides, since the architects mistrusted
the power of the inner walls to sustain the great pressure
of the second story resting upon the middle rooms." In
the fifteen hundred years of Maya architecture that we
know about, Maya construction continues to be "in reality
a monolith" (Thomas A. Joyce: *Mexican Archeology*).

The Maya also did not know the construction of the
true arch, so decisive for architectural development in
Asia and Europe and without which it would not have
been possible to erect either Santa Sophia in Constanti-
nople or Chartres Cathedral. The Maya invented the
"false arch" (Fig. 26), which does not bear any load and is

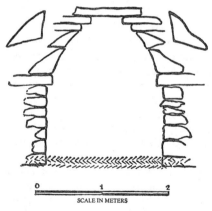

FIG. 26. False arch. Construction scheme.

a purely decorative element, not a constructive one. The
width of the chambers, which are very narrow rectangles,
depends on the length of the beams or stones that span
the walls. Nor does the "false arch" permit an enlarge-
ment of the interiors; rather, it forces them to be even

narrower, since there must be a minimum separation between the two walls so that the arch will not break and collapse. According to Totten (*Maya Architecture*), the greatest width attained is fourteen feet; in the Governor's Palace at Uxmal, which has all the aspects of a feudal construction, the chambers are thirteen feet wide. These interiors (Plate 63) are actually corridors or "true galler-

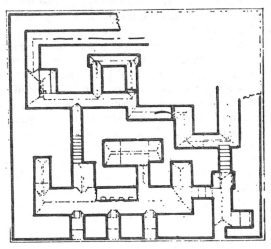

FIG. 27. Plan of the Labyrinth. Yaxchilán, Chiapas.

ies," Toscano believes, rather than rooms, divided in many cases by intersecting walls. The interior of the temple at Tzibanché was long, but so narrow "that two persons could pass each other only by turning sideways" (T. W. F. Gann and J. Eric S. Thompson: *The History of the Maya from the Earliest Times to the Present Day*). Nor can it be said that the "false arch" permitted the construction of taller buildings. This would have been possible without it and in a most simple manner, by increasing the height of the walls that held the beams, as did occur later in Chichén Itzá. But something else was achieved with the false arch: thanks to its agitated silhouette, the walls lost their rectilinear and flat appearance (at least in the upper sections), and the impression of horizontality imparted by

the flat ceiling was avoided. The resulting optical effect
was pleasing to their eyes. A laborious construction, that
presupposed a great effort and care in execution, and
whose principal purpose was to produce an effect that was
attractive, original, and—for the taste of the age—grandiose.

That taste for variations, for novel and surprising solu-
tions, is likewise manifest in planning. What procedures
are followed for this? We have already said that the Maya
do not know how to prevent the monolithic appearance of
walls. The thick and heavy stone walls—3¼ feet in Tikal
and Yaxchilán, 3¼ feet to 6½ feet in Uaxactún—are inevita-
ble; the space that can be left between them is extremely
limited. W. H. Holmes (*Archeological Studies Among the
Ancient Cities of Mexico*) observes, in his description of
the Governor's Palace at Uxmal: "We find by a rough
computation that the structure occupies some 325,000 cubic feet of space. . . . If the substructure be taken into
account, the mass of masonry is to the chamber space approximately as 40 to 1." Joyce says: "In fact, the Maya
built caves . . ." Caves, yes, but caves whose walls were
decorated in the most splendid and elegant manner. "The
typical Maya building is a solid, boxlike construction that
contains one narrow room" (Joyce). This applies above all
to the temples. A second wall, parallel to the wall of the
façade, separates, toward the rear, a second chamber,
which in general is even more narrow and divided in turn
by transverse walls into several small compartments, in
some cases (Tikal) interconnected by corridors. In Yaxchilán this method produces a narrow and relatively long
antechamber with three small chambers behind it, the
middle one being the sanctuary. In Palenque this sanctuary is decorated with stucco ornaments and forms a
solemn and impressive niche set back in another, larger
niche. Temple II at Tikal, which has to support the weight
of an exceedingly high roof crest, would be a mound of
heavy stone were it not for a hall left open in the walls
from which three corridors lead to the right and left. Certainly these "corridors"—about 16 feet long and 3¼ feet
to 3½ feet wide—are in reality the chambers of the temple. The same thing occurs at Copán, where the lateral

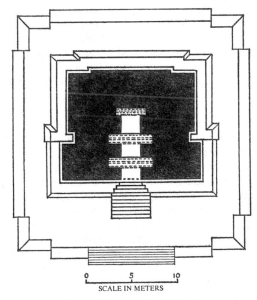

FIG. 28. Plan of Temple II. Tikal, Guatemala.

corridors are widened, so that here we may speak of rooms. In some constructions at Yaxchilán, that system of chambers and corridors forms, by its disposition, a true labyrinth, which explains the name of one of its structures —The Labyrinth. "Temples were little more than shrines or great altars" (Totten). The ceremonies that related to the cult were celebrated out of doors, in fresh air, in front of the temple pyramid, as in the north. The construction of the so-called "palaces," the majority of which were probably the residences of the priests and princes—the *halach-huinicoob,* "the true men," as they called them-selves—was more exacting. Those great lords, who con-sidered themselves as demigods or better, needed many and varied rooms. The palace at Sayil contains more than eighty chambers (Ignacio Marquina, *Estudio arquitectó-nico comparativo*). Evidently the object of such ostenta-tion was to contribute to their prestige. On the other hand, luxury had its limitations, imposed by the primitive constructive technique. To enlarge the chambers, to construct a true room, was impossible, but there was complete liberty with respect to length, and so there were built long, narrow halls, in some cases of three or four chambers, one behind the other, those in the middle having no direct light. "There are no windows in Maya architecture; only small openings at Palenque and Tulum, a few inches wide by about 12 high" (Totten). The only source of light is the entrance and the number of entrances is increased until the walls between them are almost no more than colonnades.

All the entrances open onto the terrace. The four wings of the building are grouped around a central interior patio from which the stairways rise to the terraces. In that sphere of limited space there cannot gestate the sensual experience of space, the true experience of the third dimension—as a value, as a vital tension—which can never be imparted by mere "limitations of space," by the construction of a "spatial box." In compensation, the Maya resort to decoration, to a grandiose decoration like the Bonampak murals.

In the end, the buildings of horizontal tendency and only one floor do not satisfy that estheticism. The constructions are no longer anchored to the ground; they begin to shoot upward. Thus a new effect is gained! For Teotihuacán, the horizontal orientation is axiomatic. Maya art discovers the vertical. It is not only a matter of the different aspect, the new attraction that multistory architecture offers. The restlessness of the upward impulse, the restlessness that governs that emancipation from the ground, is also essential. (In one isolated case, the so-called "Palace" at Palenque, even a real tower is built, quadrilateral in plan, a singular phenomenon in Mesoamerica.) Over the ground floor a second and a third are placed. Frequently it amounts to no more than this: one floor placed upon another. The lower part is an immediate support for the one above it and its flat roof constitutes at the same time the terrace of the upper floor, which is set back slightly from the lower floor. There is no means of interior communication such as a stairway leading from the lower floor to the second (if the word "floor" be suitable here). The tower of Palenque and, later, the "Caracol" of Chichén Itzá probably had interior stairs of wood (Totten). "In some cases, at Tikal, the upper tiers must have been reached by ladders, as no stairway leads to them" (Joyce). And Joyce adds as an interesting fact that in more than one stele of Piedras Negras a deity is shown seated in a niche "to which a ladder gives access from below." Why, we ask, was the one-story building considered unsatisfactory? In Mitla, the sacred city, the cemetery of kings and seat of the high priest, the Zapotecs conformed to one-story architecture. And they achieved spatial grandiosity in at least one case by means of a row of columns that gives double width to the chamber. In the Maya region, those in power, on whose order the buildings were erected, aspired not only to an imposing effect; they wanted their buildings to give the impression of something unheard of, something that had never existed before. Their ambition was to present a great architectonic spectacle. To the people, the residence of the *halach-huinic* must have been fabulous, something out of a dream. The lords wished to be different in every way from the "miserable plebs," to raise themselves far above them. Among the Aztecs, too, when a feudal regime began to develop following their conquests, only the great lords and the captains could have multistory houses (F. X. Clavijero, *Historia antigua de México*). This ostentation of power and of magnificence marked superior beings, who would never reside in low houses on the same level as the mob.

The most audacious and grandiose as well as the most fantastic creations of this upward impulse are the crests in Palenque (on the Temples of the Sun and the Cross) and Tikal, where the highest rises to 245 feet. In Palenque these ornamental façades or crests constitute a true architectonic body of two walls inclined toward each other in the form of a wedge, and pierced, windowlike, by niches or bays. In the Chichanchob, the "Casa Colorada" of Chichén Itzá, in Sayil, in Uxmal, in Labná, the crest is only one vertical wall above the front façade or, so to speak, the upward continuation of this façade. In the Chichanchob, there is a second wall behind the first and higher than it. This is a typical architecture of façades, in which the façade is an end in itself with no constructive body behind it. As Joyce expresses it, ". . . an elaborate false front, rising above the vertical entablature, the ornament of which it carries up to a greater height." An element of adornment, placed atop a temple of primitive construction. Several of those crests are very high—e.g., those of the temples of Tikal and very especially those of the Palomar of Uxmal—higher than the building itself. From the architectonic viewpoint, the crest is only a wall intended to bear a decoration, and it considerably augments the wall surface that can be covered with ornaments. Actually, the crests are only the cornice of an architectural work, but a cornice, an adornment, of singular magnificence, of an unparalleled audacity of conception; in the architecture of the entire world there is nothing to equal them. The subtly executed detail shows astounding richness. The architecture, generally subject to the purposes of a material or religious-metaphysical order, is here emancipated from any end except its own; it is only a manifestation of the most genuine joy in building, it is art for art's sake. What we have called the estheticism of Maya art finds here its most sublime and imposing justification. Artistic emotion, artistic will made pure form.

With these crests, Maya architecture succeeds in overcoming its monolithic character, or at least appears to have overcome it. Illusionist architecture in the strictest sense of the word. An upward flight from the lethargy and heaviness of the stone masses. Of course, the capricious silhouette and the elegant outline necessitate a considerable reinforcement of the rubblework of the lower section so that, as we have said, the chambers of the temples of Tikal are no more than narrow corridors left free in the mass of the stone. If we examine the plans from the so-called "golden age" of the seventh to ninth centuries, we immediately note the tendency to lessen the thickness of the interior walls in order to gain interior space (H. J. Spinden, *Ancient Civilizations of Mexico and Central*

*America*), a tendency that is constantly offset by the necessity to provide a firm support for the crest. Only later, in Yucatán, in Chichén Itzá, Sayil, and Tulum, when under the influence of the Toltecs the crests begin to disappear and new constructive elements are introduced into the architecture, do interiors increase in size so that they are "wider, better ventilated and illuminated" (Toscano).

Everyone familiar with the history of European architecture will recall Romanesque efforts to overcome an architecture of stone that was far too heavy for its will to form, to give it an appearance of lightness and movement. The man of the Romanesque period already felt the yearning for the transparent clarity and spatial music that would become reality in the Gothic cathedral (Amiens, Cologne). But he did not yet know the pointed arch and so his desire for immateriality was confounded by physical conditions, by the weight and solidity of traditional, i.e., Roman architecture, from which he did not know how to free himself. It is true that the building rested on the four principal columns, which had to be thick and heavy; but even so, the walls had to carry part of the load, the largest part. Thus rose the architectonic structure of Romanesque cathedrals. But the anxiety to be free of the heaviness and thickness continued to throb in man's spirit with more and more force. It was expressed in the pictorial articulation of the constructive body, in a certain curvature of the choirs (Cologne, *Apostelkirche*), in gables and stepped finials, in towers that lent movement to the silhouette. Above all, they used sculpture, just as the Maya did. Portals, columns, walls were covered with plastic ornaments and figures. A typical example is the entrance to the church of Vézelay. Extravagant creations, demons, monstrous animals, human figures weirdly twisted and coiled, fantastic, unreal, symbolic. Unable to alter the building itself, the imagination unfolds in these impassioned and expressive visions. . . .

That development of Maya architecture, which is an artistic development, would be even more evident had it not been carried out in isolation. What takes place in one particular place is not known in another, neighboring region. "Because of the separation and poor communication of the Maya area, the technical progress of Maya art is not the product of successive general experiences, but of the relatively autonomous evolution of the cities" (Toscano). What is stated here concerning technical development is equally valid for the artistic evolution. At any given moment there appear in different settlements evolutionary stages that are completely distinct with respect to advance or regression. It is useless to say to what extent this places obstacles in the path of esthetic investigation based on stylistic criticism. This is especially true with respect to the sculpture, because until now, to my knowledge, there does not exist in all the very abundant literature on this subject any study of Maya plastics that starts from comparative stylistics, nor has the substantial importance of this task been recognized, although Spinden pointed out its necessity. In attempting a synchronization of Maya and Western chronology, Spinden recognized correctly—as did A. P. Maudslay (*Biologia Centrali-Americana*) in the 1890s—that a stylistic study of Maya art would be a stupendous help, even for chronological investigation, as, e.g., in order to ascertain in what epoch the steles without dates were erected. He himself made several attempts toward this end. It would probably be of extraordinary interest to apply the methods of the criticism of style to the hieroglyphics, which after all are plastic creations, one form of artistic expression. It is impossible for us to imagine that, in Europe, the analysis of the capitals of Romanesque and Gothic manuscripts from the point of view of their artistic script would have been neglected. Of course, the experts have been occupied so exclusively in the most difficult problem of deciphering the glyphs that they have not yet been able to devote themselves to esthetic questions. At present, when the students of Maya art are consecrated to a description of the objects and their historical arrangement and have not yet approached the examination of the will to art or studies of an evaluative type, an esthetic investigation is at any rate beyond the efforts and material resources of any one individual.

We do not know of large sculptures in the round that

come from the Old Maya Empire. It is believed that there
were large sculptures carved in wood and that they were
destroyed by the tropical climate. The characteristic form
of plastic expression of the classic Maya is the stele, a
monolith of rectangular plan and often of notable height.
Its side faces are covered with figures and hieroglyphs
sculptured in relief, usually stuccoed and painted in various colors. They were erected at the end of a Katún, i.e.,
a cyclical period of twenty years; at times, more frequently
—every half Katún or, as in Copán, every quarter Katún.
In the culture of La Venta, a cult of steles already existed.
The Maya adopted it from them (Westheim: *Ideas fundamentales del arte prehispánico en México*). We do not
know how this custom arose or on what meaning it was
based. We do know that astronomical events or, better,
mythico-religious happenings, were noted on the stele at
first. On the other hand, it seems rather doubtful that they
were erected to commemorate certain astronomical phenomena. The principal argument against this hypothesis
is the five-, ten-, or twenty-year periodicity. S. G. Morley
(*An Introduction to the Study of the Maya Hieroglyphs*)
makes the very convincing observation that important astronomical or historical events just do not occur exactly
every five years. If we limit ourselves to the representation of figures, I believe we must conclude that it was a
matter of glorification (at intervals of time set by tradition) of the priests or ruling princes—if not their autoglorification, which is highly likely in view of their extremely
powerful situation—and that on that occasion a text of
glyphs was added to record transcendental, i.e., astronomical, happenings. The themes of the representations are
repeated in fairly stereotyped form, picturing either a
sumptuously garbed priest, sometimes accompanied by a
worshiper prostrate before him, or an enthroned chief re-
ceiving with an air of condescension the slaves who are
led to him.

The representations on the steles are carved in relief.
The relief is a singular type, subject to its own artistic
laws, not a variation of sculpture in the round or an early
stage of such sculpture, i.e., sculpture in the round not

yet fully mastered. Until now, many outstanding scholars of Maya culture have evidently not understood this, and so they have adopted a false attitude, since the criterion they start with is not the work's expressivity, but the degree of its approach to reality. In Piedras Negras and in Quiriguá, this latter city founded in the eighth or "Golden" century as a sort of colony of Copán, there is a series of steles in which the relief reaches such a degree of plasticity that it is almost a matter of full round sculpture, and in which, in order to give an illusion of naturalness, even the resources of perspective have been used to a certain degree. "Many of the stelae here are carved in such bold relief as to approximate sculpture in the round" (Joyce).

Such a hybrid form, which is neither relief nor true sculpture in the round, has been fervently admired by many Mayists, beginning with Spinden, who was the first to study the Maya steles even in their esthetic aspect and who, speaking of Stele 13 of Copán, says that in it, the representation of the human figure is "very superior to [the creations of] the Egyptians and Assyrians." Morley, to whom the reliefs of Uaxactún and Copán seem "awkward, stiff, and deformed," adds: "But such uncouthness in the representation of the human figure had long since passed when Quiriguá first appears in the sculptural picture of the times. . . ." It is very natural that on the basis of judgments such as these the opinion has been formed that the culminating point of Maya sculpture was reached with the high reliefs of the steles of Quiriguá and Piedras Negras. Those who deem the expressivity of Form more important than naturalistic illusionism will see phenomena of decadence in them, especially when they are compared to the stucco reliefs of the temples of Palenque, these latter authentically classic works of Maya art. Phenomena of the decadence of an estheticism that detaches itself from or does not recognize any limits, and whose observation does not signify impoverishment, but quite the contrary, intensification of artistic expressivity. Once again we see that it is not sufficient to indicate a development—and development there is in this case: greater skill in mastery of methods, greater richness of forms, closer approximation to nature—but that it is necessary to examine the facts in accordance with their spiritual and artistic value. And then, referring again to the case at hand, it may be said that evolution toward one type of work that is almost sculpture in the round without achieving the plasticity of such sculpture; evolution toward an art that worked with the resources of the illusionism of perspective instead of starting from the expressive formal elements and subjecting itself to them, makes us think of a will to art already debilitated in essence, the reflection of the spirit and social structure of a society that delighted in capricious and affected play with Form because it had already lost the elemental meaning of the creation.

Full round sculpture is the cubic structure of a mass: stone, wood, bronze—a mass that penetrates and opposes aerial space. To this tension of mass against aerial space sculpture in the round owes its plasticity. The delimitation of the mass, the silhouette that outlines it against the surrounding space, is what gives it Form. Whether an architectural or pictorial structure, a closed block or a dynamic, open form, a representation faithful to nature or alien to it, that cubic character is the decisive factor. There is nothing else, there can be nothing else—sculpture in the round is cubic sculpture. An esthetic evaluation of sculpture in the round, no matter from what age, class, or style it proceeds, can originate only in the meaning, in the creative intensity and awareness of Form that governs it. This is the criterion for creator and spectator alike. There are artists and works of art, there are entire cultures and epochs—China, the Indian Buddhas, the statue of King Chephren (in the Cairo Museum), the Negro fetishes, Teotihuacán or Aztec plastics—in which the feeling for the cubic is manifested in a vigorous and elemental way. And there are other epochs and other artists—Cellini, the neo-baroque monuments of the late-nineteenth century—in which this feeling is expressed timidly and indecisively, sacrificed to interest in the theme, in narrative detail. The norm for measuring the creative force of full round sculpture, whether it be Michelangelo's Moses or the Hera of Samos, is the degree to which cubic values, cubic structure, cubic movement, and cubic tensions are developed in it.

A relief is a creation of tridimensional corporality within a plane, i.e., within the bidimensional. It is built in the space between the fore and rear planes, which are at once an aid and a limitation. It cannot penetrate freely in aerial space, because it would lose its character as a relief. It must renounce the true cubic; the cubic values that it creates are cubic only in relation to the surface. Such submission to the plane, which makes the relief a true and special artistic genre together with and contrasted to sculpture in the round, enriches it with an element of tension that the latter does not have: the encounter between bidimensionality and tridimensionality. The relief produces that tension between the antagonistic tendencies in order to conciliate them in a formal unity, a happy balance of the cubic and the plane. This tension also governs the gradation from light to shadow, which is what really gives life and opticosensual movement to the sculpture. Sculpture in the round, a real body occupying real space, can count on the light that bathes all its sides and in accordance with which it should organize its structure in order to gain the most impressive contrast between light and shadow. Jacques Lipschitz, one of the most important modern sculptors, said in an interview with J. J. Sweeney: "In sculpture, the light falls upon the object from without. . . . The masses, if they are properly ordered, can be converted into a symphony of light. And for this end it is necessary that the plastic forms be disposed in such a manner that there arises a composition of reflected lights, shades, and concavities." The relief receives light from only one side, the front. This more artificial illumination determines its morphogenesis and ought to be taken advantage of as an expressive recourse for the movement of the mass, both in its contours and in profundity. Just as the line is a translation of the natural, corporeal phenomenon, of spatial-plastic corporeity—the only one the eye transmits—to the unreal, the abstract, so too the plane of the relief is also an imaginary, unreal, abstract element, even more artificial than the line, since cubic values are infiltrated into it despite its surface condition or better, since its surface condition must constantly defend itself against the beginnings of an evolution toward the cubic, transforming them into surface values. And just as the mural loses its monumentality in proportion to its emancipation from the surface of the wall, so too the relief loses its specific expressivity the more it sacrifices its relationship with the two planes, i.e., the more it succumbs to the false ambition of approaching sculpture in the round, or worse, of producing the effect of a painting translated into sculpture.

Reliefs that do not betray their character are those that adorn the rear faces of the La Venta altars, those of the columns and friezes of animals at Tula and Chichén Itzá, the Aztec Stone of the Sun, the round altar (No. 5) at Tikal, the Yaxchilán lintels, and the masterly stucco reliefs at Palenque of the seventh century, the apogee of Palenque. These are masterworks because of their limitation to the stated functional elements. One of these reliefs, the so-called Cross of Palenque, in the Temple of the Cross (Plates 69 and 70), represents a priest with one of his assistants, and in the center a stylized tree in the form of a cross, symbol of the earth and of rain. Wide panels of hieroglyphics frame the group. The artistic structure definitely abides by the plane of a relief; it uses the plane, so to speak, as a pictorial background. Each figure is deliberately flattened and subject to the background of the relief and never projects beyond the outer, imaginary plane suggested by the framing strip. On both sides, the rows of glyphs with their abundance of details and strong accents of light and shadow constitute a type of very decorative frame, which is the part that projects farthest optically and makes a vigorous contrast with the plastic representation of the center. The hieroglyphics are used most intelligently to compensate, above and below, for the difference in height between the smaller figure and the figure of the priest opposite, thereby avoiding a disagreeable asymmetry. The smaller figure is fitted, we might say, into a niche formed by glyphs. The central plane between the two figures almost gives the impression of a decoration. For a Maya creation its clarity and simplicity are astounding. The people of Palenque were not seized by *horror vacui*. They had a feeling for plastic nuance. Far from covering the entire surface with an indecipherable morass of details, they let the background speak, too, and understood that fullness and vacuum mutually intensify each other. Where there was danger that the background would occupy too much space, they inserted rows of glyphs, with great artistic tact and in a most unschematic distribution. The baroque arabesques of the ornamentation are balanced by the tranquil flow of the outline of the priest. Musicality of line, line filled with sensual experience, which unfolds in crescendos and decrescendos of classic nobility. A work of discipline as rigorous as the exemplary reliefs of the Old World: those of King Azhur-Nazir-Pal or the Egyptian reliefs at Sakkara.

In a book entitled *The Problem of Form in Painting and Sculpture*, read with much interest at the beginning of this century and considered the "sculptor's bible," the author, Adolf Hildebrand, a sculptor of Munich, attempted to derive all plastic creation from the relief and its morphogenetic laws. He worked out the so-called "theory of relief," according to which even a figure in the round is a relief, translated to tridimensionality and degraded, may I say, toward the cubic. Hildebrand even goes so far as to speak of torturing of the cubic. "So long as the chief effect of any plastic figure is its reality as a solid, it is imperfect as a work of art. It is only when the figure, though in reality a solid, gains its effect as a plane picture, that it attains artistic form, that is to say, perfection for our sense of vision." It suffices to say that this intellectualist theory does not capture the essence of sculpture in the round, and even disfigures it. For the born sculptor, a Michelangelo, who thinks and feels plastically, there can be no "torturing of the cubic," but only the voluptuosity of the cubic, the impulse to change mass into Form, i.e., into spiritual experience, through a creative process. Possibly there can be no "torturing of the cubic" even for the sculptor of reliefs. But, for him, creating is the constant effort to establish an organic equilibrium between tridimensionality (the cube) and bidimensionality (the plane). We have shown that at

Palenque this was achieved in a superior fashion. If we study Maya steles from Petén from this point of view, that of the creation of Form, we again come upon that restlessness, that obsession for the new and the different.

Examples of the purest art of relief are the steles of Naranjo. Stele 8, erected around A.D. 800, shows a prince or priest lifted on the back of a kneeling slave (Plate 71). The figure is seen frontally, with the face in profile. The feet are turned out at a 180-degree angle. The contrast between the modeled figures and the background plane is impressively emphasized. Considerable space was left free in the background, which helps to establish the formal structure. A structural unity integrated by a great variety of elements and at the same time extremely disciplined. The rear face of the stele is a panel of hieroglyphics, arranged in four columns of ten signs each. A true tapestry of glyphs, a modulated ornamentation, which stands out, light and transparent, among the harsh shadows of narrow vertical and horizontal bands carved deeply in the stone.

From Yaxchilán come various relief-covered lintels. One of them represents a priest making an offering to the fire serpent (Plate 72). The figures are seen in profile. There is greater distance between both planes of the relief than in the Naranjo steles and the group of figures has more plasticity without sacrificing the bidimensional character of the surface.

The reliefs at Naranjo and Yaxchilán, whose artistic security and rigor exclude every recourse that is foreign to the genre, recall the Zapotec steles, as well as Chalchiuhtlicue, the Teotihuacán water goddess, also basically a stele, a stele without inscriptions, with the outline of a human body and with a relief sculptured on its front face.

In Seibal (Plate 75), a playful impulse seizes the detail without harming the structure. The bicephalous dragon on the priest's ceremonial rod and the feather headdress become a flamboyant baroque ornament. Vegetal forms coil around his feet. A movement without respite winds and twists around his body. The details of the garment display the same playful impulse. An exquisite Gobelin carved in stone. But despite these agitated forms, the work is maintained strictly within the plane of the relief.

From Piedras Negras, a center founded somewhat later than Naranjo, there is a stele (No. 12, in the Philadelphia Museum) that gives fascinating evidence of the extraordinary artistic sensibility of the Maya. This is a representation in bas-relief, limited essentially to the carving of the contour lines, and, like the Totonac stele in the National Museum, Mexico, it is basically a drawing carved on the stone surface. But what a drawing! What certainty, delicacy, and grace in the flow of the line! It is true of course that the excessively detailed statement of the action and the superabundance of figures crammed into the tall, slender rectangle of the stele detract from its clarity and simplicity, that clarity and simplicity so characteristic of the Palenque reliefs or the Naranjo steles. We count no less than thirteen persons, captives bound with ropes, led by two warriors to a prince who sits on a high throne and glances from his lofty position at the troop approaching him. All the figures are seen in profile. The work has the definite character of a plane and its graphics is comparable to the calligraphy of Hindu and Persian miniatures. In Stele 13 of Piedras Negras we see how the realistic and illusionistic traces begin to penetrate the creation. In Stele 12, a highly acute observation is translated into abstract values, into curves and sinuosities of the drawing. In Stele 13, which represents a sumptuously attired priest, the realism of the observation is at the service of a reportage that depends on material fact.

Every detail of the clothing, even the design of the fabric, is clearly recognizable and is reproduced with meticulous exactitude. The head is seen in the more natural three-quarter view and such an attempt to approximate reality goes to the extreme of introducing in the work certain features of a representation in perspective: e.g., the left shoulder, turned toward the spectator, projects strongly, while the other is foreshortened. Another type of stele (Plate 73) seeks a novel effect by opening a niche in the center of the relief, within which is a rounded, seated figure leaning back against the rear wall of the niche—probably an image of the maize goddess. (In some of those steles we also see the ladder that, as noted in discussing architecture, gave access to the upper floors, in this case to the place where the goddess sits.) The tension between bidimensionality and tridimensionality that gives a relief its interest, quality, and category is sacrificed here because the imaginary space of the plane of the relief is transformed into the real space of the niche. The representation of the figure acquires corporeity within an ensemble that otherwise abides by the form of the relief. It is an exterior effect, not the product of an authentic and creative plastic experience. Perhaps there was, on the one hand, the desire to respect the traditional and sacred form of the stele, and on the other the desire to convert it into something new, something different and ostentatious, that would give the impression of an advance or an invention, and that it did, in reality.

Together with this "deep relief," let us call it, there appear in Copán and Quiriguá something that we might with the same reservations call high relief. Instead of hollowing out a niche in order to place a figure in it, the figure projects from the plane of the relief for the entire length of the block (Plate 75). The stele now serves almost solely as a base for the figure, which bulges in three dimensions. The face and the headdress project farthest. Perhaps the intention was to accent the head especially, to make it stand out forcefully from the other elements. In Stele H of Copán (dated A.D. 782), it seems as though the figure, scarcely touching the block, were placed on the front of the stele. There is also greater realism. The feet are no longer separated in "so unnatural" a manner, the posture is relaxed, the movement of the arms and hands is well observed; the garment, the jewels, and the design of the fabric point up the most negligible details—a figurine that could well serve as a dress model. Pomp and luxury exhibited most deliberately, and evidently this was of much importance to the artist or whoever entrusted the work to him. Oddly enough, that realism stops short of the facial features, precisely where it could characterize a particular person. "In general," writes Spinden, "a special type pre-

vails in each city. In the steles of Quiriguá there are various types, but the degree of individualization is slight.
Possibly the features of the statue-portraits varied only
slightly, as in Egypt, and the individual differences were
expressed by the clothing, ornament, or inscription."

Thomas Gann (Gann and Thompson: *The History of
the Maya . . . , op. cit.*) characterizes that evolution very
aptly: "At the beginning," he says, "the relief was low, but
it continued to change Katún by Katún until the figures
left the background, becoming almost round, and the posture of the human figure, at first rigid and conventional,
later showed considerable knowledge of perspective and
became almost perfect in its profile representation." All
very well, except that the conclusion reached from this—
that this perfection "certainly was superior to any other
effort achieved in that epoch, both in Egypt and in Meso-
potamia"—is "certainly" erroneous, because it is based on
a false premise. For if it is certain that there was perfection in technique, no less certain is the decadence in art-
istry. Toscano speaks of "the tendency toward preciosity,"
of an art that progressed "notably in elegance and elaboration of the natural models but lost in majesty what it
gained in beauty." Worringer (*Griechentum und Gotik*),
referring to the Pergamo altar comments: "The moment when this classically austere concept of the relief
is abandoned is the danger point for the Greek art of the
relief." And what he says of the Borobodur reliefs: "The
sculpture as a statuary element was completely transformed into a plastic calligraphy," may also be applied to
the Maya reliefs.

The steles of Quiriguá, a center that developed great
artistic activity in the eighth century (711–805), repeat
this evolution once again. "The anatomical proportions are
a model of perfection," says Toscano.

According to Maudslay, steles "were only public calen-
dars." We do not know whether the figures represented
on them were effigies. Spinden believes they are. "It is
extremely likely that portraits of actual rulers are to
be seen in certain carvings." This could be another explanation of the growing tendency toward preciosity, but it

is impossible to give an exact answer pro or con because the sources do not supply us with reliable data. The conventional expression of the features, which Spinden also observes, is not an argument against the theory. In the European official portrait we also find stylization of the features toward the conventional. Leaders want to, and must, appear before the world in the pose of idealized rulers, and it is natural to assume that those Maya nobles were no less vain than their European colleagues. It is very probable that it was equally important for them to be portrayed not as individuals but as superior and distant beings. Another argument in support of that hypothesis is that the erection of steles ceased after the fall of the *halach-huinicoob.*

The steles of Copán and Quiriguá likewise reveal that *horror vacui* so typical of Maya decoration. Not an inch must be left without decoration. The eye must not rest for a moment. The glance is not led to the essential but is constantly distracted. There is everywhere something new and surprising. The designs of the fabric and the jewels are reproduced in such great detail as to provide almost an inventory. Just as on the steles themselves the figure comes away from the background, so too this baroque ornamentation overflows, comes away from the frame made by the figure, spreads out over the background of the relief, and completely covers every available spot, destroying the structure of the body, whose representation is, after all, the true purpose of the work. Only the face is left free, an oasis in the jungle of ornaments. What a high degree of artistic sensibility was shown in the way the figures of the two priests were made to stand out in the Palenque reliefs! There no longer seems any appreciation of such sensibility. The thicket of ornamentation materially devours the structure of the body. The result is a disturbing lack of clarity. The mind atrophies in trying to appreciate the discretion, the discreet reserve. They cannot break up the composition into smaller proportions in order to intensify the effect. They cannot make use of the contrast between plenitude and vacuum by which what is important is emphasized and becomes expressive. The free space that isolates, that condenses by means of isolation, is deemed a lack of talent and imagination, poverty, and what is aspired to precisely is to exhibit richness, magnificence, and splendor. This is the decisive difference that separates this art from that of the Central Plateau. Teotihuacán is free of that "horror of the vacuum," isolates the objects that it represents, and develops a clear and austere rhythm. Maya art delights in quantity. Rhythm sinks and becomes inexpressive in the chaos of accumulated details. Tropical proliferation, exuberance of the *tierra caliente*. There is no doubt that one of the causes is, as in India, the excess of tropical fantasy, tropical sensuality. One of the causes, yes, but it does not suffice to explain the phenomenon, which is doubtless rooted in deeper strata: in the religious and social structure reflected by this art. A feudal art. The common people form a huge, undistinguished multitude, as in the France of Louis XV and Louis XVI, spending its toilsome, diffident life adoring the gods and the priestly and princely demigods. Its intervention in the development of that imposing passion for art and culture is limited to supplying the necessary manpower and resources.

The government of the different city-states was theocratic. An aristocracy of priests closely linked to the nobility constituted the ruling class. "The High Priest was at the same time, by virtue of his priestly rank, the highest civil authority" (Morley).

There is a study by Oswaldo Baqueiro Anduze (*Los mayas. Fin de una cultura*), an important contribution to Mayist investigation, in which the author attributes the decadence and extinction of the Maya Empire to the extremes reached by that feudalism, whose usufructuaries used the religion as a skillfully manipulated instrument by which to seize and maintain power.[2] Baqueiro Anduze begins, as the title of his book indicates, with the social structure prevailing in the last stages of the Maya Empire, but the facts he describes are a result of causes that originate in the Old Empire.

[2] See also J. Eric S. Thompson: *The Rise and Fall of Maya Civilization.*

The Maya people were filled with a profound religiosity, even more profound if possible than that of the peoples of the Central Plateau. Without that religiosity, the rise of a theocracy so immoderately avid for power would not have been possible. Faith in the gods, as in all religions, served as a foundation for a theology, an esoteric science, accessible only to its few initiates.

A primitive but convincing example of how between magic and religion priestly power is transformed into worldly and political power is given by the legend of the Aztec migration represented in the Boturini Codex. It relates that the Aztecs had found in a cave the idol of Huitzilopochtli, their tutelary deity, who, as Vaillant (*The Aztecs of Mexico*) says; "had the useful ability to speak, and to give them good advice." This means that his advice was transmitted through the words of a priest, especially in what concerned the most important undertaking of the tribe, i.e., the migration. The priests, therefore, decided whether the migration would continue. As can be seen, it is not only a matter of something concerning "the salvation of the soul," but also and above all of the material existence and its maintenance. And it is clear that those who are initiated into the secret or who are believed to be—who can communicate it to all or keep it hidden and in whose hands therefore lie the life and death of the community—are a political factor of the first order, dominating all questions concerning the individual or the tribal collectivity. And here is posed the problem of the mediator, of the omnipotence of the mediator, who by divine order and relying upon divine authority intervenes in mundane and political affairs, wields influence in these affairs, helps to determine them, or himself makes the decisions. Thus the priestly mediator appears in the social and political structure of Mayab as a figure of the first rank.

The *Tzolkin,* the very celebrated Maya ritual calendar that constitutes a system of infinite complexity, is the compendium of that theology: it is speculative knowledge, scientific investigation, and at the same time, instruction on the manner of performing the ritual. More extensive than Sacred Scriptures and the Talmud of the Jews, and

more hermetic because of the mysticism and magic ceremony with which it surrounds the religious essence,
("through the development of the symbolism and the
ritual convention there arose a great multiplicity of detail"
[Joyce]), it is as intricate, as intentionally complicated, as
iridescent in infinite facets as the Maya ornamentation that
fascinates by the imprecision, indeterminability, and unat-
tainability of its drawing.

Since it would have been impossible to establish and
evaluate the results of the astronomical investigations
without an arithmetic that allowed computations with numerical values of enormous magnitude, and a chronological system that would encompass thousands of years, it
was indispensable to invent and develop such an arithmetic; it was, so to speak, a religious necessity. And so the
Maya invented the concept of zero, discovered multiplica-
tion with the zero—elements that the European world
learned only from the Arabs—and the so-called "long
count" was established. But the calendar does not limit
itself to summarizing the knowledge of celestial phenomena. It includes the conditions of religious duties and religious conduct; it is a moral code, a social and agrarian
order, commercial law, civil code, the Magna Carta of
the Maya world, the rules governing relationships not only
between the individual and God, but also the individual
and the State. To a certain degree, it also regulated taxes.
As Antonio Goubaud Carrera observes ("El Guajxaquit
Bats, ceremonia calendárica indígena," *Boletín de Geo-
grafía e Historia de Guatemala,* September 1931), the
calendar establishes, e.g., certain taxes to be paid by merchants in gratitude for gains received or anticipated: on
the day Kahuac, for the success of projected business
trips; on the day Ahmac, in thanksgiving to ancestors for
current economic prosperity. Before undertaking a business trip—the day of good omen for the departure having
been calculated, i.e., determined by the priest—the merchant had to pay a fixed quota in accordance with the
profit he hoped to make from it. Baqueiro Anduze says
that if they did not pay those taxes, they could not oper-
ate their businesses. And the taxes, rendered to the gods,

came to rest in the hands of the priests and assured them a certain economic supremacy.

The Ten Commandments are concise and clear, understandable by everyone, and, being understood by all, they can be observed by all without further ado. Nothing of the sort can be said of the *Tzolkin*. It is complicated and difficult to understand, and admits of multiple interpretations. But the interpretation is precisely what is most important. The efficacy of the magic conjuration depends to a high degree on the exact, meticulous observation of the ritual. The slightest violation of directions endangers the results. But only the priests know the correct interpretation. It is their jealously guarded secret, their superiority over the uninitiate. And the uninitiate comprises all those who are not members of the priesthood or its close ally, the nobility. Management of the *Tzolkin*, "the control of the miraculous" (Baqueiro Anduze), is the privilege of the priests. Their knowledge is indispensable to the people, since it concerns matters of vital importance to the public. Compared with the priest, the public are minors; docile, without protest, they must submit to their guardianship. Then the priest, the expert in the ritual through which the gods can be propitiated and induced to concede happiness and well-being to men, can also cause the deity to punish and destroy. This is what gives the Maya priestly caste its extremely powerful position, which it strives—consciously or unconsciously—to display in the most obvious manner. The systematization of religious sentiment in the form of an esoteric theology is translated socially into the almost unlimited supremacy of a priestly aristocracy. Just as we speak of feudal art, so too is there feudal religion. What characterizes feudalism is not only a monopoly of goods by a privileged class, but above all that this class is in a position to manipulate the political and economic power of the State for its own interests. In the Maya world, the privileged position (also economically privileged) of the ruling classes is based on the religiosity of the masses. What Maya art reflects in such a fascinating way and at times with such preciosity is the spirit of that clerical feudalism. It is not by accident that one so often speaks of a

Maya baroque, or, more correctly, a Maya rococo. Identical conditions in the Old World and in the New gave rise to an art of identical impulses and stimuli.

On the Maya steles of the Old Empire there are not, so far as I know, any images of deities, but almost exclusively representations of priests and princes. "The principal idols to whom they sacrificed were figures of men of their own nature who had been distinguished and worthy persons, and whom they called upon, induced by the devil's slyness, to be favorable to them in wars and to give them good weather, and prolong their life. . . ." (Martín Palomar, *Relaciones de Yucatán*). Very great lords, adorned with the insignia of their power: the staff with the bicephalous dragon—one of the heads bearing the sign of the sun, the other that of death—the feather headdress, the lance, etc. Wearing magnificent garments, venerated by persons prostrate before them in an attitude of submission, they condescendingly receive the slaves brought to them in tribute. This cannot be an accident. At Teotihuacán, at Monte Albán, in both monumental and "minor" art, the substantial theme is always the figure of the deity, the divine symbol, or some mythological scene. In the steles, however, which are the official monuments of the Old Maya Empire, the gods are not to be seen. It is the same with the pottery. What do we see represented in the celebrated Maya vase in the Fenton Collection, a work of great beauty? A chief seated on his throne, surrounded by high dignitaries. In the Chamá vase (Plate 60) three princes solemnly greet a companion who wears the insignia of his dignity, a jaguar's skin, hanging from his shoulders. Compare this to one of the principal works of Mixtec pottery, the vase in the National Museum of Anthropology, Mexico, on which appear two gods, Quetzalcóatl and Tezcatlipoca. The murals discovered in one of the palaces of Bonampak, the most important of the Old Maya Empire discovered to date (Westheim: *Ideas fundamentales del arte prehispánico en México*), represent the parade of a great number of people—musicians with drums and trumpets—all seen in profile, who render homage to a high priest. On another wall we see the priest being garbed in

Photograph: National Museum of Anthropology, Mexico City.

PLATE 65. Pyramid I. Tikal, Guatemala. Maya.

PLATE 66. Stele E (detail). Quiriguá, Guatemala. Maya.

*Photograph: National Institute of Anthropology and History, Mexico City.*
PLATE 67. Stele 2 (detail). Bonampak, Chiapas. Maya.

PLATE 68. Relief (detail). Stucco. Palenque, Chiapas, Maya.

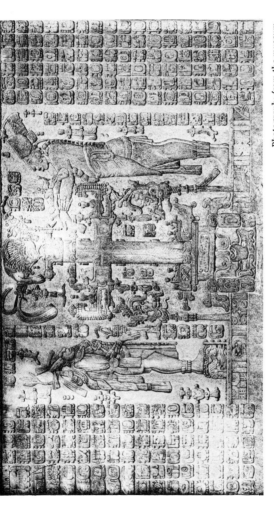

*Photograph: from the museum.*

PLATE 69. The Cross of Palenque. Stucco. Maya. National Museum of Anthropology, Mexico City.

PLATE 70. The Cross of Palenque (detail). Stucco.

*Photograph: Salvador Toscano, Mexico City.*

PLATE 71. Stele 8. Naranjo, Guatemala. Maya.

PLATE 72. Priest offering a sacrifice to the fire serpent. Lintel in Yaxchilán. Stone. Maya. British Museum, London.

PLATE 73. Stele 14. Piedras Negras, Guatemala. Maya.

*Photograph: National Museum of Anthropology, Mexico City.*
PLATE 74. Stele D. Quiriguá, Guatemala. Maya.

PLATE 75. Stele 10. Seibal, Guatemala. Maya.

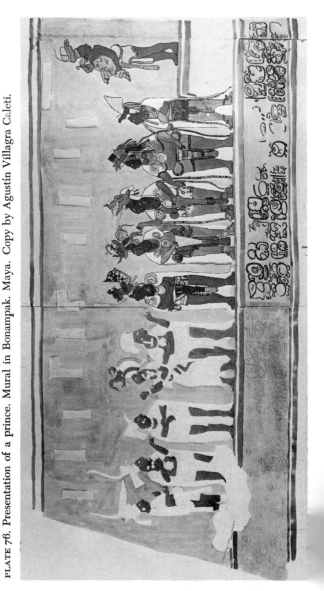

PLATE 76. Presentation of a prince. Mural in Bonampak. Maya. Copy by Agustín Villagra Caleti.

PLATE 77. Building of the Koz poop. Façade with large masks of Chac. Puuc style. Kabah, Yucatán.

PLATE 78. Palace. Chenes style. Hochob, Campeche.    Photograph: National Museum of Anthropology, Mexico City.

PLATE 79. Young maize god. Copán, Honduras. Limestone. Maya. Peabody Museum, Harvard University, Cambridge, Massachusetts.

PLATE 80. Relief (detail). Stucco. Akancé, Yucatán.

PLATE 81. Altar. Copán, Honduras.

PLATE 82. Nunnery complex. Entrance. Puuc style. Uxmal, Yucatán.

Photograph: J. Rodolfo Lozada.

*Photograph: National Museum of Anthropology, Mexico City.*
PLATE 83. The Nunnery, annex, east end. Chichén Itzá. Uxmal.

*Photograph: National Museum of Anthropology, Mexico City.*
PLATE 84. Governor's Palace. Puuc style. Uxmal.

PLATE 85. Nunnery complex. West building, detail of the façade. Puuc style. Uxmal.

PLATE 86. The Palomar (House of the Doves). Puuc style. Uxmal.

Photograph: Enrique A. Cervantes.

Photograph: Ernest Rathenau, New York City.

PLATE 87. Nunnery complex. West building. Puuc style. Uxmal.

*Photograph: Ernest Rathenau, New York City.*

PLATE 88. House of the Magician. Puuc style. Uxmal.

his ceremonial robes, and on the third wall, a person presenting a prince to an illustrious gathering (Plate 76). Evidently this is a fiesta celebrated in honor of the rain god. The god, of course, does not appear there in person, but the upper panel is decorated with masks of Chac and everywhere, as emblems, there are all types of aquatic animals. Another chamber is decorated with a masterful representation of a battle, a glorification of the conquering prince. We have already expressed the supposition that Maya art is in large part a glorification—or autoglorification—of the ruling caste. This caste makes a show of its rank, that of *halach-huinic,* and of its being sublime, superhuman, worthy of adoration, everything implied by the term *Roi Soleil,* translated into Maya. The subject must shudder before the power and the splendor of the great lords. What Baqueiro Anduze says about the Maya theater ". . . official art, that wishes to convince the people that they live in the best of all possible worlds," can also be applied to the plastic arts: they want to convince the people that their rulers are the best in the world.

The inscriptions, in so far as they can be deciphered, refer to astronomical happenings; and astronomical happenings are a manifestation of the divine. Does the inscription perhaps establish a relationship between the demigods represented and the divine? Was this relationship perhaps intended to show to what degree the *halach-huinic* belonged to the world of the gods, and how far he was from the mass of the people? These inscriptions occupy a great deal of space. They are no less detailed than the prolix inscriptions that the baroque potentates had placed on their castles, monuments, mausoleums. No inscriptions have been found at Teotihuacán. On the Zapotec steles, as Alfonso Caso notes (*Las estelas zapotecas*), and also on the Aztec monuments, glyphs are few; there are only those indispensable ones that indicate historical dates or events. Teotihuacán art, being as it is a collective religious art, is clear, sober, objective. Theology, on the other hand, is eloquent, resorts to metaphor, ambiguity, psychological slant, to the insinuating melody of the word. An art for the masses ought to indicate and underline fact.

A feudal art delights in paraphrase, in attractive representation, in esthetic adornment. The Maya glyph is also calligraphy, an artificial and artistic calligraphy full of arabesques, of an original and refined graphics. Referring to the codices, Morley states: "In the Maya texts, the glyph in itself is a perfect painting." He speaks of "very considerable modifications, so that the final composition of the sign not only constitutes a balance and harmonious design but also exactly fills the given space." In writing, also, a subtle refinement and a fastidious lack of clarity! The twenty day signs are essentially the same among the Nahua, Zapotecs, and Maya. The Nahua and Zapotec signs are precise and perfectly intelligible. "This is not true with the Maya," Seler says. "Here the nature of the signs is only insinuated, in those cases where it is not ambiguous: a closed eye and a bare tooth signify 'cranium' or 'death'; two wavy lines that cross each other and represent the broken surfaces of the stones used to kindle fires signify 'flint knife'. . . . But frequently a symbol is used instead of the concrete sign, a metaphorical expression, so to speak: in place of 'house' a face covered with a mask as a symbol of 'night,' because at night the sun enters his house. In place of 'deer,' a hand in the position that signifies 'eating.' In place of 'vulture,' the 'bald' (i.e., old) bird, a symbol of the pitcher of pulque, because only the old men were permitted to drink pulque. To sum up, the majority of names are obviously symbolic, the result of interpretations; they form part of an esoteric priestly science." So, then, the Maya codices—as far as we can draw conclusions from the three that escaped Landa's destructive furor—whose sheets are covered with innumerable images of gods, each one of them with many attributes and of varied meaning, constitute in effect the esoteric science of a ruling caste whose taste and estheticism are reflected in their style and artistic writing.

Is not the prolixity of inscriptions on the steles one more proof of the baroque preciosity of the Maya? In a documented study (in the magazine, *Yucatán Ilustrado*, January 1929), Ermilo Solís Alcalá shows that the upper class took pleasure in using a private language, metaphorical

and incredibly affected. Euphemism, intellectualist preciosity of an elite of the learned, whose affectation pleased
only themselves, the initiate. For whom, we ask, were
those detailed inscriptions intended? Not for the people.
The art of reading and writing "was taught only to the
persons of noble lineage," writes Morley. They were
therefore not directed to the masses. But, perhaps they
were directed precisely to them in order to impress them,
to show them that to the great lords there was no secret,
not even the secret of the writing that served to establish
the sacred, divine matters . . . ?

In the reliefs of the Palenque temples we see in the
center—in a scheme that is repeated in almost stereotyped
fashion—the emblem of the deity between long rows of
hieroglyphics that flank it. But at the side of the divine
symbol, the priest who celebrates the ceremony stands
erect, tall and dominating. The ritual act celebrated by
the priest: here is the theme, not the god himself, not his
divine omnipotence. It is as though they wanted to say:
the principal thing, the substantial thing, is the celebra-
tion of the ritual; God is great, yes, but no less great (and
absolutely indispensable, since he directs the divine will)
is the mediator, who appears there full length, majestic
and imposing. Totten states that the relief in the "Temple
of the Beautiful Relief," now known only through Wal-
deck's drawing, represents "the seated figure of possibly
the ruler or High Priest of Palenque." It is a glorification
of the priests, priests not at all humble, but on the contrary, very proud and conscious of their power; glorification of the ruling class even in the temple, and especially
in the temple, with the purpose of presenting their power
as part of the divine omnipotence.

Without a doubt, Palenque is a rather special example,
but it is nevertheless a most instructive one. It is true that
the temples generally contain images of the deities; it
could not be otherwise. Vaillant observes: "But there exists
almost no sculpture in the round representing a god that
could have been placed on the central altar." Although
the mediator occupies so predominant a place in the reliefs of the Palenque temples, the façades of the palaces

of Puuc, or Chenes, style (Kabah, Uxmal, Sayil, Hochob, Labná) are decorated—and at times covered to the last inch—with large masks of the rain god. How shall we explain this? Behind those sumptuous façades lived and governed the *halach-huinicoob*, who derived their control and their right to control from their divine ancestry. They, the *halach-huinicoob*, the "true men," were descendants of the gods and had come down to live temporarily among common men in order to direct them and their destinies, to transmit to them, as mediators, the benevolence and benediction of the gods.[3] It is stated that the *Popol Vuh* was written because, after the Conquest, the Spaniards promised the Maya nobility an exemption from taxes on the condition that they present the credentials, as it were, of their nobility. In its final section, probably added by someone else, the *Popol Vuh* enumerates the different lineages, names, titles, genealogy, and goes back to the history of creation to show the divine origin of those families, the only title of nobility that counted for anything in Mayab. "They take great pains to learn the origin of their families," writes Landa.

The common, ordinary men live in primitive huts. They are accustomed to this; it is natural. But the emissaries of the gods, the great men, the powerful men. . . . As the *Popol Vuh* says, man has been created to maintain the world, to maintain the gods, and, in the interpretation of the nobles, to maintain themselves, to offer them riches and luxuries, to build sumptuous palaces for them. Art and architecture—here as at Versailles—create distance. The more grandiose the artistic standard, the more natural will the role of subject, of commoner, seem to the people. Libertinism is also an important feature in the picture of

[3] The *Relación de Mechuacán* states that when the Spaniards arrived in Michoacán, the Tarascans called them *tucúpacha*, "gods," *tepáracha*, "great men or gods," and also *acácecha*, which means "men with caps or hats," and they called the women *cucháecha*, "ladies or goddesses." They believed that the Spaniards had descended from the sky and that the clothes they wore were human skins such as the Tarascans themselves wore in their fiestas. . . .

the customs of that esthetic world. When we read the description in Landa's work of the orgiastic festivities with their feasts, music, dances, excesses—diversions of the great men of Mayapán—we once again recall Versailles.

Louis XIV adorned Versailles with the emblems of war because he was eager to be admired as a war hero, too. This ostentation of warlike heroism was no more justified than the legend of divine origin spread by the Maya princes. The wars undertaken during his reign were fiascos and led to disastrous consequences. If the Maya palaces are so magnificently decorated with the large masks and images of the gods, does this not show a similar anxiety? They boast of their divine ancestry in the same way that European manorial houses display the noble escutcheon over their entrances. The common people are supposed to experience a chill of veneration. Those beings who live among them are of superior race; gods made men, and the masks and divine images exhibited so ostentatiously on their palaces are like ancestral portraits. What Baqueiro Anduze states in attempting to explain the anthropomorphic tendency of the Maya theogony corroborates this thesis. "A god," he says, "or a priest, represented by a tiger, does not signify the deification of the tiger, but that that god or that prince shares in the most distinct characteristics of that animal: indomitable courage, implacable ferocity, powerful energy. In time, the word 'tiger,' i.e., *balam*, would acquire an esoteric significance in the religious terminology. . . ." In other words, those lords not only boast of their divine origin, they also attribute to themselves the properties, the omnipotence, the invincibility of the gods. This is manifested in the names *Balam* or *Chac* that they assume, in the ceremonial and decorative trappings with which they surround themselves. The large masks of the gods on the façades of their palaces are not only ancestral portraits; at the same time, they indicate the superhuman qualities of the *halach-huinic*. "These lords are the equals of the gods," we read in the *Libro de Chilam Balam de Chumayel*. And just as in ancient Egypt the gigantic pyramid that was erected over the corpse of the Pharaoh served to preserve forever the mortal remains and the memory of the powerful lord, and was also considered a protection for the living against his perilous return from the dead, it may be that by placing images of the divinity on their walls the Maya too wished to establish a taboo. No one would dare to rebel against those whose intimacy with the gods was such that the latter were even domiciled in their homes. That would be more than rebellion; it would be a challenge to the gods themselves. . . .

The eagerness to show off power and magnificence intervenes in the conception of many works, determining the morphogenesis in a decisive way. This will to beauty, directed to grace and nuance, reaches culminating points in the sculptures of the young maize god (found in Temple 22) and the altars of Copán. The image of the maize god (Plate 79) is a work of delicate lyric sensibility and noble reserve that by its marked realism is strongly differentiated from the creations of the Teotihuacán world, where such secularization of the divine would have been inconceivable. In the altars of Copán (eighth century, A.D.) with the bicephalous dragon that twists in baroque turns and erupts winding into space like an agitated and exalted ornament (Plate 81), is expressed another of the creative impulses of Maya art: the tropical fantasy that roams in wandering fashion, bold and magical—a charm and an enchantment—and is crystallized in mystical visions. In the reliefs of the frieze at Akancé (of the transitional epoch), a whole Mount Olympus of zoomorphic gods undertakes the march from the heavens: birds, bats, jaguars, rodents; fantastic divinities, mysterious and restless. Goyaesque fantasies (Plate 80). Goya etches the hallucinations of his subconscious on a sheet of copper; the artist of Akancé projects his mythical fantasies onto the walls, a mural decoration at once morbid and monumental, sharply outlined by the aggressive light of the tropical sun.

In the ninth century, the Maya world slowly disintegrated. Within a period of fifty to eighty years, the great cultural centers of Palenque, Uaxactún, Copán, and finally Tikal were depopulated. No longer were buildings raised, steles erected. The superb temples, the magnificent palaces, were deserted; the jungle devoured them.

Why were these settlements, the fruit of centuries of work, abandoned, and so precipitately? The most diverse hypotheses have been put forth to explain that strange phenomenon: epidemics, earthquakes, climatic changes, exhaustion of the soil. Two conjectures prevail currently, that abandonment of the Maya cities was due either to the expulsion of the inhabitants by the Pipil, a warlike Chichimec tribe established in the Puebla region before they entered the Maya area, or a rebellion of the rural population against the *halach-huinicoob*, their masters and exploiters.

The emigration, led by the dominant priestly caste, was directed toward two different points, the southeast and Yucatán. As a result of internal struggles in the peninsula, groups of Mexican mercenaries were summoned to the assistance of the Cocomes, whose tyranny had provoked the trouble. Among the mercenaries were those Toltecs expelled from Tula, who brought a new cult, a new culture, and a new art to Yucatán. A renaissance. But was this a renaissance of Maya art, or of Toltec?

## 12

## Chichén Itzá

The migration of the Maya tribes toward the Peninsula
of Yucatán, where the Olmec and Nahua groups had penetrated from the north during the so-called transition period, gave rise to tensions, rivalries, and even battles, almost unknown until then in the peaceful land of Mayab.
The excessive ambitions of one family, the Cocomes, con-
tributed greatly to creating a state of hatred and discord.

It is supposed that Uxmal was founded in the ninth or
tenth century, A.D., by the Xiúes or the Tutul Xiúes. (It
is not known for certain if this latter name were only the
title of their rulers.) Landa relates that the Cocomes
called the Xiúes "strangers" and that they had come to
Yucatán "from the direction of midday." It seems that
that "direction of midday" corresponds to what is today
Tabasco. Until now it has not been possible to ascertain
whether the Xiúes were a Maya people or a Mexican
group that were gradually being "Maya-ized" in Tabasco.
The Maya chronicles said: "they do not speak our language well." They were not Toltec: this only is certain.

Uxmal and the new Chichén Itzá, neighboring and contemporary cities, developed completely distinct styles in
architecture and plastics. The Xiúes did not adopt the
new constructive elements that the Toltecs had created in
Tula and introduced later into Yucatán, nor does the enigmatic figure of the Chac Mool appear in Uxmal. The artistic tradition of the so-called Old Empire predominates
there. A modified tradition, enriched by new expressive
resources, the style designated by archeologists as "Puuc
style." They preserve the false arch (Plate 82), which explains why the chambers of the Governor's Palace—one of

the most splendid constructions of Mesoamerica, 321½ feet long—are only 11½ feet wide. The Palomar (House of the Doves) (Plate 86) owes its beauty to its roof crests. The friezes appear exclusively on the upper part of the façades, another Maya inheritance. Those friezes of Uxmal, whose open disposition contrasts with the restless and exuberant forms of the classic Maya, are rows of rectangles in which stand out representations in relief seen over a background of latticework formed by perforated rhombi. The immense frieze of the Governor's Palace is a complicated mosaic of some twenty thousand stones, a stone carpet whose different elements: latticework, frets, masks, human and animal figures—are incorporated into the unity of the ensemble and subject to the rhythm that breathes in that unity. In the simple and monumental frieze of the East Building of the Nunnery Complex, there stand out from the latticework background six trapezoids, each composed of eight bars that end at both sides in serpentine heads. An owl's head, decorated with a great plume, is placed on the top part of each of the trapezoids.

In the second half of the fifteenth century, Uxmal was suddenly abandoned. Although in 1451 the Xiúes had triumphed over Mayapán and had even destroyed it, they did not return to their splendid capital. At the same time, the Itzá abandoned Chichén Itzá, went away toward the south, and established themselves on the shores of Lake Petén. Why? All these events are still enveloped in mystery. It is possible that the Xiúes succumbed to the superior forces of some invading people. What is known with certainty is that they founded a new capital, which they called Maní. The arrival of the Spaniards put an end to the epoch of Maní, an epoch of decline and decadence.

Maní is the place of unfortunate fame where Fray Diego de Landa, then Provincial of Merida, motivated by an excessive religious zeal, organized in 1541 that auto-da-fé in which five thousand idols and twenty-seven Maya codices were destroyed. Of these latter, three have been saved. It was the same Landa who wrote, years afterwards, the *Relación de las cosas de Yucatán*, the best and most complete information on the old Maya culture.

Chichén Itzá, the center of the Itzá, left us examples of their architecture in the Nunnery, the Temple, and the Chichanchob (Red House). After the arrival of the Toltecs, a radical change took place in this architecture.

A chief named Kukulkán, which means "plumed serpent," a translation of the Nahua word Quetzalcóatl, came to the peninsula with the Toltecs. The sovereigns of Tula followed the custom of adding to their own names the name of Quetzalcóatl, their tribal deity. Quetzalcóatl was also the name of the last prince of Tula, who disappeared enigmatically without leaving a trace, as enigmatically as the legendary disappearance of the chief, Kukulkán.

Kukulkán is believed to have had a strong and vigorous personality, a figure who calls to mind the *condottieri* of the Italian Renaissance. Summoned to Yucatán as chief of the mercenary troops, he soon became the decisive political factor. Landa relates that the Indians claimed that, when the Itzá found themselves in Chichén Itzá, a great lord named Kukulkán appeared there, "and the principal building that is called Kukulkán shows that this is true." Kukulkán made Chichén Itzá an imposing center of religion and culture. There are those who consider him the founder of Mayapán, although it is more likely that this seat of the Cocomes existed previously and that Kukulkán only enlarged it and embellished it with magnificent buildings.[1] It is likewise maintained that he brought about the League of Mayapán, that alliance of the different Maya princes which was basically nothing less than their submission to the Cocomes.

Kukulkán presented himself in Yucatán as the descendant of a deity—something not unusual in that peninsula—and demanded that he be venerated as such. The legend that crept into oral tradition makes him the Quetzalcóatl of the Maya.

*Chi* means "mouth," *chen* a *"cenote,"* [a pool or under-

[1] It appears that the destruction of Mayapán, in the year 1451, happened so suddenly that in the recent excavations organized by the Carnegie Foundation few remains of those splendid constructions came to light, remains more interesting to archeology than to art.

ground reservoir], and *Itzá* is the name of the Maya tribe that founded the city in A.D. 534. The sanctuary that made Chichén Itzá the place of pilgrimage for all Mayab, to which the faithful traveled from afar and which gave the city its name, was the Sacred Well or Cenote. The Sacred Well, near the site where the Temple of Kukulkán was erected, is a pool that looks like a well, with vertical walls approximately 67 feet deep. A sanctuary to the rain god in arid Yucatán! Whenever droughts threatened, sacrifices were offered to him there, the victims usually being women and children who were thrown into the well in a solemn ceremony that took place at sunrise. If the victim were still alive at midday, he was considered, as in the medieval ordeals, to enjoy the special protection of the gods. He was then taken out of the well and showered with divine honors. The *Libro de Chilam Balam de Chumayel* tells that Hunac Ceel was one of those who was able to come out of the well alive. "Then they began to declare him the principal chief. He had not been the ruler before that time."

Intrigued by this tradition and convinced that there must be offerings at the bottom of the well, Edward Herbert Thompson began to explore it in 1894. After years of hard and fruitless effort, the idea that obsessed him was confirmed. He found the treasures he had dreamt of, which are today in the Peabody Museum of Harvard University (made known by T. A. Willard, *The City of the Sacred Well*): jewels of gold, works of copper, jade, and mother-of-pearl, stone sculptures, arms, pottery, masks, etc.[2]

The Toltecs who arrived in Yucatán did not adopt the religion of the Maya. They brought their own, the cult of Quetzalcóatl-Kukulkán, and decided to impose it on their new country. They were militant believers and fanatic missionaries, determined to make converts among the aborigines. The most grandiose of the constructions that they built in honor of their tribal deity was the Temple of Ku-

_____
[2] In 1959 the Peabody Museum returned to Mexico some of these pieces: four discs of gold.

kulkán, called "The Castle" (Plate 90). Its four stairways, one on each side, lead us to believe that it was the place where human sacrifices were offered to Kukulkán. The practice of human sacrifice had previously existed among the Maya, especially in Chichén Itzá, the city of the Sacred Well, but only the Toltecs made it the base and foundation of the ritual. Thus, as the Catholic Church erects its symbol, the Cross, wherever it goes, so too the Toltecs plant everywhere the symbol of Kukulkán, the plumed serpent. Now there is no edifice on which the snake with the quetzal feathers does not appear, in the most diverse places and in the most varied forms.

There is no doubt that this insistence also arose from a political intention. The Toltecs used the plumed serpent to make a show of their power and authority. As is natural, this was of the greatest importance to them. They had been called in as auxiliaries to repress an uprising and in the meantime the situation had changed: the mercenaries had become the ruling class. *Cujus regio, ejus religio:* this maxim from the days of the Reformation, which in Europe was always more a theory than a reality, was almost implied in pre-Columbian America: the defeated people had to adopt the gods and especially the tribal deity of the conquerors. To their way of thinking, the victory was infallible proof that the gods of the victorious tribe were more powerful than those of the vanquished. "The winner's gods must be good gods, this is how the cults of Mexican origin spread through the length and breadth of Middle America. Just so, the Christian religion had a ready acceptance in Indian America when the missionaries were backed by such redoubtable exponents of our gentle faith as Cortes, Pizarro, and their coadjutors" (Vaillant: *The Aztecs of Mexico*). As evidence of victory, the Aztecs brought the statues of the deities of the conquered tribes to Tenochtitlan. They had a prison for the dethroned gods in the Great Temple of their capital, a building intended exclusively for them (this was the fourteenth building in the Temple complex, according to Sahagún), perhaps to suppress any incipient rebellion, since the conquered people were impotent without their gods. The new masters of Yucatán had no better way of displaying and securing their power than by imposition of their faith. In that way they legitimized their power and made it an irrefutable fact.

Once the Toltecs of Tula were established in Yucatán, their ambition was to make their new city, Chichén Itzá, a greater and more grandioso center than the lost Tula. The Cocomes accepted the cult of Kukulkán. "They said of him that the Kings of Yucatán descended from him, whom they called Cocomes, which means Judges," relates Torquemada. The princes who resided in Mayapán, courtiers of the Cocomes, followed their example; they too were converted to the new religion. "The people of Yucatán boast that their nobles descend from him [Quetzalcóatl]," says P. Clavijero (*Historia antigua de México*). One ought to be on the side of power, and Kukulkán was power. Those who count for something, or wish to, bask in the light of the new leaders. Perhaps in that way they will attain new prestige, new splendor. . . . The cult of Kukulkán was, so to speak, the official religion, official church. It was, as we would say today, propaganda of the government and for the government, and it used all the means at the government's disposal. The people had to conform, externally, with the new religion, but privately they continued to adore the old gods. As the princes were not allowed to leave Mayapán and return to their own land, and as they were obliged to live far from their court and their subjects, the people believed that "their master was the victim of a kidnapping because of the systematically imposed cult of Kukulkán in Mayapán" (Baqueiro Anduze).

The situation worsened and resentment increased proportionately. The tyranny of the Cocomes was becoming insupportable. The other members of the League, who officially enjoyed equal rights, began to rebel. Disturbances and uprisings broke out. Consequently, the oppression of the chiefs who "watched over order and safety" increased.

The Cocomes depended on the new merchant caste, which had grown considerably and had succeeded in exercising influence in the political sphere as well. Commerce and trades flourished, and even something that could be called industry: the textile industry and boat building. Importation and exportation prospered. But that wealth—the wealth of a privileged class—meant misery for the people. The more the industrialists and merchants learned how to increase their sales, the more they intensified—indeed, had to intensify—the pressure they exercised on the lower classes. Their enterprises were based on free labor, on the work of slaves. Slaves had always been one of the most important articles that they imported in exchange for other merchandise, but now this importation did not suffice to fill their enormously expanded requirements. It became necessary to recruit workers and, with the help of the Cocomes, to turn their own people more and more into industrial slaves. To these social and political tensions were added resentments of a religious nature. The people were certain that the cause of such great misery lay in the abandonment of the ancient gods in favor of the new cult, the foreign religion imported from abroad. In 1451, Mayapán was destroyed. When after the fall of Chichén Itzá (in 1461) the Itzá had to migrate again and turned southward to the region of Petén, their former territory, they returned also to their ancient faith (until they were converted to Christianity in 1697). "There are indications that the exodus of this people brought to an end the strong Mexican influence at Chichén Itzá and that in its place there was a resurgence of old, underlying, Maya cultural elements, a resurgence of earlier forms" (Pollock). "After this destruction [of Mayapán], the said feast [of Kukulkán] was celebrated only in the province of Maní," Landa points out.

The Toltecs not only created a new cult in Chichén Itzá, they also brought to Mayab the expressive elements of a new art and a new architecture.

Their constructions: the Pyramid of Kukulkán (The Castle), the fifteenth-century Temples of the Tigers and the Warriors, differ completely in aspect from those of Palenque, Tikal, Yaxchilán, Kabah. In their structure and ornamentation the Nunnery and the Red House are of the most noble Maya baroque. The Castle and the Temple of the Tigers, on the other hand, impart a feeling of classicism, a very pure, very harmoniously balanced classicism. With the exception of certain details that are peculiar to Mesoamerica, such as the serpentine columns instead of the Doric or Ionic and the lack of a triangular pediment, their structure equals and is no less harmonious than the best creations of European classicism. The silhouette is clearly outlined, the constructive body is a closed block. An ornament in the form of a G constitutes the horizontal edge of the roof line. The steps of the stairway, parallel to the finial, are flanked by sloping panels that are perfectly incorporated into the structural mass. Two pillars divide the elongated rectangle of the entrance. Supreme clarity and calm.

The Toltecs brought a new constructive element, the column. They frequently used the pilaster as a constructive element to support the roof beams and thereby overcome the monolithic character of Maya architecture. While the latter had to resign itself to building long, narrow corridors, there now appears a type of chamber of suitable dimensions, not only long, but also wide. The most typical example and the most perfect solution is the Temple of the Warriors. The plan is almost square. In accordance with the requirements of the ritual, the temple is divided into two rooms: the vestibule, with the serpent columns[3] at the entrance where the stairway ends, and behind the vestibule, the sanctuary with the altar. The vestibule, with its two rows of six pilasters each, measures 61 feet 4 inches by 29 feet 1 inch; in the sanctuary, 61 feet 6 inches by 29 feet 8 inches, there are two rows of four pilasters each. The two chambers are separated from each other by a wall 2 feet 7³⁄₁₆ inches thick, in which a passage is cut. The roof beams rest on the pilas-

[3] Speaking of the mastery of the artistic creations at Tula, Sahagún mentions the columns of the Serpentine Order, ". . . of which they left one that is still there (in Tula) and can be seen today, although they did not complete it, that they call *coatlaquetzalli*, pillars in the shape of a snake, with the head resting on the ground and the tail and rattles above."

ters, whose faces are decorated with reliefs. "This was a new method of construction among the Maya," Totten notes. Maya architecture had been untiring in the invention and elaboration of novel decorative effects; the new architecture of Chichén Itzá is based on a new system of construction.

The decorative cedes first place to the structural. The ornament is now only one of the accents within a broader architectural unity; it is no longer allowed to flow excessively and without restrictions. The tropical night's dream has been followed by an awakening. What is expressed in the architecture is an awakened knowledge, the solemn gravity of a faith that knows nothing—wishes to know nothing—of the demigods whose megalomania had relegated the true gods to second place. The age of the demigods has now ended. The estheticism, the mellow grace, are now only a style that has gone out of fashion. No longer do they build palaces, but homes for the gods; temples and ball courts, these latter for the divine sport.

As at Teotihuacán and at Tula, the horizontal is the dominant. The stairways of the Pyramid of Kukulkán, one on each side, rise without interruption to the platform on the top. This of course imparts a strong vertical feeling to the stepped pyramid, but the temple, wide and not very high, counteracts this upward tendency with great energy. The two strongly salient fasciae that surround the entire building and form its upper edge accentuate this extension of width, so that the effect of the whole is, as in the Pyramid of the Sun at Teotihuacán, much more horizontal than vertical.

The Caracol, a building of circular plan whose construction was begun in the early period of the Toltec invasion, is not a tower of bold upward impulse, but a cylinder of classicist contour (Plate 96). On this building, too, the broad horizontal fasciae break up the vertical, giving the impression of a wide and heavy architectonic body. Was it an observatory? Was it, as is generally believed, a temple consecrated to Kukulkán, a souvenir of the round or oval temples of Quetzalcóatl on the Central Plateau? "What we do know, however, is that round buildings appear suddenly in Yucatán without indication of earlier developmental forms, that they are all connected with the invading wave of Mexican culture, and that they are associated with a culture hero, Kukulkán-Quetzalcóatl, who is reported to have come from Mexico . . . we can hardly doubt that he is to be identified with the wave of Mexican culture that is known to have entered the peninsula, and that it was the Mexican conception of Quetzalcóatl that inspired the circular buildings found there" (Pollock).

No longer seen is the picturesque, fantastic spectacle of the Maya roof crests, rooted in a different vital feeling, a different religiosity. There is no place for them in the sober and austere concept of the world that now holds sway. Those crests of Tikal and Palenque, with their stirring ornamentation, merge pictorially with the atmosphere; lights and shadows play an impressionistic game around them. Their charm is in the evanescent, the indefinite, the unseizable. The silhouette of the Temple of Kukulkán, like those of the Temple of the Tigers and the Temple of the Warriors, stands out sharply above the horizon with a precise outline. The friezes on the façades of the Temple of the Tigers (Plate 35) unfold between two strongly accented horizontal fasciae. Above the portico is a frieze that represents tigers and shields, the emblems of the warriors whose sanctuary this is, and above this frieze there is another, of abstract forms, circles and spheres, incorporated into a meander. Compare this decoration and this architecture with the decoration and architecture of the old Chichén Itzá buildings!

The base of the Temple of the Warriors is decorated with a frieze in relief that extends across the entire width of the front façade, forming a low, elongated rectangle: eagles and tigers in rhythmic succession. This frieze is a faithful copy of that found on the Pyramid of Quetzalcóatl at Tula. On the Skull Altar annexed to the ball court there is a frieze of skulls that is an almost exact copy of the one decorating the wall of the interior patio of the temple of Tula, the only differences being that at Chichén Itzá the frieze consists of three rows one above the other, that at Tula of one row; and also, at Tula, the skulls appear between the jaws of serpents. Once again—as at Tula and at Teotihuacán—the solemn and insistent repetition of a single motif with each individual form sharply carved and replete with definite symbolic significance. There is no capricious impulse or lack of clarity in the representation here, as in the steles of Copán and Quiriguá, where the ornament spreads exuberantly around the figure represented, diluting and devouring the structure. The high reliefs of the steles have also disappeared, those figures that are on the verge of liberating themselves from the rear plane, to assume a quasi corporeity. The reliefs on the innumerable pilasters in front of the Temple of the Warriors, those of the Temple of the Tigers, and of the Temple of Kukulkán—representations of warriors with lances and feather headdresses—the stylized serpents of the columns of the vestibule of the Temple of Kukulkán—also adopted from Tula—are bas-reliefs whose clearly outlined details are subjected to the planes of the relief. The monumental accent in the Temple of Kukulkán is the jaguar throne. A divine, majestic, and demoniacal symbol. It is, in its grandiose expressivity, at the same time sublime and terrible.

Of enormous interest for a psychographic investigation is the plastic frieze of the Temple of the Warriors (Plate 94). Here we see a Maya motif adopted: the large masks with the trunk-shaped so-called Roman nose. But in contrast to Kabah, where the large masks are crowded together and interspersed, staring at the spectator with thousands of menacing, hypnotizing eyes and creating an ensemble of surrealistic aspect, those masks at Chichén Itzá do not cover the entire surface, as at Kabah, nor do they disintegrate it into a series of fragments of plastic corporeity with their strong bosses and recesses. They appear only at the corners of the temple, framed, as it were, and neutralized by wall surfaces whose smoothness makes a striking contrast to the rich and animated decoration. In the center of those wall surfaces is another relief: the symbol of Kukulkán, the head of the plumed serpent with a human head appearing between its open jaws. This serpent head projects as strongly as the heads of the deities in the Pyramid of Quetzalcóatl at Teotihuacán. The ornamentation of large masks, restless and complicated on the Maya buildings, is here delimited by precise outlines and forms part of the architectural structure. A new surface rhythm evolves. Movement and rest, fullness and space, decoration and background, mutually accentuate and increase each other's effects.

Spinden (*A Study of Maya Art*) enumerates the following as characteristic elements of the Nahua influence on Maya architecture: serpentine columns, balustrades with serpentine ornamentation, merlons atop the walls of the temples (such as we see in the codices and in the small Nahua ceramics that represent temples), the sloping bases of the temples, platforms with colonnades, flat roofs, ball courts, atlantes; and in Maya sculpture and ornamentation: the Chac Mool, the solar disc as a religious symbol, the speech volute (which in Maya ceramics appears occasionally, but only "in connection with animals, not men"), the large masks with plumes seen from below, the processions of groups of warriors with their corresponding glyphs. Seler (*Gesammelte Abhandlungen*) also mentions as characteristic the representation of the eight phases of the planet Venus in the relief of the Temple of the Chac Mool in Chichén Itzá, where on one side is the symbol of Venus and on the other the eight year signs, a representation that Enrique Juan Palacios terms "a specialty in the centers of the Toltec domination." But there is much more than this. It is a matter of the inoculation of another and different mode of expression, of the manifestation of another and different spatial feeling, and this is what is decisive.

The new cult is also expressed in the formal configuration. The orientation of the temples, their deflection of from sixteen to seventeen degrees from the east-west axis, is a peculiarity of Toltec architecture. The Chac Mool, which will become typical of Yucatán—a horizontally disposed figure with legs drawn up and head turned to one side, supporting on its stomach a basin or tray—is "Toltec style" (Walter Lehmann: *The History of Ancient Mexican Art*). The model of this representation has been found at Tula. The Toltecs built architectonic ensembles made up of ball courts, temples, and altars. The verticality that had penetrated earlier Maya architecture disappears, and in its place is a marked horizontal tendency. The incipient realism disappears. A monumental stylization is sought. There is no doubt that some Maya elements are adopted. We have already mentioned the large masks of Chac on the façade of the Temple of the Warriors. But that imposing and monumental art that rises in Yucatán after the Toltec invasion is dissimilar in its essence. True, Chichén Itzá is more grandiose than Tula; in Chichén Itzá the artistic creation used more abundant resources, developed on a larger scale, had a more vigorous spirit. The art of Tula experiences a grandiose resurgence in Yucatán, a strong intensification of its creative power. And once again the question is raised: is this a Maya or a Toltec renaissance? No one can doubt that Palenque and Tikal are, with respect to their creative goals and artistic attitude, radically different from the Temple of Kukulkán at Chichén Itzá.

Earl H. Morris (*The Temple of the Warriors at Chichén Itzá*), who excavated the Temple of the Warriors, believes that considerably before the conquest of Chichén Itzá by the Toltecs there was already a cultural contact between the Maya and the Toltecs. "But be that as it may," he says, "to judge from the buildings in the northern end of the city, a pure Maya culture might never have existed at Chichén Itzá." In the course of the history of art it frequently happens that the conquering people adopt the superior culture and art of the conquered: the Persians accepted as their model the architecture and plastic arts of the Babylonians; the Romans tried to assimilate Greek culture; and the Aztecs, that of Teotihuacán. Here this did not happen. Did exclusively religious reasons prevent it? Was the religious fanaticism of the Toltec invaders, who were determined to impose their cult of Quetzalcóatl in Yucatán, the only factor? Or must we seek the explanation in the sphere of the art itself, in an artistic will that rejected—that had forcibly to reject—the tradition it encountered?

## 13

## *The Zapotecs: A Race of Architects*

They were a race of architects, says Alfonso Caso of the Zapotecs. And truly, they were great builders, not because they built magnificent structures—they did not—but because they felt and understood the architectonic from its very roots, from planning and from construction. Zapotec architecture is monumental in its conception.

They built Monte Albán and Mitla, sanctuaries, tombs, fortresses. Their architectonic ensembles are simple and great.

Monte Albán, their religious center, is an architecture of empty spaces. The buildings define and constitute a spatial unity. The individual construction is conceived as part of this unity and is absorbed by it. Just as the Greek column is a member of a constructive body, to which it imparts structure and physiognomy, and as this structure determines the number, height, and diameter of the columns and even the distance between them, so, too, at Monte Albán do the empty spaces govern the mass, the form, and even the location of the pyramids, temples, and altars. The stone buildings are only the imposing skeleton of an organism that lives and breathes in light. What these constructions enclose and the manner in which they merge in a sonorous and grandiose accord is precisely what constitutes the experience of Monte Albán. A unique and singular plan because of the way it is conceived and realized. In all continents, in every age, there are few, if any, urban ensembles that reveal a more homogeneous spiritual organization or a more powerful impulse. The "religious objectivity"—a formula we coin to designate the fundamental posture of pre-Columbian art—acquired here a spirit of sublime majesty, "as though they (the Zapotecs) had wished to express with stone, on earth, the ideas of eternity and greatness with which they conceived the divinity" (Leopoldo Batres, *Exploración de Monte Albán*).

Whole centuries and different epochs collaborated to erect Monte Albán. The buildings of the Zapotec era give us the impression that generation after generation followed a single plan. A single spirit, a single creative intention, a single artistic *ethos,* presided over the construction of this city during its different stages. Tradition that never degenerated into eclecticism, that remained alive because the zeal for monumentality and the greatness of the artistic concept remained alive.

Those builders were not satisfied with raising the complex of temples on top of the mountain, 1181 feet above the City of Oaxaca, founded in 1529 by Cortes. They transformed the summit of this mountain into a plateau 3117 feet long and 1476 feet wide. Two ravines on the northwest and southwest corners of this high plateau were each converted into roads leading to each of the groups of pyramids. The whole mountain underwent a radical change; we have already quoted Holmes's statement about the pyramid. "The mountain on which Monte Albán was erected was reconstructed, not once, but several times" (Alfonso Caso). The environs were also transformed on a large scale. The homogeneity of the ensemble does not begin at the walls of the Great Plaza but covers much more: around the ceremonial city extends a complete sacred zone, scattered with tombs and pyramids built over subterranean funerary niches.

While Chinese architecture attempts to adapt the edifice, with the most subtle sensibility, to the landscape that surrounds it (the curved roof of the Chinese pagoda repeats the gently rolling line of the hill that stands out above the horizon); while the contemporary planner strives to adjust his plan to the conditions of the terrain so that his reinforced-concrete desert preserves at least a fractional part of the charm of nature's own creation; the urbanistic ensemble of Monte Albán is non-nature par excellence. Its builders not only did not respect the natural conformation of the terrain, they rejected it as a disorder that man had to put in order.

The center of Monte Albán is a rectangular and entirely level plaza (called the Great Plaza), surrounded on four sides by pyramidal constructions. It is subdivided by geometrically distributed groups of pyramids that in turn encircle patios or plazas. The basic structure of these ensembles of temples is an edifice of rectangular, lengthened plan that rises above a terrace and is flanked by lateral constructions that form a right angle with the principal building. This makes a patio open on one side only, with a raised altar in the center; patios and more patios, a whole system of empty spaces mutually complete, interpenetrate, and communicate with each other; a multiplicity of elements that integrate an organic unity, a spatial symphony. Separate, at the side of the Great Plaza, a ball court.

All axes are parallel to each other (Ignacio Marquina: *Estudio arquitectónico comparativo*). To the north is the platform of the principal temple, which measures 538,195 square feet; leading to it is a stairway 131 feet wide, the largest stairway of Mesoamerica. Behind the temple was found a series of constructions related to the cult. There still exist the remains of the columns from the temple itself, cyclopean columns 6½ feet in diameter, constructed of stone ashlar.

Between this temple at the north end of the plaza and the one at the south are aligned various pyramidal constructions that do not exactly follow the central axis, a crime against art by Zapotec standards. That deviation from the axis was probably caused by the Observatory (Structure "J"), which dates from pre-Zapotec times.

Structure "J" itself is a strange building. While all the other architectonic complexes are oriented sensibly toward the cardinal points, this Observatory deviates from them (Alfonso Caso: *Exploraciones en Oaxaca*, 1936–37 Season). Its plan (Fig. 29) is an irregular polygon, the only pre-Columbian construction of irregular plan. "Another of the characteristics of this structure is that its plan does

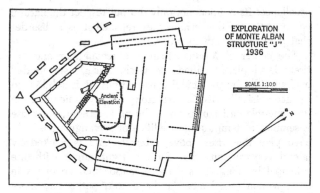

FIG. 29. Plan of Structure "J." Monte Albán. *By Bazan and Acosta.*

not present a quadrangular or rectangular form as do the other structures, since the rear part ends in an angle" (Caso). It is very likely that the plotting of the center pyramids constituted a serious problem for the planners of Monte Albán: they could abide by the central axis and create a rectangular plaza to the east, but within this the Observatory would have been inharmonious as an alien body; or, in order to avoid free space so poorly balanced, they could deviate from the central axis and form, with the new constructions, a second axis that would include the Observatory. For love of spatial unity, the latter solution was chosen.

To see how the Zapotecs were able to compensate for this defect is highly interesting and helps us to understand their concept of planning. The temple on the north side was not built in the center of the plaza like that on the south, but a little to the west so that it lay exactly on the axis of the central pyramids. Facing these and in front of the pyramids situated at the western limit of the terrain, several smaller pyramids were built at the right and left extremes that, on the one hand, together with the central group, limit a rectangular plaza of great homogeneity, and on the other give rise, in front of the same central group, to a sort of street, long and narrow, that corresponds to another, identical "street" on the other side of the central complex.

The great North Temple, the splendid dominant of the urbanistic ensemble, is arranged in such a way that the axis of its east wall coincides with that of the central pyramids. On the other hand, its central axis coincides with that of a wide plaza that opens between the temple and that central group. In this way they avoided the disagreeable impression of an unaxial, asymmetrical ensemble and gained a ground plan richer in accents, more audacious, more grandiose, and yet no less severe. The central constructions are "of scant height," (Marquina) lower than the outer ones. Thus, even in the dimension of height there is a conscious organization of the proportions, of the similarities and contrasts. A better conceived and more inspired plan would be hard to visualize.

The temples were the victims of time, as happened almost everywhere. The traces of the foundations indicate a very simple distribution of the interiors. But what we can still see—the pyramids themselves (Plate 98)—is imposing, vigorous, and monumental. The architects who worked there started, in their conception of the work, from the constructive. There are no accessories. The architectonic body is expressed through the articulation of its mass, through its elemental plasticity. Collective art that says what it has to say in clear, decisive language. With what energy the panels and slopes stand out! What grand rhythm is unfolded here! And it is only that. Anything additional would have dwarfed the grandeur, would have reduced the sublime to the proportion of the human, of the relative. In the Pyramid of Quetzalcóatl at Teotihuacán, the panels are decorated with a series of heads of Quetzalcóatl and Tláloc, incorporated in the undulations of the serpent. That plastic ornamentation is lacking in Zapotec Monte Albán. What speaks there is the structural mass, the architectonic Form, and its voice is great and impressive.

It is true that at Mitla the walls of all the buildings are covered with a mosaic of small incrusted stones that form the most diverse variants on the stepped fret (Plate 34),

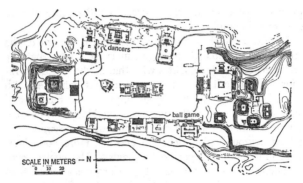

FIG. 30. Site plan of Monte Albán. *By H. Herrera, A. García,
and J. R. Acosta.*

an ornamentation that does not exist in any other part
of the world. But unlike Monte Albán, Mitla was not a
city of temples, a religious center for the masses. Mitla
was a very sacred place, surrounded by myths, legends,
and mysteries, inaccessible to common mortals, more a
concept than a reality: Lioobáa, "house of happiness,"
(Seler) as it was called in the Zapotec language. Mitla
was the city of the dead, the cemetery of the Zapotec kings
and noblemen. The word "Mitla" may be derived from
Mictlan, the Nahua name for the lower world. The hieroglyph by which Mitla is designated in the Aztec Tax Roll
(Mendoza Codex) is a skull by a mortuary bundle. Burial chambers have been discovered beneath the palaces
of the king. "In no other part of the world were the living
and the dead so close." It was a "community of living and
dead," observes Count Harry Kessler (*Notizen über Me-
xiko*). Francisco de Burgoa (*Geográfica descripción*) relates that when a member of the royal family died the
king went to Mitla to spend the mourning period there.
Mitla was, furthermore, the seat of the high priest, *uija-
táo*, "the great prophet," considered the "living image of
the deity, or his lieutenant" (Seler). In a state of ecstasy
"he put himself in contact with the gods and transmitted
their replies to the devout public. . . . At the great
feasts that were celebrated with sacrifices or at the burial

of some king or great lord, he directed the lesser priests or ministers to assist him in arranging his catafalque and his garments and the many incense burners that they used, and he descended with a large retinue [to the temple]." No common mortal was allowed to see the high priest, and he was convinced that if anyone dared to look at him face to face, that person would fall dead at once "as a punishment for his audacity" (Burgoa). The "circumstantial evidence" that Burgoa mentions is the arrangement of the architectonic ensemble that was probably the abode of the high priest: four buildings grouped around a patio and completely cloistered from the outside. Access is through a narrow lateral passage at the rear of the Salon of the Columns, which communicates with the interior patio, not in a direct line, but at a right angle, so that no profane glance could actually penetrate to the interior, not even from the ceremonial hall. On the other hand, the high priest could go to this hall without being observed from without.

It is a distribution that appears only in this group of buildings. The others have the typical structure of Monte Albán. They are five in all: a palace where the king resided when he was in Mitla and four other buildings for the assistants of the high priest, the royal retinue, and the captains (J. Eric S. Thompson: *Mexico Before Cortez*). These constructions are "exceedingly formal, in profile as well as in ground plan" (William H. Holmes, *Archeological Studies Among the Ancient Cities of Mexico*): a block of quadrangular form with flat roof and walls, broken only by the pilasters of the portico. The roofs were of wood. On top of the beams was a layer of stones covered with mortar or stucco. The interiors were not subdivided and each building contained only one chamber. In some places there were small niches halfway up the walls. Possibly idols were placed there, and in one of them may have been found the celebrated relic of Mitla, the so-called "heart of the world": a stone 4⅛ inches high, in all probability a piece of translucent jade, on which were carved a bird and a serpent (Thomas Gann, *Mexico, From the Earliest Times to the Conquest*). According to the report of a Spanish priest, the stone was pulverized on the order of a missionary friar.

That very simple, very objective architecture bears the fret ornamentation that has made Mitla world famous (Plate 34). Above a base about five feet high, all the walls—interior and exterior—are decorated with frets worked in an incrustation of mosaic. The stepped fret is the sign of lightning, of the fire serpent. In its perfect abstraction it is the most elevated and expressive form, a form of religious symbolism, and, therefore, the motif suitable for decorating a place as sacred as Mitla. We have already spoken of the magic conjuration in the serpent motif (see Chapter 7, "The Stepped Fret"). "The esthetic value of the undulating serpent is of great power; one undulation continues into another, like the living vibration of the animal, from the head to the tail. . . ." (Eulalia Guzmán).

There are fourteen different motifs in these stone mosaics, which demonstrates the absence of schematicism and the ingenuity and fecundity of that spirit of abstraction. To form the design of the mosaic, the easiest and simplest way would have been to join stones of different sizes and set them flush on a flat surface. But, strangely enough, this procedure was not followed. Examining the walls carefully, we make the astounding discovery that the profile of the ornament was carved with unparalleled effort and skill on each of the countless stones that comprise the mosaic. The relief that was fashioned in this way is strictly subjected to its two planes. It is said that in just one of the patios more than eighty thousand small stones were used. This was precision work, executed with such exactitude that not only are the fore and rear planes of the "relief" vertical, perfectly in line, but so exact is the fit of the stones that it was not necessary (except in a few places) to join them with mortar. The artisans did not want to cover these mosaics with stucco. It was their ambition to work with such skill that a smooth surface with imperceptible joints would result. On the other hand, they painted their work in strong, brilliant colors. The white ornamentation stood out from a red background.

Perfection of workmanship, sufficient in itself to fill us with admiration. And in all the history of art we know only one case of equal, unconditional consecration to the work: the Gothic cathedral, carved by the stonecutters leaf by leaf and tendril by tendril so that the dream of a filigree work rising straight toward heaven might be given Form.

But the admiration we feel before the decoration and the craftsmanship at Mitla must not make us oblivious of the fact that that decoration constitutes at the same time an essential element of the architectural structure. It is not only an embellishment of the wall, an ornamental accessory. It is for those buildings what the triangular pediment is for the Greek temple: a means of articulating the wall. Because of the mosaic panels, the flat, smooth, monotonous walls broken only by the porticos acquire corporeity. The frets, following one after the other, not only develop their ornamental rhythm: the disposition of the panels, one next to the other and one above the other, gives rise to an architectonic rhythm that imposes on the flat, or, so to speak, incorporeal wall—which in itself is only the delimitation of the mass of a block—an organic articulation, and gives it movement and animation. This is not a matter of an exhibition of ornament and decoration; the mosaics are incorporated into the architecture as a formal element that is part of the structure itself and thanks to which the architectonic structure is what it actually is.

The panels decorated with frets are framed between bands in the form of a meander[1] that cover the entire width of the walls without any interruption (Plate 99). Square blocks frame the corners, whose rigid solidity seems intended to oppose the inherent vehemence of the rhythm of the frets and the meander. And the meander, with the meticulously carved detail of the frets, is limited in turn by wide horizontal bands that likewise extend the entire width of the wall surface. Studying the horizontal

[1] It has been said that the abstract form of the meander hides a symbolism. Quite possible. It evokes the Zapotec glyph for "mountain" as well as, to a slight degree, that for "sky," the open jaws of the tiger.

cornice of the roof of the Temple of the Tigers at Chichén
Itzá, we find an identical disposition: stone bands around
the entire construction, between which the ornamentation develops. However moving, ingenious, and varied the
forms of the Mitla frets may be, they are completely subordinated to the architecture. They are not allowed to go
beyond their frame. Even in the "Salon of Frets" (Plate
34), where such framing was renounced, where the frets
expand without interruption on the four walls of the narrow patio like a stone Gobelin, there is a horizontal articulation thanks to the diversity of the designs that were
organized in three bands, one above the other, that mutually limit each other. It seems to me that herein lies an
essential and characteristic difference between the ornamentation at Mitla and that of the Old Maya Empire—
which we have called a tropical night's dream—as it appears on the façade of Kabah, in the steles of Piedras
Negras or Quiriguá, covering the architectonic structure
with a picturesque morass of forms that materially devour
it. In Mitla, the wall speaks; it speaks as an integral part of
the architecture. True, it is sumptuously decorated, but
the ornamentation is incorporated into the ensemble, maintains a strict discipline, abides by its role of ornament,
and accentuates and enriches the architecture with its
movement, its rhythm, its plasticity. If the singular grandiosity of the Mitla ornamentation is to be admired, the
constructive force that made this adornment a structural
element is to be admired even more. Creators whose innate architectonic sensibility was so powerful that it never
failed to manifest itself, not even when one time the reins
of ornamental fantasy were slackened in order to create
a decoration worthy of a sacred place.

That tectonics likewise confers tension and monumentality on the sculptural work, on the representation of the
human figure. The most characteristic example of such
transformation of the human figure into an architectonic
body is an image of Xipe, the maize god (Plate 101), rescued from Tomb 58 of Monte Albán (National Museum
of Anthropology, Mexico). It is a brazier of fired clay—a
ritual object that exists in all pre-Cortesian cultures—in-

tended to hold the sacred fire and to burn copal in. A seated figure, whose legs are two columns that flank a cylindrical body. The pectoral, perhaps a representation of a butterfly with its symmetrically extended wings, is entirely flat in front but adapted to the curvature of the body in back. In his left hand, resting on his knee, the god holds by the hair the head of a sacrificial victim; in his right, lifted with great impetus, he holds a sphere. The head of Xipe is also a sphere in which there are three circular holes: the mouth and the two eyes. The nose is not even suggested. There is nothing else. Only the spherical roundness of the head and the three circular holes. But, what expressivity the sculptor achieved! A cry is heard from the mouth, a titan's cry, powerful and penetrating. This figure of Xipe, of a late epoch, not the beginning but the end of an evolution, is of elemental, vigorous plasticity, a mass that penetrates space in all directions. A figure scarcely ten inches high, but, nevertheless, monumental. A body constructed with geometric-cubic forms. We resort quite intentionally to the word "construct," for what is manifested here in sculptural form is really architecture. It possesses the corporality, the corporeal solidity of the pyramids of Monte Albán. It is what a "race of architects" can express, can create, when it employs its structural discipline to shape the human form and the sublimity of the divine. It is not Teotihuacán; it is not a translation of the cubic experience to the plane; it is not eagerness to "horizontalize" the work; it is not that purified abstraction made pure spirit. It is corporeity shaped with the abstract, fundamental elements of Form. And neither is it Maya, because of its will to Form, which recognizes and aspires to the tectonic and nothing but the tectonic, that will to Form before which such popular criteria as "more naturalistic" or "less naturalistic" appear absurd. Consider the Copán maize god, certainly a work of great nobility and an authentic masterpiece of its kind. But, from the angle of expressive resources and expressive will, how far is the Zapotec creation from the sculpture of Copán! No less far than a Chinese Lohan from the Romanesque saints of Vézelay, Aulnay, Moissac. The geo-

metric-cubic structure that lends monumental expressivity
to the representation of Xipe—the vivacity, the intensity
of the living—is found in innumerable small sculptures, in
the jade or jadeite figurines whose solid block character
we generally associate with preclassic art. And actually it
is possible that here it is a matter of an ancient tradition
that did not evolve, that was not sacrificed to modernity.
We find it also as an internal discipline in the Zapotec
funerary urns (Plates 102 and 103), adorned with the
figures of gods.

The origin of the Zapotecs is surrounded by legendary
mists that we have not yet been able to penetrate. Of
their history we can reconstruct with certitude only the
two centuries preceding the Conquest. The only source is
the seventeenth-century writings of Fray Francisco de
Burgoa, *Palestra historial* and *Geográfica descripción;* but
it seems that Burgoa could not always distinguish between
truth and poetry. The political capital was Zaachila and it
is conjectured that the Zapotec kings took their name from
the city.

When the Zapotecs arrived at Monte Albán, probably
around A.D. 200, it was inhabited by an Olmec tribe, by
the men who had carved on the walls of a building those
very famous "Dancers": priests and hunchbacks performing ritual dances around the sanctuary (Westheim: *Ideas
fundamentales del arte prehispánico en México*). Bodies
in dynamic motion, as tall as a man, sculptured in relief
on large pieces of stone (Plates 4 and 5). Tachygraphs,
written with great confidence, with only one line, that
limit themselves to the lines of the contour. Expressive
form. Extraordinary, the force of expression and the energy with which the observed reality is translated into
plastic creation. A lineal graphism saturated with emotion.
The cubico-geometric form that will characterize the later
epochs is not yet developed. If I may be permitted a
comparison with contemporary artists, I would say that
the style of those works of Monte Albán I has an affinity
with the lyric expressionism of the *fauves*, Matisse, and
of Gauguin. There is no doubt that the "Dancers" do
evoke the "Dance" of Matisse, not only in theme, but

especially in vision, in expressive modality. Pottery contemporary with the "Dancers" shows great artistic perfection. That culture "flourished in an age when the great Maya civilization had not yet risen," and "before the Toltecs founded their great empire" (Caso). Caso says that the rocks in Monte Albán were drilled to their bases without encountering any trace of a primitive culture. The Zapotecs, who later began to rebuild Monte Albán, had a high artistic and cultural level. They already possessed writing and the calendar, and knew how to erect structures of certain importance. Where and how this culture was developed is not known. Only this much is certain: it was not developed at Monte Albán.

The territory of Oaxaca is a mountainous plateau, difficult of access and easy to defend. At Quiotepec, situated on a hill that dominates the confluence of two rivers, are still preserved the traces of a fortress built by the Zapotecs in a spot wisely selected from the strategic point of view. It is a region apart, that the Zapotecs had to share with another tribe, the Mixtecs. The eastern part as far as the Isthmus of Tehuantepec was Zapotec; the Mixtecs—"according to Aztec tradition, they proceeded from the Toltecs" (Luis Pericot y García, *La América indígena*)—were established in the west, in a zone of high mountains. In Náhuatl, the word *"mixteca"* means "inhabitant of the country of the clouds." A continuous war for leadership resulted from this proximity. In the eleventh or twelfth century, the Mixtecs succeeded in expelling the Zapotecs from Monte Albán and Mitla, where they established themselves and began to develop their own culture. The dominion of the Zapotecs was limited to their capital, Zaachila. For the Aztecs, with their zeal to widen their own sphere of power, the region of Oaxaca was of particular importance; it was the strategic and commercial gateway to the rich cacao-producing countries on the Pacific coast of the Isthmus of Tehuantepec. Chocolate was not only an excellent drink, appreciated somewhat like caviar in Western civilization, but the chocolate bean constituted in that moneyless economy, that economy of barter, a sort of substitute for money. In 1494, the year

"Two-Rabbit," the Aztecs conquered Monte Albán. There is a representation of this campaign in the Telleriano-Remensis Codex. In the year 1495, the Aztecs also occupied Zaachila, but without subduing the Zapotecs. They therefore agreed to make a pact with the still-powerful people, whom they would never be able to dominate, a pact in which the Zapotecs promised to pay tribute to the Aztecs. To ensure the fulfillment of the agreement, a Mexican garrison was established in Uaxyacac, today the City of Oaxaca. While the Aztecs were undertaking an armed expedition to Guatemala, the last Zapotec king attacked and defeated the Aztec troops stationed in Oaxaca. When Cortes arrived in Mexico, he allied himself with the Zapotecs against the Aztec Empire—one of the diplomatic feats of the conqueror of Mexico and an unfortunate alliance for the Zapotecs. Cortes, "the protector," behaved like all "protectors." In 1521, after subduing the Aztecs, he sent to the Oaxaca region Francisco de Orozco, who crushed the Zapotecs and the Mixtecs.

Since 1902, when Batres made the first explorations at Monte Albán, that succession and superposition of three cultures—preclassic, Zapotec, and Mixtec—whose traits were not distinguished from each other until recently, gave rise to what in the archeological world has been called "the enigma of Monte Albán." The natural confusion was complicated by the conjectures of many who wanted to confirm the theory that the region of Oaxaca was a sort of cultural colony of the Maya. Alfonso Caso's merit lies not only in his having explored and reconstructed Monte Albán, but also in his having elucidated the character and participation of the different cultures that created this important center. It can be affirmed, therefore, that today there no longer exists an "enigma of Monte Albán." None of the archeological problems of ancient Mexico has found a clearer, more precise solution than this one, in which there is only one point still obscure, the same obscure point that we come upon in any study of pre-Columbian cultures: their origin. Caso (*Culturas mixteca y zapoteca*) distinguishes five epochs, using the ceramics as a basis for this. The first is the so-called "archaic," the period of the reliefs of the "Dancers"; three Zapotec epochs follow, which cover almost twelve centuries and whose apogee is Epoch III of Monte Albán; the last is the Mixtec. After the explorations of 1936 and 1937, whose sensational results were the discovery of the jewels rescued from Tomb 7 and the murals in Tombs 104 and 105, Caso could state with quite justified pride: ". . . at last, division by epochs in Monte Albán has been confirmed anew" (*Exploraciones en Oaxaca*, Fifth and Sixth Seasons, 1936–37).

To arrive at this conclusion, a scientific discipline and an archeological perspicacity were required that (as in much of the investigative work in the field of Mexican archeology) reminds us of Sherlock Holmes. The problem consisted of determining definitely just what pertained to Zapotec culture and what to Mixtec, similar, but oriented toward the north, toward Nahua territory. Caso began with the objects whose Zapotec provenance was certain: the funerary urns and the glyphs of their inscriptions. The Zapotecs had an arithmetical system in which the number five was represented by a bar, as among the Maya, while Teotihuacán and the Aztecs expressed it by five points. The Mixtecs used both methods of notation, points and bars. But the Zapotecs possessed their own glyptic writing, their own year sign, and their own day signs, "different from those of the Mexicans and Maya." The Mixtec day signs, as far as we have been able to decipher them, i.e., fourteen of the twenty signs of one month, coincide with the signs of the magical calendar of the Nahua people. The Zapotec hieroglyphic for the year was the "face of the god Cocijo or Tláloc, who has a mask with serpentine attributes in front of his mouth," to which was added a disc or rectangle with a drawing that probably represents a turquoise (Caso: *La Tumba 7 de Monte Albán*). The Mixtec year sign has the form of an A intersected by a ring, a sort of horizontal O. This A form, as the Aztec calendar shows, signifies the rays of the sun, and the horizontal O is the nose of Cocijo. Among the Zapotecs, the hieroglyphic for the sky, which figures in the upper part of all their religious and mythological representations, is the wide-open jaws of a tiger with the fangs showing and the lower lip drooping, a glyph that the Mixtecs did not have. This means that all objects on which this hieroglyphic figures must be of Zapotec origin, and that all those whose inscriptions are composed of different signs cannot be Zapotec, since it would be a hitherto unheard-of phenomenon for a people to have two different "alphabets." On this basis, Caso (*Las estelas zapotecas*) could prove that all the steles found in the Oaxaca region are Zapotec; that all the codices proceeding from there are Mixtec and not Zapotec, among them the Nuttall Codex, a historical account that lists the exploits of two princes, "Eight-Deer" and "Four-Tiger"; that the jewels found by him in Tomb 7 are Mixtec work while the construction of the same tomb is Zapotec; that the frieze of murals in Mitla, whose miniaturelike delicacy contrasts strongly with the violent rhythm of the frets, is a later addition of the Mixtecs. (Seler: *Gesammelte Abhandlungen,* who notes its affinity with the Borgia Codex, calls it "an open book projected upon the wall.") Long before the explorations at Monte Albán were begun and before the study of the glyphs could solve this problem, Seler had intuitively recognized (in his book, *Wandmalereien in Mitla,* published in 1895, and in his essay of 1904, *Les Ruines de Mitla*) that those murals could not proceed from the Zapotecs, whose "architectonic style" was, in his opinion, characteristic and unmistakable, but that they belonged to a civilization related to Nahua culture. He interpreted them as an apotheosis of Quetzalcóatl, central figure of Nahua myth, while the tutelary deity of the Zapotecs was Cocijo. One of the panels of the main wall represents the abode of the sun, the region of sunrise. Another panel shows the bird that sings at the hour of dawn, i.e., Quetzalcóatl disguised as a bird-man. "There is found more than once," says Seler, "the image of the god who abandoned his kingdom and traveled toward the east to die there—the great god Quetzalcóatl, the priest-god, the creator god—in his original conception, without doubt, the god of the moon who in his waning phase goes to die in the rays of the rising Sun, and, resuscitated, appears in the evening sky in order to continue on his course again." Very well, since a basis now exists for clearing up the derivation of the different objects, and since there is now manifested the dissimilar character of two modes of creating that are similar to each other but arise from different creative intuitions and different hypotheses, it is fitting to say that while we must consider the Zapotecs a nation of architects, the Mixtecs were the craftsmen of Mesoamerica, whose works need envy nothing among the most beautiful creations of Asia and Europe.

Subtle craftsmen of admirable sensibility, who give all their work the highest perfection and delicacy. "An extraordinarily refined culture" (Caso). Their codices, the Nuttall and Vindobonensis, are miniaturist painting, masterful in the organization of the surface, in the distribution of space, in the selection of colors, and in the graphism of the lines. At Mitla that fine, restrained, shaded painting is translated into mural decoration. It is an authentically decorative ornamentation in the original sense of the word: ornamentation meant to decorate a wall surface, delighting the eye and the fantasy with delicate tonalities and harmonies. Painted Gobelins. Precisely because they are that, they constitute the most energetic contrast with the mural painting of the Zapotecs and the Teotihuacanos, whose great and vigorous language expresses a sublime symbolism. The thirty-five carved animal bones, which from the archeological and artistic points of view are probably the most important manifestations of Mixtec art, translate that same exquisite and delicate miniaturist painting into the idiom of sculpture. Reliefs—narrow rectangles scarcely wider than a thumb—that relate the myth and mythical happenings. One scene follows another, but this is not a simple plastic narration such as in the illustrations of a book. Just as in the rhythmic repetition of the mural ornament of the frets, it is here an integrated unity of homogeneous structural elements, absorbed by a rhythm that throbs in the ensemble, "distributed symmetrically in accordance with a vertical axis" (Guzmán). Caso (*Thirteen Masterpieces of Mexican Archaeology*) calls the Mixtec ritual ceramics "the most beautiful that was produced in Mexico." The proportions are balanced with

the greatest subtlety; the coloring, actually no more
than a few tones—white, black, a reddish brown—has an
ineffable charm. It is possible that the golden treasures that
Dürer saw at the court of the Emperor Maximilian and
that won his high admiration, were also Mixtec work. (He
mentions them in one of the letters from his trip to the
Low Countries in 1520.) To Fray Bartolomé de las Cases,
the objects sent to the Emperor Charles V appeared "as
if they were a dream, and not made by the hand of man."
Also proven to be Mixtec was the silver fish with incrustations of gold that Charles V presented to the Pope, and
which Cellini investigated thoroughly without being able
to determine how it was made. The conquerors, in their
greed for gold, had most of the works thrown into the
crucible and destroyed. They were used to pay public
debts and to finance military expeditions.

A characteristic feature of both Oaxacan cultures, Zapotec as well as Mixtec, is the funeral ritual. The Toltecs
and the Aztecs cremated their dead; the Zapotecs and
Mixtecs buried them. "The Zapotecs abhorred cremation,
considering it destructive of the soul" (Thomas A. Joyce:
*Mexican Archeology*). We must distinguish between "pri-
mary burials" and "secondary burials." This means that
the deceased was first buried provisionally, as it were.
Later, when only the bones of the corpse remained, they
were buried with solemn ceremony in a tomb constructed
in the interim and decorated with plastic ornamentation
and mural paintings. That second interment usually took
place at the end of four years, during which time the dead
man, accompanied by the dog that had been buried with
him as his guide and protector, found himself on the road
to Lioobáa, the lower world. Before this final burial, the
bones "were painted red, the funeral color, and afterwards
were interred in the grave" (Caso: *Las culturas mixteca y
zapoteca*). Over the skull was placed the mask, and to the
side the mortuary offerings: vessels with food and drink,
the clothing, jewels, and arms of the deceased, idols, and
other precious objects. This reminds us of Egypt, but
certainly there is a radical difference here. In Egypt, the
basis of funeral customs is the cult of the personality,

the ambition of the Pharaohs to continue playing their roles and instilling respect and admiration even after death. There is nothing of all this among the Zapotecs. It is quite significant that in no Zapotec or Mixtec grave is there anything that can be considered a portrait of the deceased, nor any representation whatever that commemorates his life and deeds. The decoration of Tomb 105 of Monte Albán III, the epoch of the apogee of Zapotec culture, represents a procession of nine divine couples, symmetrically disposed, gods and goddesses walking in solemn rhythm on the wall surface. Nine was the number of the gods of the lower world, and according to the Vaticanus A Codex, each one of these gods had a wife. Above the cortege of deities, as well as in the other representations of those murals, we see the large, engraved sky glyph, the jaws of a tiger, wide open and with a full set of teeth. It is the symbol that rules that sacred art and that cult of the dead.

The tombs that they began to build in the epoch of Monte Albán II, i.e., at the time of the arrival of the Zapotecs, are a peculiar and characteristic chapter in Zapotec architecture. Those subterranean constructions show the clear, simple, and objective structure of all Zapotec buildings. Besides the simple chambers with flat ceilings and without a doorway are two other types: a quadrangular, oblong chamber spanned by a false arch, a constructive element probably adopted from the Maya region; to this type belongs Tomb 4 where, as we mentioned when discussing the pyramid, a pre-Cortesian architect succeeded—the one and only time—in constructing a species of authentic arch. A second type is characterized by two lateral wings and the cruciform plan that results from such disposition; in the majority of cases the ceiling is flat. In both types of tomb, niches for offerings are cut into the walls, usually three in number, but at times five. In an antechamber were the so-called "funerary urns," ceramic works in the form of divinities, on whose rear side was a vessel intended, in all probability, for the burning of copal. The urns are usually images of Cocijo, whose hieroglyphic is the Zapotec year sign. Cocijo is shown as a seated human figure; in front of his face, over which crawl snakes, he wears a mask. The nose in the form of an eagle's beak stands out powerfully. The forked serpentine tongue hangs down to his chest. Representations of other deities are also common: of Xipe, of the maize goddess, and of the goddess "Seven-Serpent." A singular work was found in Tomb 77: an urn with an amazingly characterized head of a man, distinguished by the vigor of the conception and the closed form of its plastic structure. In one of those monuments, Tomb 104, is seen outside, in a niche over the portico, a seated statue of the maize god (Plate 105). Do not those spirits in the antechamber of the tomb remind us of the Chinese "guardians of the sepulcher," guides who point out the road to the tomb of a great lord or who perhaps show his spirit the road back from the tomb . . . ?

The funerary urn is in the Zapotec world what the stele is for the Old Maya Empire: the typical sculptural form. Despite the multiple attributes that characterize the deities, despite the rich jewels that adorn them and that are reproduced to the smallest detail, the funerary urn is sculpture of a "nation of architects," structural and tectonic, sculpture in which the details are subordinated to the mass and totally incorporated into the unity of the whole. Perhaps it is not by chance that much sculpture has been found in the Mixtec region, but until now, no funerary urn.

After conquering Monte Albán and Mitla, the Mixtecs not only took possession of the temples but installed their own prominent dead in the Zapotec tombs. They left the chambers as they found them and reused them. That was carried to such extremes that a tablet found in Tomb 104 is at first sight completely enigmatic, having a Mixtec inscription on the outer side and a Zapotec inscription on the inner. The Mixtecs simply appropriated the slab they found there, which so perfectly suited their purpose of closing up the entrance that they turned it around and put another inscription on the back. The same thing happened at the celebrated Tomb 7, one of the few that the archeologists did not find sacked and from which they rescued, in 1932, those most valuable and unusual jewels

PLATE 89. The Church. Chichén Itzá, Yucatán. Maya.

*Photograph: National Institute of Anthropology and History, Mexico City.*

PLATE 90. The Castle, Pyramid of Kukulkán. Chichén Itzá. Toltec- Maya.

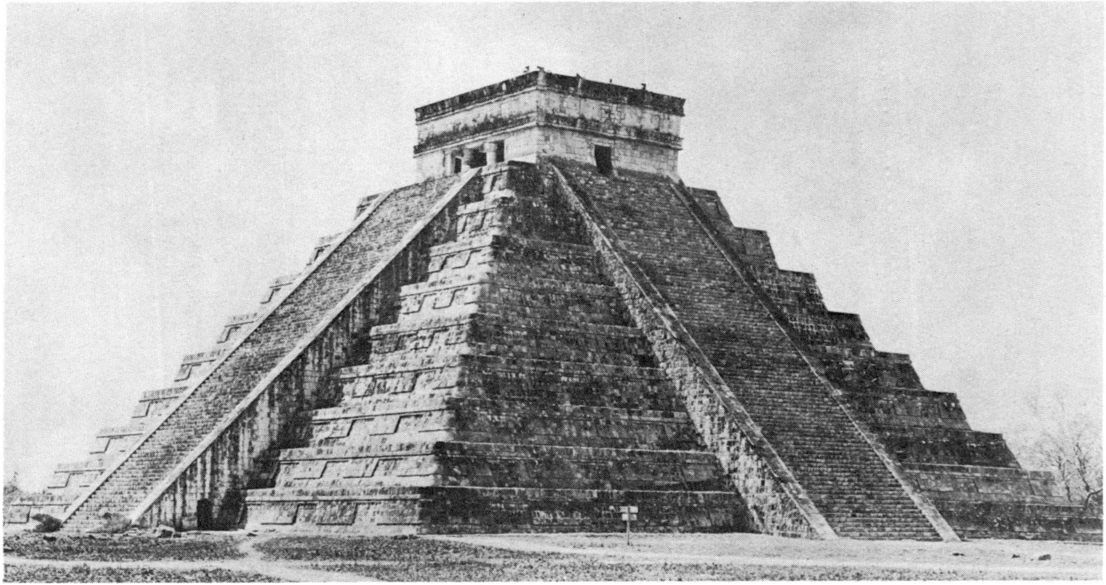

PLATE 91. The Chichanchob. Chichén Itzá. Maya.

Photograph: Ernest Rathenau, New York City.

PLATE 92. The Nunnery complex and the House of the Magician. Uxmal.

Photograph: Enrique A. Cervantes, Mexico City.

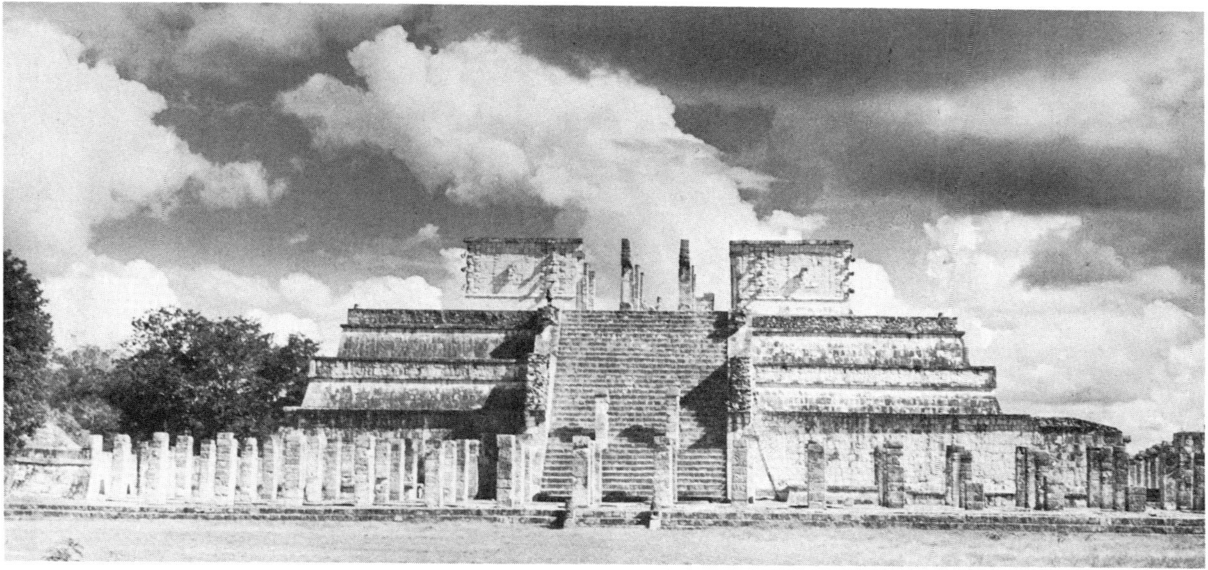

PLATE 93. Temple of the Warriors. Chichén Itzá. Toltec-Maya. *Photograph: A. G. Formentí, Paris.*

*Photograph: Ruth Deutsch de Lechuga, Mexico City.*

PLATE 94. Temple of the Warriors (detail). Chichén Itzá. Toltec-Maya.

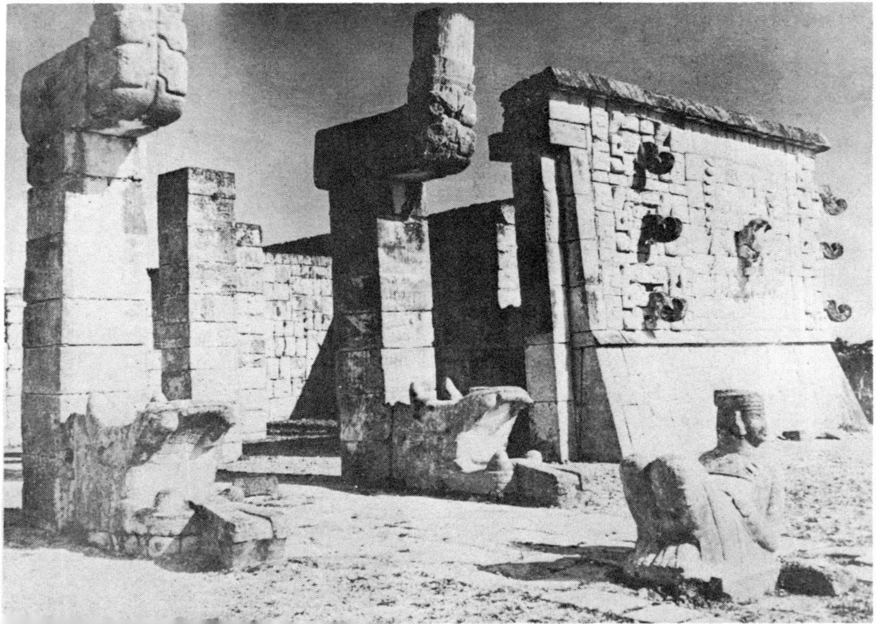

*Photograph: Ruth Deutsch de Lechuga, Mexico City.*

PLATE 95. Warrior's head. Relief from the ball game (detail). Chichén Itzá. Toltec-Maya.

Photograph: National Institute of Anthropology and History, Mexico City.

PLATE 96. The Caracol. Chichén Itzá. Toltec-Maya.

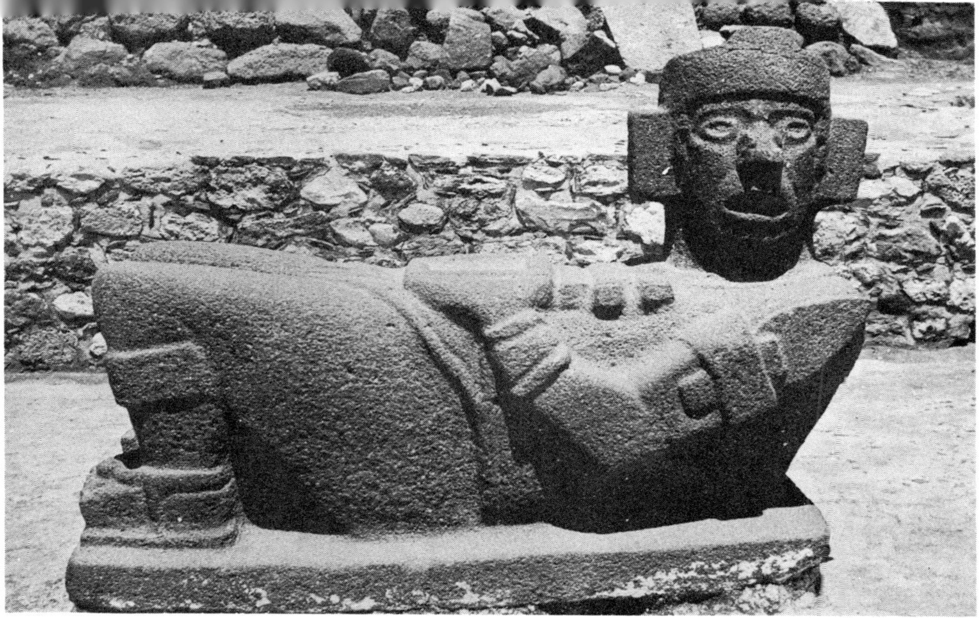

PLATE 97. Chac Mool. Tula. Toltec.

PLATE 98. Monte Albán. Zapotec.

Photograph: Ernest Rathenau, New York City.

PLATE 99. Principal façade of the Palace of Columns in Mitla. Zapotec.

*Photograph: Ernest Rathenau, New York City.*

PLATE 100. Stele. Monte Albán. Zapotec.

PLATE 101. Brazier, image of Xipe Tótec. Ceramic. Zapotec. National Museum of Anthropology, Mexico City.

PLATE 102. Funerary urn. Ceramic. Zapotec. Kunsthistorisches Museum, Vienna.

PLATE 103. Funerary urn. Ceramic. Zapotec. Kunsthistorisches Museum, Vienna.

PLATE 104. Musician blowing a shell. Ceramic. Zapotec. Kurt
Stavenhagen Collection, Mexico City.

*Photograph: Ernest Rathenau, New York City.*

PLATE 105. Niche over portico of Tomb 104 with the figure of the maize god. Monte Albán. Zapotec.

PLATE 106. Funerary urn. Ceramic. Zapotec. Kurt Stavenhagen Collection, Mexico City.

PLATE 107. Funerary urn. Ceramic. Zapotec. Kurt Stavenhagen Collection, Mexico City.

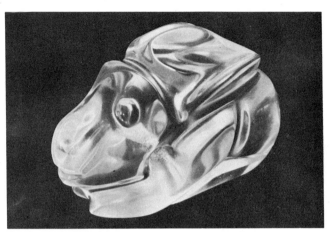

*Photograph: from the museum.*
PLATE 108. Rabbit. Rock crystal. Mixtec. National Museum of
Anthropology, Mexico City.

*Photograph: from the museum.*
PLATE 109. The Great Coatlicue. Stone. Aztec. National Museum of Anthropology, Mexico
City.

*Photograph: from the museum.*
PLATE 110. Coatlicue. Stone
Aztec. National Museum of
Anthropology, Mexico City.

*Photograph: Walter Steinkopf, Berlin.*
PLATE 111. Frog. Stone. Aztec. Völkerkundemuseum, Berlin.

*Photograph: Walter Steinkopf,*
*Berlin.*
PLATE 112. Coyote. Stone.
Aztec. Völkerkundemuseum,
Berlin.

PLATE 113. Océlotl-cuauhxicalli, vessel for hearts in the form of a tiger. Stone. Aztec. National Museum of Anthropology, Mexico City.

*Photograph: from the museum.*
PLATE 114. Océlotl-cuauhxicalli, vessel for hearts in the form of a tiger. White onyx. Teotihuacán. British Museum, London.

*Photograph: Irmgard Groth-Kimball, Mexico City.*
PLATE 115. Seated figure of a man. Stone. Aztec. Kurt Stavenhagen Collection, Mexico City

Photograph: Irmgard Groth-Kimball,
Mexico City.

PLATE 116. Seated figure of a
woman. Stone. Aztec. National
Museum of Anthropology, Mexico City.

Photograph: Irmgard Groth-Kimball,
Mexico City.

PLATE 117. Figure of a woman.
Ceramic. Colima. Kurt Stavenhagen Collection, Mexico City.

PLATE 118. Vase with serpentine legs. Ceramic. Tarascan. Diego Rivera Collection, Mexico City.

PLATE 119. Mother with a child. Ceramic. Tarascan. Guillermo M. Echániz, Mexico City.

PLATE 120. Armed warrior with a club. Ceramic. Nayarit. National Museum of Anthropology, Mexico City.

PLATE 121. Dancers. Ceramic. Colima. National Museum of Anthropology, Mexico City.

PLATE 122. Eagle from the frieze of the Xochicalco pyramid.

(valuable and unusual even from the artistic point of view) presently filling the display cases of a large exhibition room in the Oaxaca Museum. There is no doubt that the architecture and the decoration of the tomb are Zapotec. The three urns, of which the center one represents the fire god and the other two Cocijo, are also Zapotec. The slab above the portico bears a Zapotec inscription. Even the small objects—vases and grinding stones—are Zapotec. But the jewels, as Caso demonstrated, are Mixtec. One of the most beautiful pieces, the pectoral with the mask of the death god, bears the Mixtec year glyph. There is only one explanation for this: the Mixtecs reused the Zapotec tomb. It is as though at this location either happenstance or the course of history wished to show, through the coexistence of Zapotec architecture and Mixtec goldwork, the radical difference between the two neighboring cultures.

The Oaxaca region is situated approximately halfway between Teotihuacán and Copán. It is contiguous with Nahua territory on the north and the Maya zone on the south. Although well protected against enemy invasions by its privileged situation on a high tableland, this did not prevent it from developing a commercial and cultural interchange with both the north, Teotihuacán, and the south, the Maya territory. Cultural and artistic elements infiltrated from both sides. Concerning the murals of Tomb 7, Caso writes: "The similarity of this painting [Zapotec] with objects of the Teotihuacán culture is indubitable." With even more reason can this be stated with respect to the Mixtecs who, as their writing and day signs show, were oriented toward the neighboring Nahua civilization. It has been said that the dividing line of the cultures (Nahua and Maya) passed through the Oaxaca region; that the West, Mixtec, belonged in spirit and religion to the Central Plateau while the East, Zapotec, was under Maya influence. As the Zapotecs adopted various elements from Teotihuacán, it is certain that they also accepted suggestions coming to them from the Maya sphere. But fundamentally this is not a matter of "influences." What happened, as Joyce says (*Maya and Mexican Art*), was that "the Zapotec potter, while accepting inspiration from outside, has not been dominated by it, but has turned it to his own use in the production of works of art which are 'characteristic' in the sense that they bear the unmistakable stamp of his own peculiar psychology." What Joyce states with respect to the ceramics can be applied to the architecture, and perhaps with greater emphasis.

In Zapotec art there are various elements that can be considered of Maya origin: the bars that represent the number five, the false arch, stylization of the feather headdresses, and especially the steles.[2] But we must not attach too much importance to isolated details, objects, motifs. To be able to speak of artistic influences and artistic dependency, we must ascertain the will to art and the direction in which it operates.

An object suitable for an investigation of this nature is the stele. The Zapotecs adopted it from the Olmecs, from whom the Old Maya Empire likewise adopted it, but—a highly significant fact—it does not exist in Mixtec culture, which has greater affinity with the Central Plateau. Are the Maya steles and the Zapotec steles identical, then? Only in their exterior form: it is in each case a monolithic slab whose faces are decorated with representations or glyphs in relief, and it is erected in the vicinity of a temple or an altar. But beyond this. . . . We have said that the Maya stele is a glorification or autoglorification of the *halach-huinicoob*. The Zapotec steles (assembled in Caso's book, *Las estelas zapotecas*) are nothing of the sort. As in the tomb paintings, mythico-religious happenings, myths of the gods, and divine feats are represented. All the reliefs have on their upper part, if this has not been

[2] Walter Lehmann (*Aus den Pyramidenstädten Mexikos*), a disciple of Seler and an eminent connoisseur of Mesoamerican cultures, cites as one of the proofs of this "Maya influence" the lack of ball games in Monte Albán. It was believed then that the ball game was unknown in the Old Empire and that the Toltecs introduced it in Yucatán. Meanwhile, ball courts have been discovered in Copán, Palenque, and Yaxchilán. At any rate, Lehmann's argument fell by the wayside upon the discovery of a ball court at Monte Albán in 1936—three years after the publication of his book.

destroyed, the sky glyph. In a certain place at Monte Albán near the temple called "Four-Doors" and only in this place, eight steles have been found in whose reliefs we see some prisoners of war, close to glyphs that evidently signify places. But even these steles, whose reliefs probably represent Zapotec victories, bear the sky glyph. They are monuments consecrated to the gods, to whose aid the triumph was due. The Zapotec steles manifest a totally different religious feeling from that of the Maya and an equally different artistic thinking. They are bas-reliefs, not carved as deeply as those at Naranjo and Yaxchilán, but that architectonic discipline that gives full-round sculpture its support and its form also fills these reliefs on the Zapotec steles. There never appears—as at Quiriguá and Piedras Negras—that hybrid form between relief and full-round sculpture; in no way is such a "development" of the relief aspired to.

In a comparison of the esthetic order, we must not limit ourselves to a cheap artistic philology or confuse the search for motifs with a true understanding of the creative impulses and of the will to art. In the final analysis, what and how much may have been adopted in any one place is not important, compared to the use that was made of what was adopted. The Etruscans borrowed many elements from the Greeks, with whom they maintained a constant interchange of goods, and even from the aboriginal Italian population, but nevertheless, no one has used this as a basis for doubting the originality of Etruscan art. For the archeological classification of objects it is important to list and interpret the existence of the same motif in the ambit of different cultures; but an esthetic investigation must start from the creative spirit realized in the work. To study Zapotec art, and even more, to ascertain the place it occupies in the world of Mesoamerican cultures, we must consider as a decisive factor the architecture of Monte Albán, the considered equilibrium of that planning, the breadth of the urbanistic ensemble, the solid, organic corporeity of the pyramids, the simplicity of its structure that needs no accessories because it is rich, vigorous, and expressive.

The Zapotecs—no matter what they adopted or where they adopted it from—were bold and original artists, who impressed their own spirit on everything they created, revealing in it a will to art that is rooted in the architectonic and that tends toward the monumental. Zapotec art is not Maya art, nor is it Teotihuacán. It is Zapotec.

## 14

## The Aztecs: People of Huitzilopochtli

The monumental work of Aztec art is the Great Coatlicue of the National Museum of Anthropology, Mexico (Plate 109), found in Mexico City on the spot where once was located the Great Temple of Tenochtitlan. It is monstrosity monumentalized to the sublime. The history of world art knows only one similar case, only one visionary creation where monstrosity has been shaped with identical vigor: Dante's Inferno. Of course, Dante, the Mediterranean man, introduces traits of Greek humanism into his Gothic vision. The grandeur of his Inferno, one of the representative works of Western spirituality, is classic grandeur; it still preserves a relationship with the human world. European art, oriented toward classic antiquity, starts from man and leads to man. It is based on the concept and the measure of man. The art of ancient Mexico—and not only in a monumental creation like the Great Coatlicue—starts from myth and leads to myth. It brings man to a sphere of the divine impossible to capture with human concepts and human measurements.

Coatlicue is one of the most demoniacal figures of the Aztec Olympus, more demoniacal than Huitzilopochtli and Tezcatlipoca.[1] Goddess of the earth, she represents the source of the primordial generation, that mystery that made Goethe conceive of the "kingdom of the mothers."

[1] Cf. Justino Fernández: *Coatlicue,* the first volume of a trilogy that intends to develop an aesthetics of Mexican art on the basis of so many characteristic works for each era (the Great Coatlicue for pre-Hispanic art; the Retablo de los Reyes for the art of New Spain; "El Hombre," a mural by Orozco in the dome of the Hospicio Cabañas, Guadalajara, for contemporary art).

From her womb comes all being, all that lives and breathes, all that has form: gods, men, animals and plants, the sun, the stars, everything. She existed before all beginning. She gave birth to the sun, begotten in an immaculate conception. Myth relates that while cleaning the steps of the temple Coatlicue saw a ball of feathers fall from the sky, which she placed in her bosom. When she wished to offer it to the gods, it had disappeared, and she felt herself impregnated. Her four hundred (i.e., innumerable) children, the stars, indignant at the "dishonor" and counseled by their sister Coyolxauhqui, the moon, decided to kill their mother. But then from the womb of the goddess came a voice that said, "Fear nothing." And Huitzilopochtli appeared, armed with his lance and shield, wearing a green plume on the crown of his head and another adornment of plumes on his feet. He threw himself at his brothers, killed them, and with the fire serpent cut off his sister's head. On a sculpture of the National Museum of Anthropology, Mexico, that represents the severed head of Coyolxauhqui, little bells hang from the head, an allusion to her name, which means "She who has bells on her face." The legend of that nocturnal struggle is engraved on the lower part of the head.

Coatlicue is not only the great birth-giver from whom all earthly life proceeds; she is also the great destroyer, the beginning and end of all earthly being. The earth mother devours her children like Saturn, that surrealist Saturn that the aged Goya painted on the walls of his solitary dwelling. Nothing and no one escape her. Therefore, she is also called "consumer of filth." Her garment is made of serpents, the animal that crawls on the earth, which is her body: "the one with the skirt of serpents" is another of her names. This explains the belt of serpents at the foot of the Tenayuca pyramid, one of whose temples was consecrated to the solar god (Plate 23).

The Great Coatlicue is a block of quadrangular plan, a cyclopean monolith, architectonically built, showing the contour of a human body. This contour is only vague insinuation; there is no intention to "associate" the goddess with the human figure. The sculptor wished to express something greater, something that would transcend all human concepts. To relate it to the human would be to belittle it, to take away its strength. And so the outline is intermixed with details that reveal its nonhuman, super-human condition. Instead of a face, the goddess has two serpentine heads between whose gaping jaws appear the fangs and forked tongue. The severed head alludes to her lunar character. (In ancient Mexico, the earth deities are at the same time lunar deities.) The stumps of the arms also terminate in serpentine heads, and serpentine heads are the hands. Instead of feet, she has the claws of a beast. The serpents are streams of blood. A collar of human hearts and severed hands circles the neck of the goddess and falls on her breast. The rear side of the figure (actually, one cannot speak of her "rear" side because she has two "front" sides) is not her back, but a variation of the front, composed of almost identical elements. The details that characterize the deity, her omnipotence and her properties, and that attest to an acute observation, are strongly emphasized. It is almost as though the sculptor had wanted to sacrifice the surrealistic aspect of the conception to the realistic representation of the details. So it appears. But in reality—I have already insisted on this several times—that contrast is one of the principles that govern creating in ancient Mexico. Caso, speaking of the Great Coatlicue, says that "the enduring characteristic of indigenous art [is] the reality in detail and subjectivity of the whole." Perhaps it would be better to say the visionary character of the whole.

The term "surrealism" applies to this work of art not only because the Aztec sculptor did not follow the Aristotelian precept that he "copy nature"—nor can the spectator be guided by it—but above all in view of a certain affinity between the procedure used in the creation of the Great Coatlicue and the artistic method of today that surrealism resorts to. To a general contour that represents or suggests a human figure are incorporated, and not just added as decoration, foreign elements, extrahuman elements like serpentine heads, animal claws, etc.

In my book, *El pensamiento artístico moderno*, I say of surrealist art: "Realistic elements, fragments of reality, are gathered together—*le plus grand nombre de restes optiques* (Breton); they are torn from their relationship, they are situated in an ingenious and creative relationship; in a relationship that surprises us by the strangeness of its contrast. That is called *dépaysement*." Of course, we must not approach with modern esthetic concepts that Aztec work created from an entirely different vision of the world. The surrealism of our day springs from an intellectual skepticism before the chaotic turbulence of a world that is organized on a rational base, before the evidently problematical rational thinking and a rational scientificism.

It is the reaction provoked by that rationalism and its ambiguity; it is a flight toward the subconscious, after having proven that science, incapable of penetrating the depths, captures phenomena only unilaterally. Its mysticism is, in many cases, an intellectual mysticism. André Breton (*Manifeste du Surréalisme*) speaks of the "objective accident." That "accident" does not exist for pre-Hispanic man: precisely what we call accident, the inexplicable within an otherwise logical occurrence, is foreseen in his cosmic order, is not considered nonnatural or supernatural, but, on the contrary, natural. We can designate the artistic attitude of ancient Mexico as "mythical realism" (Westheim: *Ideas fundamentales del arte prehispánico en México*, Chapter "Realismo Mítico").

Contemplating the Great Coatlicue, we ask ourselves what that great pile of details signifies. What does it mean, not from our mentality, but from that of the artist who conceived the work at the order of a collectivity, and interpreting the thinking and feeling of the collectivity? It can only have the purpose of exalting the concept of the earth goddess to an inconceivable grandiosity far beyond all human measure. The earth sustains man, the earth devours him. It is not kind. What Knut Hamsun expresses in the title of his novel, *"Markens Grøde,"*[2] may also exist in that world, but it does not count.

She, the earth goddess, mother of all that is created, determines the length of that intermezzo between two eternities that is called life, that brief moment given to the individual to walk in light. There is no conjuration to offset her acting; there are only periods of grace that can be wrung from her by force of adoration and constant sacrifices. In this concept of the human destiny is manifested most characteristically the tragic fatality that projects its shadow over the life and the thought of Aztec man. It is not the Buddhist nothingness, the losing of oneself in the Nirvana. It is the absurd law that obliges man to let himself live by destiny, by a destiny implacable and without kindness, without any other meaning beyond its demoniacal law.

Coatlicue is more than one figure among many in a crowded pantheon. She is the incarnation of a fundamental religious-philosophical concept, of a whole conception of the world: a death precedes every birth. In that great Aztec work nothing is analyzed. None of the many legendary and frightful actions of the divinity is related. There is no story; there is no action. In majestic calm, immobile, impassive—a fact and a certainty—the goddess stands before the spectator: a monument, a symbol, a concept. And all the plastic resources—decorative and symbolic at the same time—all the details, represented with clarity and precision, the serpentine jaws and bodies, the human hearts and the severed hands, the animal claws: everything has the one purpose of accentuating and dramatizing the tremendous power of the earth goddess so that the spectator, i.e., the believer who devoutly approaches the image, re-creates it in his imagination. There must take place here what the poet was once exhorted by Stephane Mallarmé: *laisser au lecteur le soin de recréer.* The end pursued is not limita-

[2] This has been published in English as *The Growth of the Soil,* but the author's allusion is more aptly conveyed by the Spanish translation of *Bendición de la tierra,* or, *The Bounty of the Earth.* [Translator]

tion of the fantasy (it has already been discussed in
Chapter 3, "The Spirituality of Pre-Cortesian Art") by
bringing the work closer to reality, but excitation of the
fantasy. Insinuation from the metaphysical in order to
free the visionary power of those for whom the work is
an incarnation of the divine. If, according to Lessing, the
"purification of passion" was the goal of Greek art, here—
as in the sacred dance, which transports the dancer to
a state of mystic ecstasy—it is a matter of unchaining a
psychic religious force, a detachment from self, of being
extinguished in the spiritual experience, of the mystical
ecstasy of a world for which the divine is manifested as
the inconceivably monstrous. Plutarch, a frequent visitor
to irreligious Rome, thought the gods should be loved,
not feared. He said that to believe in the gods would free
man from fear and fill him with an overflowing happiness. Ferdinand Gregorovius (*Glanz und Untergang
Roms*) believes that the Olympian gods, as they lived in
Plutarch's imagination, "are only petrifications; they can
adorn an art gallery, but it is not possible to transform them
philosophically into ethical and intellectual powers." When
the Aztec artist represents Coatlicue, Mictlantecuhtli, the
no less frightful death god, or Xólotl, the guide of the
sun in his path to the lower world, he does not try to
carve a museum piece to arouse esthetic emotions. He
forms a religious experience that proceeds from a more
profound sphere and reaches to an ambit far beyond the
purely esthetic.

The Great Coatlicue wears a skull as a pectoral. In
other images of the goddess, the skull substitutes for the
head (Plate 110). Nevertheless, the true gods of death
are the lords of Mictlan, realm of the dead—Mictlantecuhtli and his wife, Mictecacíhuatl. But the earth gods
are likewise death gods (and also lunar deities). We
must remember that the lower world begins immediately
beneath the surface of the earth.

All thought, even artistic thought, revolves around
death. One of the poems of Netzahualcóyotl, prince of
Texcoco, reads:

*All the world is a tomb from which nothing escapes,*
*nothing is so perfect that it does not fall and disappear . . .*

. . . . . . . . . . . . . . . . . . .

*What was yesterday, today is no more,*
*and what lives today cannot hope to exist tomorrow.*

The skull is the favorite object of representation, not only in Aztec, but in all pre-Columbian art. To celebrate the fifty-two-year cycle, the end of a past epoch and the beginning of a new, a commemorative slab on whose four sides were carved human bones and skulls was placed in the Great Temple of Tenochtitlan. These are the dead years, the years that have been lived. Nothing of the atmosphere of a new year, of hope for the future. Innumerable skulls, large and small, are carved from the hardest and most valuable of minerals, rock crystal. The display cases of the world's museums are full of them. The most notable is in the British Museum. A macabre fantasy? A tragic sentiment? Salvador Toscano (*Arte precolombino de México y de la América Central*) speaks of a tragic art. It depends on the interpretation. It depends on whether our interpretation, which considers death a horrific end, the definitely irreparable, coincides with that of the Aztecs, which is doubtful. The Aztec was familiar with death. Death was man's closest relative; it belonged to life as the shadow belongs to light; it formed part of the meaning of life. "Death engenders in him neither fear nor hope. The world is subject to the will of the gods and cannot subsist without the sacrifice of man" (Alfonso Caso: *Thirteen Masterpieces of Mexican Archaeology*). And is it not impossible that the skull had been precisely the symbol of life, just as Coatlicue, "she who devours everything," is the symbol of the earth? (Westheim: *Ideas fundamentales del arte prehispánico en México*).

The religion of the Aztecs is the most sanguinary and fanatical of all Mexican religions. Huitzilopochtli, their tribal deity, god of war and of the sun, is a blood drinker. The heart, the symbol of life, is consecrated to him; he is fed with blood. Blood is the only food that can give the sun the necessary strength to traverse the firmament every day. The plastic representations show how the sun absorbs the blood through his long, tonguelike rays. Huitzilopochtli is insatiable, greedy for sacrifices, for prisoners of war. Prisoners of war, conquered enemies of the Aztec people, brought triumphantly to the country: this is his favorite food, and he must be fed daily. His altars, the steps of his temples, are bathed in blood. Human multitudes are immolated by his priests. According to a drawing in the Telleriano-Remensis Codex, twenty thousand men were sacrificed on the day of the inauguration of the Great Temple of Tenochtitlan.

On the cult to Huitzilopochtli, on that faith in the power and invincibility of their tribal deity, the Aztecs derive faith in their own power. From this comes their invincibility complex and the impulsive force that makes them warriors and imperialists, that fills them with warlike furor. Their awareness of being the executive instrument of that vigorous and militant god is one of their war potentials, perhaps the decisive one. They owe their rise and their greatness to Huitzilopochtli. They are proud of being "the people of Huitzilopochtli," "the people chosen by the sun" (Caso). He gives them boldness, that boldness that builds empires. León-Portilla (*Los antiguos mexicanos a través de sus crónicas y cantares*) states that the warlike mysticism was not "imposed" on the Aztecs until the fifteenth century, by means of the propagation of the cult to Huitzilopochtli by Tlacaélel, the conqueror of Azcapotzalco (1439).

They are an imperialistic people. Their whole way of thinking is imperialistic.[3] The most renowned caste after the king, the priests, and the merchants (*pochteca*), is the warriors of Huitzilopochtli, the Eagle Knights, and those of Tezcatlipoca, the Jaguar Knights. Their duty is to provide food for the gods, the most important social

[3] From the point of view of the psychology of the people, it is interesting to note that the Aztec glyph for the number twenty was a flag or standard. Twenty men, as Bernal Díaz observes, were the smallest unit of the Aztec army (the "banner" of the Middle Ages, the Roman "century").

function, since the community cannot exist without the strength of the gods, and this must not diminish. They are, in the strictest sense of the word, soldiers of god.[4]

When they wage war, they serve the gods. They have their own sanctuaries, adorned with their emblems. While still in the cradle, the Aztec male child was given his warrior's destiny as an assignment that would rule his entire life. "And since you were born for war," says the benediction given to the newborn, "die in it defending the cause of the gods. . . . Grant, O Lord, that this child go to the heavens where celestial delights are enjoyed and where go the soldiers who die in war."

To the Aztecs, "war is a form of worship" (Caso). The cosmic model is the struggle that the sun must undergo night after night against the powers of darkness: the moon and the stars. "The earthly wars are only an imitation of these celestial combats" (Preuss: *Mexikanische Religion*). It is therefore very understandable, adds Preuss, "that the Mexicans painted the men who were to be sacrificed, destined to be food for the sun, with the characteristic painting of the gods of the stars," i.e., they put on them black masks with white circles for the eyes, the symbol of the star. The Aztecs intentionally left a measure of independence to some of the tribes that they could have subjugated, so that there would always be an opportunity to wage war and take prisoners. In a conversation with Cortes about the Tlaxcaltecas, Montezuma said that that was the reason why they had not been conquered. He was alluding to the so-called "flowery wars," an institution established by Montezuma I Ilhuicamina (1440–69). It is well known that not all of the Aztec wars were "flowery," that there were also wars of conquest, deliberately planned and with quite realistic

[4] Parenthetically, their great adversary, who would end by destroying their kingdom—Hernando Cortes—did he not also present himself as a soldier of God? And he himself was convinced that he was. On conquering a colony and its riches for the Crown of Spain, one of his guiding impulses—the decisive one for him—was the desire to spread the Christian faith in the New World and bring eternal salvation to millions of souls.

earthly and political goals: expansion of their empire, sub-
jugation of other tribes, and spoils. But although these
wars broke out hard upon political considerations, we can
assume that the ultimate cause—the most profound—the
hidden motive force was always the worship of Huitzilopochtli. Since the Aztecs believed that their incessant
sacrifices had maintained and augmented the force—the
power-giving force—of the tribal deity, they thereby inferred that their duty was to continue fervently to provoke wars and offer sacrifices. And we ask ourselves: was
that, as so often happens, an imperialism converted into
a cult, or an imperialization of the religious? Samuel
Ramos, in his book, *El pensamiento en América,* compares the Aztecs with the Romans. He points out their
great political acumen, their bellicose temperament, and
the stupendous rapidity with which they were able to
build a vast empire, their organizing talent and capacity
for engineering works. There are even further parallels.
Just as the Romans tried to absorb the superior culture
of the Greeks, the Aztecs tried to assimilate Toltec culture. Nevertheless, there is a fundamental difference, fundamental precisely in what concerns the artistic evolution:
the totally different attitude toward the religious. The
Romans were unbelievers and for them religion was an
institution of the State and nothing more. "The official
religion of Rome was subordinated to the interests of the
State, with the tendency to adopt more and more a purely
formalistic character" (Arthur E. R. Boak, *A History of
Rome*).

Both the organization and the practical and material
amplification of the empire constituted the goal of all
efforts, in which the metaphysics of the Roman spirit
culminated. Based on this fact, Élie Faure (*The History
of Art*) says: "In Rome, the true artist is the engineer,
just as the true poet is the historian and the true philosopher the jurist." The mission of art is to glorify the State
and the great statesmen—emperors and generals. The great
productions of the spirit of Roman art are the monumental
works of engineering: bridges, aqueducts, highways, triumphal arches, theaters, baths; and a highly objective,

highly realistic and rationalistic portrait sculpture in the busts, coins, and precious stones. The Aztecs, religious fanatics, were not only believers, but their entire existence —their living and working, their social conduct, their wars —revolved around the religion and was absorbed in it. Even the State was first and foremost a religious community, created by the gods and for the gods. The warrior on the field of battle did not die for the State, but for the gods, in order to participate in the supreme happiness, to be incorporated into the following of Huitzilopochtli. The famous Roman "circuses," the games of sport, the gladiatorial contests, the horse-and-chariot races, the wild-animal hunts, the theatrical functions, were public spectacles, a popular carnival. The Aztecs held no festivals of an earthly nature for the diversion of the people. The innumerable and sumptuous celebrations with their sacred dances were acts of adoration, of conjuration of the gods. They were performed according to the sacred rites and revolved around a culminating point: the sacrifice, which provoked a frenetic ecstasy in the masses and gave them the conviction that they had served the gods, had obtained their benevolence. There were no portrait sculpture or triumphal arches. They did not know the glorification of man, and if one time a deed was glorified—quite an extraordinary case—as on the Stone of Tízoc, it was a matter of a monument intended to be placed in the temple in praise of the gods, in proof of gratitude to the divinity for aid granted. Referring to the songs that treat of war, Ángel Ma. Garibay K. (*Historia de la literatura náhuatl*) says that "they do not sing of victories, but celebrate the religious duty of contributing to the existence of the world by giving sustenance to the gods." This attitude also explains for us the significance of the Stone of Tízoc. Roman art, profane art, is important and creative only when it is profane. When Augustus invented his conventional gods Rome and Augustus—the so-called Imperial Religion—and ordered statues made of these new gods, the result was conventional works long forgotten by the history of art. Aztec art is religious art, even when it incorporates realistic features in the creation.

When that nation of warriors entered the Valley of
Mexico and even for a long time thereafter, they were
obliged to exhaust all their material and spiritual energies
in order to secure their threatened existence. Cultural development was not yet possible. The representatives of
high culture in the Valley of Mexico were the Toltecs.
The Aztecs, impressed by their cultural superiority, elevated spiritualism and creative power, tried to adapt
themselves to these.

The artistic production of Tenochtitlan was in the
hands of guilds composed for the most part of Toltec
families. As their first king, the Aztecs elected Acamapichtli, grandson of the sovereign of Culhuacán. Atotoztli,
mother of Acamapichtli, was a Toltec princess (Tezozómoc: *Crónica mexicáyotl*). To their minds, this meant
that the king was a descendant of Quetzalcóatl, i.e., of
divine lineage. In view of that ancestor, the Aztec kings
were thought to be of Toltec origin. All the nobles of
Tenochtitlan were obsessed by the ambition to descend
from the Toltecs. As is inferred from the Ramírez Codex
and from the work of Durán, each of twenty principal
men decided to give one of his daughters to the king as a
wife, "since he was of the lineage," as it says in the *Relación de Genealogía.*

A comparison of the statues of the Great Coatlicue and
Chalchiuhtlicue is enlightening. We can show a certain
coincidence in various formal elements and a very marked
contrast in what is essential. At the same time, we discover
one of the stages on the road that leads from Teotihuacán
art to Aztec art. Both works, built as architectonic blocks
with clean silhouettes, are articulated in horizontal zones,
although the Aztec sculptor did not yet understand the
guiding principle of Teotihuacán art—the elimination of
the vertical character, its transmutation into a horizontal
tendency—but only adopted it superficially. In both works
the intention was to create a conceptual image, a symbol.
But despite the structural similarities, the vision that governed the creative act is completely different. Teotihuacán religiosity differs from the Aztec. By this I do not
mean to say that the latter was less authentic; this is not

even probable. It is true that the Chalchiuhtlicue reveals a greater faculty for abstraction. Teotihuacán religiosity comes from more profound strata than the Aztec and covers a wider sphere. There is in it a deep wisdom, what the Christian mystics called "contemplation," the yearning and the gift of penetrating to the subsoil, may I say, to the pith of the religious experience. Materiality is refined and takes on the quality of an abstract concept. The form of expression also shows that conceptual character. A perfect spiritualization in the plastic resources as well, among which there is none that does not constitute a purely and exclusively functional formal value. All sensuality is extinguished in that transubstantiation. The fantasy of the Teotihuacán artist, as expressed in Chapter 2, "Collective Art," is formal fantasy, plastic fantasy. Thanks to the strong condensation of the expressive language, monumentality is attained. Aztec art does not reach contemplation. From its works, frenetically, bursts a savage instinct; from its works, the religious furor cries out. Great, strange, and fascinating creations, that express experiences more emotional than spiritual. The vision still contains sensuous elements, remains of representation not yet transmuted and that, therefore, cannot become absolute Form. It is an imagination that, certainly, aspires to the conceptual and the symbolic but that cannot or will not completely sacrifice the material fact. With that imagination—that in Coatlicue adopts a character of macabre and monstrous fantasy—it tries to impress, to impress even the senses. To this end and within the monumental ensemble of the composition, it offers those details that fascinate not only as Form, but as real phenomenon. Chalchiuhtlicue is free of this: in her, what is indispensable is barely suggested, and even that slight insinuation is transformed into function, more formal than material value. Referring to the Aztecs, Caso speaks of the "barbaric originality of a young and energetic people."

That "barbaric, young, and energetic people," who so rapidly reached power and riches, like the Romans, greedy to display at once a zeal for culture corresponding to their recently won greatness, abided by the Teotihuacán tradition of the Valley of Mexico and managed to assimilate certain formal elements, a certain artistic posture, but not the spiritual disposition characteristic of Teotihuacán. Probably the Aztecs were more talented than the Romans; their "Teotihuacanism" was more authentic than Roman Hellenism. It cannot be said that they adopted a repertory of forms, which in any case would have been foreign to their mentality. But they aspired to the monumental effect, and in order to achieve it they needed a suitable artistic strategy.

Teotihuacán is their guide and lodestar in this undertaking, but at times—and we point this out when discussing Coatlicue—they adopt only the exterior form without assimilating the creative spirit of Form. In this connection, the most illustrative example is the Océlotl-Cuauhxicalli, the vessel for hearts in the form of a tiger, 9 feet long and almost 3 feet high, found in Mexico City (National Museum of Anthropology, Mexico) (Plate 113). Let us compare this Océlotl-Cuauhxicalli, solemn and ceremonious in style, by its size and importance a characteristic work of Aztec art, with the Océlotl of Teotihuacán. What power of abstraction in this latter creation! How much purity in the conception of the Form that gave birth to the vision, a vision of the supra-earthly! The Aztec work, although imposing, seems rather decorative, a stylized impression of nature. The mane, the teeth, the claws, all are stylized. Monumentality is achieved through omission and simplification. The jaws become ornament, a very decorative cursive line. The mane too is composed of the same decoratively arranged cursive lines. The body mass is rounded off in a succession of crescendos and decrescendos. The sureness and homogeneity of the stylization of this work reveal creative power, although not true originality, but rather a great talent for achieving a unitary disposition of the formal elements and for making use of the plastic means to gain an impressive effect. Monumentality, there is no doubt, but a studied monumentality, not that barbaric eruption of the elemental that attracts us with mysterious force, with magic fascination, in the Coatlicue.

Stylization, an essential resource of Aztec art, its expressive element par excellence, does not prevent the object from reflecting the excellent observation of nature, nor does it impair the monumentality of the whole. Joyce (*Maya and Mexican Art*) speaks of "the supreme energy which characterizes the Aztec, combined with their receptiveness." (In small sculpture, too, they achieve that monumentality.) They develop a type that must be considered specifically Aztec, not only because of its frequency: the figure of a seated man with his legs drawn up. A masterful example is the "Standard-Bearer," or "Sad Indian," long ago a decorative figure on the stairway of the Great Temple of Tenochtitlan. The thighs and arms are closely joined to the trunk, the arms crossed on top of the thighs: this produces a mass of closed block. The legs are like columns. The head, another closed mass, whose gaze is directed forward, rises above that block, that constitutes a sort of pedestal for it. This pedestal is not at all rigid, nor does it show the decorative stylization of the Océlotl-Cuauhxicalli: a great sensibility is revealed here that articulates the mass, imposing a rhythm on it, and that characterizes the thighs, calves, feet, well observed in their details. In the seated feminine figures, the skirts covering the legs give the lower part of the bodies an even more closed form. Vigorous simplification; the energy of a young, virile, self-conscious art that succeeded in overcoming its inferiority complex before Teotihuacán culture.

The realistic element, already contained in the surrealism of the Great Coatlicue, begins to project strongly here, repressing the magico-psychic forces that make that work such a grandiose expression of Aztec religiosity. Observation of reality, subjected to the architectonic, submitted to a formal discipline. In the literal sense of the word, this is not realism; it is a stylization that starts from the experience of the reality and that in certain works—like the head of Coyolxauhqui with its broad surfaces—recalls the art of India.

Based on all those tendencies, Aztec art develops a plastic idiom very much its own, clear, concise, lapidary as the Aztec hieroglyphic. The Aztec hieroglyphic is not mysterious like the Maya glyphs, where signs of esoteric meaning are inserted into the heads of the gods. It is as impressive as the Roman capital letter and actually more decorative. The creation myth is related on the relief of the Aztec Calendar Stone with precision and moderation. It is impossible to tell a story more objectively, more clearly. The fifteen groups of figures carved on the circular surface of the Stone of Tízoc have the same clarity. And let us consider the clear and expressive Aztec animal sculpture of tigers, turtles, frogs, locusts, dogs, coyotes; the serpents, with and without feathers, and those grandiose serpents whose coiled bodies form a monument, a pyramid whose vertex is the head: observation of nature transformed into rhythm of the mass and rhythm of the Form.

We must remember that the Aztec Empire accomplishes, in the brief period of its brilliant ascent, a radical transformation of its social structure. Along with the *calpulli* system that never completely disappears rises the ownership of large landed estates, a result of the partition of conquered lands among the worthy generals. A military aristocracy develops, that of the Eagle and Jaguar Warriors, rich and powerful institutions that begin to exert influence in the State and evidently in artistic production as well, as indicated by the style that Aztec art creates, the clarity and concision of its expressive idiom, the base of realism without rhetoric, that nevertheless strives for a representative, monumental effect. "An art of soldiers." This phrase coined by Worringer to describe Roman art (*Griechentum und Gotik*) could apply to Aztec art as well. Of course, the Eagle Knight, the Jaguar Knight, is not a Roman legionary risen to the rank of general. In him breathes the magic of the cult of Huitzilopochtli. He is a soldier of God, detached from his own ego. It could be called a militarized religious art.

This feudalism of the Eagle and Jaguar type is different, more robust, than the theological feudalism of the Maya, inclined to a precious esotericism. It is also different from the feudalism of the eighteenth-century French nobility, for whom the battlefield and the dangers of war were almost no more than ancestral glories. Until its fall, the Aztec Empire never ceased to fight and to conquer. Perhaps we could compare the Aztec warrior with the Gothic knight. Gothic realism is likewise impregnated with a radically religious vital feeling. The head of the Eagle Knight (National Museum of Anthropology, Mexico) is a symbolic image; it symbolizes a concept. The warrior whose face appears through the open beak of the bird-god is an incarnation of the energy and warlike impetus of Huitzilopochtli.

Before its overthrow, the Aztec Empire displays a dazzling luxury, a pageantry and pomp that yield nothing to the splendor of the Old Maya Empire. Bernal Díaz del Castillo enthusiastically describes the superb buildings in which the Spaniards were lodged as guests of Montezuma in Tenochtitlan: ". . . in palaces magnificently constructed of stones, whose roofs were of cedar, with spacious patios and rooms with the finest cotton hangings. All was adorned with works of art painted and admirably restored and bleached, the multitude of birds making it all the more delicious." Refinement in the style of living, reflected also in the artistic manifestations. A trivial naturalism appears. The ceramics of Period IV, the period of Montezuma II, renounces the great and sacred tradition: geometric ornamentation, symmetry, rhythmic repetition, linear abstraction. Imitation of nature becomes the fashion, "drawings of birds, fish, and plants, executed with the careless exactitude that characterizes Japanese brush drawings in sepia" (George C. Vaillant: *The Aztecs of Mexico*). What a long way from the magic formula of the stepped fret and the monumental conception of the Great Coatlicue to this final stage!

But that is not characteristic. It is characteristic only of the final period, whose forces are already growing weak, sensing the presentiment of the imminent catastrophe. Its worldly grace is a symptom of decadence. Aztec art had been great and original when its wandering fantasy, powerful and barbarically bold, was absorbed by its meditation on life and death.

## 15

## *The Tarascans: Profane Art*

The Lienzo de Yucutácato relates that when the Tarascans arrived in the region of Michoacan, they gave a village the name of Nonoualco, which means "land where one is silent," i.e., a land of foreign language. The Tarascans had their own language and kept it over the years. They also had their own artistic language, which is in no way a simple dialect but entirely different from the plastic idiom of the other Mesoamerican peoples: an art of their own in both content and formal repertory. To this cultural horizon designated by archeology as "Western Mexico" also belong Colima, Jalisco, and Nayarit. The art of each of these regions certainly presents variations in details—its own particular stamp—which results in large measure from differences in workmanship and which permits stylistic classification. But all express the same fundamental attitude.

While the art of Teotihuacán, the Toltecs, Aztecs, and Zapotecs has an essentially religious orientation and one subject—the representation of the divinities and of the cosmic happenings—a worldly attitude predominates in Western Mexico. In the ceramics of this culture, of which innumerable examples are preserved, it seems that the gods did not exist. What it represents are men and women, animals and fruit. A surprising phenomenon is the numerous "genre scenes." There are warriors with their arms: slings, wooden swords, clubs, and axes. Ballplayers in their special outfit. Chiefs, musicians, acrobats, men and women dancers. Women nursing their children, stripping ears of corn, grinding maize, making tortillas, combing their own hair or that of another woman. Love scenes. Chiefs borne on litters by four bearers; often their wives sit close to them and sometimes a dog accompanies them. Others are seated on stools protected, in some cases, by canopies. Groups of dancers, dancing around the musicians, to the sound of drums and tambourines. Domestic scenes: the rectangular house with its steep roof painted in a rich ornamentation; the husband, wife, and children squat in the entry. Animals of all kinds—dogs, monkeys (there is a figure of a monkey yawning with his mouth wide open), turtles, ducks, herons, parakeets, spiders, fish, sharks—that in the majority of cases are in the form of a vessel, like the representations of squash and different fruit. There are the most diverse objects: arms, musical instruments, fans, obsidian mirrors. The characteristics notable in the human figure are the often extravagant headdress and the finely executed body painting that indicated social standing. Profane art, which delights in the description of daily life and seems to ignore what for Teotihuacán and the whole Nahua world was the only thing worthy of being represented: the supra-earthly and the transcendental. "One of the deep enigmas of our pre-history," says Salvador Domínguez Assiayn of the Tarascans (in the magazine, *Universidad Michoacana*, Vol. III). Lucio Mendieta y Núñez (*Los tarascos*) notes that "the Tarascan [language] lacks metaphysical words." Diego Basalenque (*Arte de lengua tarasca*), who did serious research in this field, "did not succeed in collecting a dozen words that could serve as elements to express a superior mentality." Until now no traces have been found of hieroglyphics or indications that the Tarascans had developed writing. "The Michuaques were a people of very primitive mentality," affirms Seler (*Los antiguos habitantes del país de Michoacán*). If he is correct, that "very primitive mentality" coincided with an astounding creative power.

Our most important source of information on the Tarascans and their neighbors—with whom they fought constantly without being able to subdue them—is the *Relación de Mechuacán*, written about 1540 on the order of the viceroy, D. Antonio de Mendoza, by a Franciscan monk who dedicated himself to collecting the traditions of the indigenous peoples. Unfortunately, the first part of this chronicle is missing, in which the religious celebrations and the origin of the gods are discussed. In all probability the Council of the Indies seized it and perhaps even destroyed it, fearing that the description of pagan rites might favor idolatry. A deplorable loss. Perhaps those folios contained the solution to the "deep enigmas" Domínguez Assiayn refers to. It is also a loss for esthetic research, all the more so in view of the scarcity of information given in this respect by the other sources, such as Fray Pablo Beaumont's *Crónica de Michoacán.* A more complete knowledge of the religious thought of the people of Western Mexico would have explained how that art arose which, like the Tarascan language, is an enclave within ancient Mexico.

Among the funerary offerings found in the Tarascan zone itself, as well as in Colima, Jalisco, and Nayarit, there are numerous figures of dogs. Astounding figures, in which the facts supplied by a sharp observation of nature are transformed by a bold creative conception. At times the dog is provided with a human mask, a proof that there existed among the Tarascans as among all the peoples of the Central Plateau the belief in a journey to the lower world that the deceased, led by the dog (the disguise of Xólotl), had to undertake. It is not at all necessary for the Tarascans to have adopted this belief from the neighboring tribes; this may well have been a tradition preserved from archaic times: that dog to guide the deceased has also been found in graves near the Cuicuilco pyramid.

Seler notes that "in its essential features" the Tarascan calendar must have been identical to the Mexican calendar. The theogonic system, the adoration of the sun and of the moon, the human sacrifices, the ball game, also show considerable affinity in many areas.

José Corona Núñez (*Mitología tarasca*) was able to reconstruct the Tarascan pantheon. The oldest deity, and the one who enjoyed the greatest veneration, was Curicaueri, the fire god. His son, the tribal deity of the Tarascans and also called Curicaueri, was the sun god. (The sun is the ball of fire in the firmament.) Like the Aztec Huitzilopochtli, he was symbolized by the eagle and the humming-bird. The Tarascan word for "hummingbird" is *tzintzuni*. This explains the name of their capital, Tzintzuntzan, which means "where the hummingbird is." Objects of special veneration were Xarátanga, moon goddess, and Cuerauáperi, "the Creator," mother of the gods. Corona Núñez also proved the existence of three symbolic animals of the death god: the mole, the squirrel, and the weasel. Seler's investigation reaches the conclusion that "between the Mexicans and the Michuaques existed a profound affinity with respect to the religious concepts and also in large part with respect to the practices of the cult." A certain relationship in artistic manifestations might therefore be expected, but quite the opposite is true. How is this explained?

It is possible and even probable that the Tarascans adopted many of the rites practiced by the peoples of the Valley of Mexico but that their "very primitive mentality" did not develop an identical religiosity; that there were priests, temples, and a ritual, but that the masses held magico-religious conceptions from very remote times. This is implied by the character of the artistic creation. Tarascan art, like that of all the high Mesoamerican civilizations, developed over the base of a culture that the archeologists designate as "preclassic." In numerous works pertaining to that art we can easily show the ensemble of traits that might be called "ingenuous realism."

The Tarascans develop a craftsmanship of vigorous expressivity that succeeds in transmuting the natural Form in accordance with a very marked stylistic sensibility of its own. They learn how to model the body in its three dimensions. They strive to represent a man or an animal in complete mobility by capturing the twists, turns, and intersections of the body, by creating dynamism. There is none of the form of the closed block, none of the hieratical solemnity of the Teotihuacán, Aztec, and Zapotec figures. The Western Mexico way of seeing is an impressionistic one; the goal of its art is to catch what the moment yields. It is a proof of great confidence, of exquisite artistic tact, that a certain small size is never exceeded, that the playful and improvised character of the work is never lost from view. The geometric-abstract forms that the Teotihuacán sculptor used to construct the Chalchiuhtlicue, and that the Egyptians also used, constitute one of the bases of monumental creation. Had the Tarascan "action sketches," which try to imitate the animation of the natural model, been amplified to natural size or larger—the fatal ambition of much contemporary sculpture—the result would have been that banality that not even Rodin could always avoid.

The Tarascans do not succeed in developing spiritually the archaic fundamentals on which they rely. They only intensify the observation of reality that characterizes the creations of the preclassic culture. Not without reason has Tarascan art been designated as an "evolved archaic." Teotihuacán also builds its art on the groundwork of the preclassic culture, but its traditional mode of expression is colored with the magico-religious thought that it developed and to which Teotihuacán art owes the greatness of a style of monumental symbols, suitable to give plastic form to metaphysical representations. This does not happen with the Tarascans. Their art has another horizon. Its beginning and end is what is perceptible by the senses. This is its starting place and its goal.

Seen as a whole, Tarascan art is happy, full of the exuberant joy of living. It does not embrace that awe before the demoniacal breath of the gods who never cease to menace the existence of the world and of man. One of their mythical traditions is significant. When the gods learned of the radical change caused by the arrival of the Spaniards, they broke out in complaints, protesting that after the creation of light it had been agreed that the end of the world would not be repeated; that the earth would now live in peace, in the established order. Such was the security in which the Tarascan world was living. Their art reveals a great confidence in man himself, also unique in pre-Hispanic Mexico. It did not create anything comparable to the Aztec representation of Coatlicue. It is true that the goddess Cuerauáperi, "The Creator," a sort of Tarascan Coatlicue, plays a role of some importance; but the tragic feeling of life, which is the element that really animates pre-Columbian myth and to which the myth owes its profundity and tension, is lacking. When Aztec art represents the serpent or the jaguar, these are not only divine symbols. The quaking aroused in the believer by the concept of "serpent" or of "jaguar" is always perceived in their configuration. Concepts of this type are missing from the Tarascan world. Its art lacks this dimension: it accepts the real fact as real. Without reserve and without metaphysical interpretation, it joyfully abides by the exterior appearance of the object and represents it with manifest delight in the variety it offers to the eye. For it, life is interesting, not enigmatic, not demoniacal. Filled with an innate optimism, free from anxieties and sorrows, it creates its attractive works. Characteristic of this art is a certain air of ironic superiority that is often expressed in caricature. The sexual is not only accented but very often exaggerated, and with enjoyment. The pipe in the form of a phallus seems to have been a very common object. Paul Kirchhoff (Catalog of the exposition, "Arte precolombino del Occidente de México") found a certain type of clothed masculine figures "that leave their genitals uncovered." He also mentions men who "wear an artificial phallus, as well as some individuals who exhibit phalli of extraordinary dimensions." Another peculiarity of the art of Western Mexico is the male figure who wears, suspended below the navel, a marine shell (Plate 120), a fertility symbol generally reserved for woman. From the artistic point of view, that caracole is an appendage that destroys the unity of the body, which leads to the conclusion that it was very important to add it. Kirchhoff states that masculine homosexuality was publicly recognized. He mentions "figures of men with women's garments and performing feminine occupations." Many of the attractive artistic jewels that thrill the connoisseur in the display cases of museums and in private collections are burial offerings created not to delight the living but to accompany the dead to the lower world. The intense cult of the dead is a characteristic trait of Western Mexico. The burial of a prominent person motivated a display of considerable pomp. Besides the sub-

terranean mortuary chambers there were true mausoleums, of which we shall speak later when discussing the
architecture. Among the Tarascans, as among the Nahua
people, the dead were cremated. In the case of a great
personage, his wives, slaves, and the hunchbacks and
dwarfs who had been members of his suite in their capacity as beings given magical virtues by the gods followed
him to the beyond, i.e., they were sacrificed during the
funeral ceremonies. As in other places, his arms, jewels,
and other objects of value were buried with the deceased.
While the peoples of the Nahua group customarily fas-
tened a mask to the mortuary bundle, which was more a
"portrait of the personality" than an effigy, ceramic figures
are found in the Tarascan graves that may be considered
authentic portraits of the dead. The material corporeity is
immortalized, is conserved "magically . . . i.e., by means
of the transmutation of the carnal body to the sculptural
image" (Toscano: *Arte precolombino . . .* , op. cit.). The
supposition is probably true that many of the masculine
and feminine figures that came from the mortuary chambers were portraits of those who had been close to the
deceased or who had lent splendor to his existence:
women, warriors, musicians, men and women dancers, his
totemic animal. Further, given the belief that in the beyond the deceased continued to lead his life just as he had
in this world, and that he should not lack any of the pleasures he had enjoyed, this existence was frequently reproduced in miniature works that appear to be toys. It was
hoped that the dead person would believe that he was in
his accustomed surroundings. Involuntarily there come to
mind the Egyptian reliefs on the tomb of Methen, in Abu-
sir and Sakkara, that describe in complete detail the world
that the deceased had abandoned. But the same purpose
that those monumental reliefs served in Egypt is filled in
the world of Western Mexico by attractive clay miniatures.
    Neither the descriptions of daily reality nor the per-
sonality cult are found in other spheres of the pre-Hispanic
world, with the exception of the reliefs carved on the steles
of the Old Maya Empire that we can perhaps consider to
be portraits. The mundane character revealed here is not

only contrary to the mentality of those people, but they rejected it with all their strength. The mural painting in Tomb 104 of Monte Albán is a solemn procession of the nine Lords of the Night. In the niche above the same tomb, the maize god is enthroned as guardian. The funerary urns are adorned with the figure of Cocijo, tribal deity of the Zapotecs, or Xipe, or, at times, with the goddess Seven-Serpent. All the representations speak of the myth and of the gods, never of the person of the deceased or of his deeds or the circumstances of his life. This difference is important. From it we must deduce that in the region of Western Mexico, despite the many ritual customs adopted from elsewhere, the fundamental religious attitude was very different from that prevailing in the other cultures of ancient Mexico.

The chronicles report that the totemic cult was extensive among the Tarascans. Corona Núñez writes that the Tarascans "believed that they were the descendants of great rocks. Perhaps this is their oldest totemic belief." And it is fitting to ask if the innumerable animal figures —among which are many that resemble surrealist works, like that fish with the head of a man, or that torso of a masculine figure whose legs terminate in serpent heads, both from Colima and both from the collection of Diego Rivera—are perhaps representations of totemic animals, in contrast to the animal figures of the Nahua peoples, which symbolize deities.

The name "Tarascans," according to Orozco y Berra (*Historia antigua y de la Conquista de México*), was given by the Spaniards to the settlers of the region of Lake Pátzcuaro. When in 1522 the conquerors began to penetrate Michoacan, the last sovereign of the nation, Calzontzin, and the members of his court, tried to win their friendship. They gave their daughters to the Spaniards as wives and called them "sons-in-law," a word that in their own language is *"tarasco."* As the Spaniards heard this word frequently, they believed that it was the name of the tribe, which is actually—in the "Tarascan" language— *Purépecha.*

The experts' opinions differ with respect to the origin of

the Tarascans. It is known that in the region of Michoacan they found a primitive, Náhuatl-speaking population, the Teca, that they subdued them and founded their capital, Tzintzuntzan. The territory with its lakes and great rivers is rich, the climate favorable, the soil fertile. There was no lack of water and fishing was a source of sustenance. (The word *michoaque* means "inhabitant of the place of the fish.") There was obsidian, a valuable raw material for making knives, arms, and mirrors, also used by the Tarascans for working jewelry. In Tomb 25 at Tzintzuntzan, Daniel Rubín de la Borbolla found a valuable labret of this material with incrustations of gold and turquoise mosaic (now in the Morelia Museum). Life does not seem to have been difficult in that world. The chronicles speak of riches and well-being. According to them, the treasures that Nuño Beltrán de Guzmán snatched from Calzontzin were considerable, although not even remotely sufficient to satisfy his insatiable hunger for gold. The *Relación de Mechuacán* states that in "the house called of the Eagle," the sanctuary of Curicaueri, which was also the king's treasure house, there were kept two hundred silver shields, many headdresses, also of silver, with which they adorned sacrificial victims, and four hundred—a number that in the Mesoamerican languages means "innumerable"—discs of the same metal. The artistic representations also point to a high standard of living. The ceramics that have been preserved represent men and women with rich adornments: nose rings, earplugs, labrets, bracelets, and ankle rings. High mountain ranges and wide rivers (the Lerma and the Balsas) offered protection against invasions. Excellent warriors, the Tarascans were never dominated by other peoples. The Aztecs failed in repeated attempts to penetrate their region.

In résumé, conditions were propitious for the development of an artistic production of great enterprise. But, paradoxically, the Tarascans never achieved monumentality. They created neither an imposing architecture, such as that of the Zapotecs in Mitla and Monte Albán, nor a monumental plastics.

Eduardo Noguera (*La cultura tarasca*), who completed

explorations in Zamora and Jiquilpan, believes that the architecture is without any doubt "inferior to that of the majority of the pre-Cortesian peoples." The technical execution is likewise more primitive than in other sections. As one of the reasons for this, Rubín de la Borbolla mentions "the nonexistence of vital construction materials," e.g., lime and suitable sand. We must mention, nevertheless, an interesting development in the architectonic sphere. The Michoacan pyramid, called *yácata*, differs in structure from all the other Mesoamerican pyramids. One of its sections is a long, narrow rectangle, and this is in front of another, round section. Both constructive bodies served as the base for several small constructions that had a conical roof. The plan of the whole is in the form of a T to which a circle is added. How is this invention explained in a nation that in all else gave so few indications of architectural initiative? It results from the cult of the dead. The round section of the pyramid, added to the sanctuary and joined to it by a narrow corridor, was, as is inferred from the *Relación de Mechuacán*, the sepulcher of a prominent person. In the center his mortal remains were buried and the offerings were piled up. The graves of the persons who had formed his suite were arranged radially around these.

Rubín de la Borbolla says that the rectangular sector of the pyramid of Tzintzuntzan was "excessively long," about seventy feet, and so narrow (only 5 feet 8 inches) that there was not sufficient space to erect a temple above it. "It is possible," he says, "that the upper surface of the rectangular Tarascan pyramids had been used to place the statues of their gods." None of those statues of the gods have been preserved. Perhaps they were not made of stone? The *Relación de Mechuacán* mentions the Tarascan custom of carrying their gods on their backs when they went to war. Corona Núñez writes: "They did not carve colossal statues."

Their artistic sensibility and their authentically creative imagination, on the other hand, are manifested exuberantly and grandiosely in the minor arts. The Tarascans are, in ancient Mexico, the inventors of featherwork, that singular craft that seeks to achieve the nuance, the delicate subduing of colors. They also invented the "lacquer" technique whose beauty lies in the brilliance and contrast of strong colors. They were excellent metalsmiths who could create masterworks in copper, later in gold, and occasionally in silver. Sahagún and Muñoz Camargo praise the artistic perfection of the fabrics woven by the Tarascan women. And above all, they were marvelous ceramists, who ennobled the humble material by means of Form and color. They decorated their vessels with abstract, geometric designs—figures, too, at times—and with harmoniously shaded colors, a decoration that reveals an inexhaustible inventiveness and a refined taste. The pottery of Chupícuaro is distinguished by the peculiar luminosity of its purple. It is not strange that Tarascan ceramics has become a coveted item for the type of collector who seeks intimate charm, subtlety, refinement.

What gives those figures their particular character is a certain hypersensibility, a certain decadence that is manifested in them. This decadence may be another of the reasons why Tarascan art, despite an unquestionable creative power, could not raise itself toward the monumental. An intense sensuality is evidenced in the images of men and women. The observation of nature seems to have been more a pleasure than a matter of conscientious study (which it was among the Japanese). These Tarascan figurines reveal a brilliant intuition that plays in very free variations with corporeity, changing real Form into expressive Form. The dimensions are modified. Some details are exaggerated and others suppressed, capriciously and arbitrarily, it would seem. This art does not limit itself to a simple copying; it always re-forms, re-creates, but in such a way that the work retains a memory of the object that inspired the artist's fantasy. An art that springs from a genuine artistic impulse. It is not metaphysical, and only a very tenuous bond unites it with the physical.

# Index